You Can't Steal a Gift

Gene Lees

You Can't Steal a Gift

Dizzy, Clark, Milt, and Nat

FOREWORD BY NAT HENTOFF

Yale University Press New Haven and London

Designed by Rebecca Gibb. Set in New Caledonia type by Achorn Graphic Services.

Library of Congress Cataloging-in-Publication Data

Lees, Gene.
You can't steal a gift : Dizzy, Clark, Milt, and Nat / Gene Lees ; foreword by Nat Hentoff.
     p.   cm.
Includes index.
ISBN 0-300-08965-1 (alk. paper)
1. Jazz musicians—United States—Biography. 2. Gillespie, Dizzy, 1917–1993. 3. Terry, Clark, 1920– . 4. Hinton, Milt, 1910–2000. 5. Cole, Nat King, 1919–1965. 6. United States—Race relations—History. I. Title.
ML394.L393 2001
781.65′092′273—dc21
2001003444

A catalogue record for this book is available from the British Library.

The paper in this book meets the guidelines for permanence and durability of the Committee on Production Guidelines for Book Longevity of the Council on Library Resources.

For Phil and Jill Woods
and Roger and Jorjana Kellaway

Contents

Foreword

by Nat Hentoff

Increasingly, most of the writing on seminal jazz figures is based on second- or third-hand sources. Gene Lees, however, is one of the relatively few chroniclers left who has known the musicians he writes about long and well.

Moreover, he is not just a jazz critic or journalist. Lees is a musician, singer, and lyricist with his own distinctive body of work. Unlike most of those who write about jazz, Gene is one of the family, and so, when he interviews musicians, he literally speaks their language. Clearly, that leads to deeper communication.

Also, unlike some critics who try to burnish their own reputations by earnestly discovering "new stars" and new forms of the music—one writer has advocated the diminishing importance of the soloist in jazz—Gene keeps adding to our knowledge of those creators who have shaped the music over time.

What this book vividly reveals, in addition, is that Lees, while literate musically, understands that, as Charlie Parker said: "Music is your own experience, your thoughts, your wisdom. If you don't live it, it won't come out of your horn." And living the music can be perilous.

"It's like going out there naked every night," a bass player once told me. "Any one of us can screw the whole thing up because he had a fight with his wife just before the gig or because he's not with it that night for any number of reasons.

"I mean, we're out there *improvising*. The classical guys have their scores, whether they have them on stand or have memorized them. But we have to be creating, or trying to, anticipating each other, transmuting our feelings into the music, taking chances every goddamned second. It can be exhilarating too, but there's always that touch of fear, that feeling of being on a very high wire without a net below."

Gene Lees knows, from the inside, the fierce commitment that jazz makers have to the music. Their nightly risk-taking requires such intimacy with the instrument that, as William Butler Yeats once wrote, you can't tell the dancer from the dance.

Louis Armstrong spoke for his peers, and for those who yearn to be in that company: "I don't feel no different about that horn now than I did when I was playing in New Orleans. That's my living and my life. I love them notes. That's why I try to make them right. Any time of the day, you're liable to see me doing something toward that night."

Even John Coltrane, who practiced for hours every day, experienced more than a touch of fear one night. At the Five Spot in New York, where off-duty musicians would line the bar to hear and watch the intense interplay between Thelonious Monk and Coltrane, I saw Coltrane come off the stand one night looking utterly dejected. I asked him what had happened.

"Monk's music is so all of one piece," he said, "so interconnected, that on that last number, I got lost. I felt as if I'd fallen down an empty elevator shaft."

Lees knows the uncertainties as well as the joys of the jazz life. And being an insider, he knows a continuing source of uncertainty—the political economy of jazz. How to survive the career-determining producers at record companies, the club owners, the bookers and impresarios, and the critics.

Throughout this book, you will find stories about the challenges of the jazz life, on and off the stand, that, I expect, cannot be found elsewhere in the jazz literature. At least I didn't know them before.

John Coltrane used to try to discourage me from writing liner notes to some of his recordings. And I'd say, "John, I have this gig." Being a kindly man, he'd agree to talk about his music, but he kept saying, "If the music can't speak for itself, no writing can help it."

In one vital respect, he was wrong. A writer like Gene Lees, who has the trust of the musicians he writes about, can lead listeners to the musicians' experiences that are at the continuing core of their music. A writer can't alchemize bad or shallow music, but he or she can lead listeners to want to know more about the music because they become so intrigued by the lives of the players. Gene Lees does exactly that.

I once asked Duke Ellington what he most wanted of his listeners. "I don't want them," he said, "to analyze musically what I'm doing. I want them to listen with their feelings, their memories. You see, it works both ways. When Johnny Hodges is playing a ballad, and I hear a sigh from one of the people on the dance floor or in the audience, that becomes part of our music."

It's of no use to notate a sigh: but once a listener is drawn to a particular way of music, learning more about the person, the actual person, making that music, can lead to deeper dimensions of listening.

This has been true for listeners from the beginning of jazz, and Gene Lees—through the musicians in this book—makes you want to hear more of their music, which transcends categories that critics too often place on jazz, dividing the music into styles that are "modern" or "avant-garde" or "old-time."

One of the most continually resourceful musicians I've known, Eric Dolphy—who expanded the range and depth of a number of reed instruments—was considered on the cutting edge of jazz. But one night, during a jazz festival in Washington, Eric Dolphy heard, for the first time, the Eureka Jazz Band of New Orleans, playing as the marching bands had when Louis Armstrong was coming up.

"I stood right in the middle of those old men," Dolphy remembered, "and I couldn't see much difference from what I'm doing, except they were blowing tonally, but with lots of freedom. You know something? They were the first freedom players."

And among the long line of freedom players who followed are the musicians in this book.

Gene Lees captures another part of the essence of jazz. Cornetist Jimmy McPartland recalled: "People used to ask Bix Beiderbecke to play a chorus just as he had recorded it. He couldn't do it. 'It's impossible,' he told me once. 'I don't feel the same way twice. That's one of the things I like about jazz, kid. I don't know what's going to happen next. Do you?'"

Preface

Sometime about 1985, the magazine *Toronto Life* asked me to write an article about the most famous jazz musician Canada has produced, and one of the most famous in any field of music, namely Oscar Peterson. I had known Oscar slightly since 1950 and well since 1959, when I became editor of *Down Beat*. As we did this new interview, Oscar said that he would like to make some comments about racial discrimination in Canadian television commercials. But, he added ruefully, it would be a waste of time, because the magazine would never print them. I told him he was wrong; I knew the magazine better than he did. He made his comments, I quoted them, the magazine printed them, and thus began a campaign in which Oscar ultimately triumphed, redressing the balance of ethnic representation in Canadian TV commercials. And the article led to my writing a full biography of Oscar. The point is that he *thought* the magazine would not print what he said.

I came to know almost all the jazz chroniclers and critics of my own generation, most of those of the generation before me, and a lot of those younger than I. I have never known one who was not deeply concerned by issues of civil rights in the United States and, in even closer focus, the treatment of black Americans. That racism is the most critical problem in American society should be, but isn't, obvious to everyone. The boom in building "free enterprise"—that is, profit-making—prisons, and the concomitant expansion of "law enforcement" personnel, is conspicuously an imperative to lock away in modern oubliettes the black male population, especially that part of it in the full strength of youth. The mere possession of a marijuana joint is enough to get you warehoused for several years if you are from the black ghetto. If on the other hand your father is a "respectable" taxpaying white man, chances are you will not spend even a week in the pokey for this petty offense, maybe not even a day.

Given that all, or certainly most, of the chroniclers of jazz have had an interest in black civil rights ranging from the sympathetic to the impassioned, it is odd that more comment on race and racism does not turn up in interviews with black jazz musicians in magazines. Why is this? Do they, like Oscar Peterson on that occasion in Toronto, think the magazines will not print their views?

In view of my own concern for this matter, and my conviction that its racial division constitutes the most crucial social issue of the United States—in the past, in the present, and into the future—I have gone out of my way *not* to raise the subject whenever I have interviewed black jazz artists. I do not wish to exhibit an intemperate curiosity. I certainly do not want to project anything that might be construed as a patronizing sycophancy. Above all, to use a lawyer's courtroom term, I do not want to lead the witness. I am always interested in what it is the interviewee *wants* to say, and thus I like to let him or her lead me.

Despite this policy, I have never interviewed a black musician who has not at some point himself raised the subject. This was true even when I was working for *Down Beat* at the start of the 1960s. And it certainly has been true since, in 1980, I started the *Jazzletter*. Perhaps it has been because the subjects of my portraits for the most part have known me for years and, more important, know that because it is my publication I have control over what goes into it. No one can veto or censor me.

I have said repeatedly that I have no trouble understanding, at least in an empathetic way, blacks who hate whites. What truly does baffle me is those great spirits who *don't*.

The *Jazzletter* freed me from the restrictions of length implicit in the nature of magazines. If I wanted to let a piece run longer than the three or four thousand words common to magazine articles, I could do so by spreading it across several issues of the publication. This evolved into a form I think of as the minibiography, and through its use I have been able to reflect on the lives and legacy of dozens of artists who might all too easily have slipped through the interstices of history. Five volumes of these essays have previously been published; this is the sixth.

Lies Across America by James W. Loewen, a book published in 1999 by the New Press in New York, examines many monuments and markers across America and tells the true stories behind the lies engraved thereon. One of the segments, on the statue to a supposedly heroic Chicago cop who participated in the Haymarket Riot of May 1886, is actually hilarious because that figure has the distinction of being the most knocked-over and blown-up monument in American history. I recommend the book. I intend to read Loewen's *Lies My Teachers Taught Me*. The one thing Henry Ford and Voltaire would have agreed on, had they met, was Ford's statement that history is bunk. Voltaire put it more elegantly. He said that history is a fiction that has been agreed upon.

One of Loewen's passages is particularly illuminating to me.

It explains why I find it so fascinating, and urgent, to set down, for example, Milt Hinton's memories and for that matter my own memories of certain events. Loewen writes: "I have found useful a distinction that societies make in east and central Africa. According to John Mbiti, Kiswahali speakers divide the deceased into two categories: sasha and zamani. The recently departed whose time on earth overlapped with people still here are the sasha, the living dead. They are not wholly dead, for they live on in the memories of the living, who can call them to mind, create their likeness in art, and bring them to life in anecdote. When the last person to know an ancestor dies, that ancestor leaves the sasha for the zamani, the dead. . . .

"Historical perspective does not always accrue from the passage from sasha to zamani. On the contrary, more accurate history—certainly more detailed history—can often be written while an event lies in the sasha. For then people on all sides still have firsthand knowledge of the event. Primary source material, on which historians rely, comes from the sasha. To assume that historians and sociologists can make better sense of it later in the zamani is merely chronological ethnocentrism."

Simon Schama, in the preface to his *Citizens: A Chronicle of the French Revolution* (1989), makes a similar point: "Historians have been overconfident about the wisdom to be gained by distance, believing it somehow confers objectivity, one of those unobtainable values in which they have placed so much faith. Perhaps there is something to be said for proximity. Lord Acton, who delivered the first, famous lectures on the French Revolution in the 1870s, was still able to hear firsthand, from a member of the Orleans dynasty, the man's recollections of 'Dumouriez gibbering on the streets of London when hearing the news of Waterloo.'"

As Loewen makes clear in his book, you must evaluate monuments in terms of when and by whom they were erected, for they bear the prejudices and convenience of their own time and of their builders. And this is true of history, not simply the erection of monuments. Thus the Haymarket statue bears the prejudices of the police, who were responsible for it, and does not tell you that it was not the protesters who rioted but the police themselves. The monument makes these killers into heroes. Distortion exists too in some of the "histories" of jazz. Memory may be fallible, but I have found the recollections of musicians more compelling, and usually more credible, than some of the writing on jazz, past and current.

For one of my earlier collections of musicians' memories, *Cats of Any Color* (1994), I compiled a group of my essays on men whose lives in one way or another had been affected by the racism of the United States. Fully two-thirds of the book dealt with white racism. The last third dealt with the phenomenon of anti-white black racism, manifest in a certain minority of younger black musicians, the policies of the Lincoln Center jazz program, the writings of Stanley Crouch, and other evidence, including a statement by Spike Lee that blacks were incapable of racism. (I think you'd have trouble selling that in Rwanda.) The press to a large extent dwelled on the last part of my book and hardly mentioned the first two-thirds.

This book is not an extension of *Cats of Any Color*. It is almost its opposite, the obverse of the coin. It comprises essays on four great men, on the magnificence of the legacy they bequeathed to their country and indeed to the world, and the munificence of their humanity. All are men who had every reason to embrace bitterness—and didn't.

We all have our heroes. These are four of mine.

Sudden Immersion

In the first week of May 1955, I traveled by train from Montreal to Windsor, Ontario, crossed into the United States on a bus, handed my permanent-residence papers to an immigration officer, and proceeded into downtown Detroit with an odd and tremulous feeling that I was leaving all that I was and ever had been behind. I was going to take up life in a new country and a new city: Louisville, Kentucky. I was twenty-seven. I bought a pair of shoes that day. The young salesman asked my name. I told him. He called me by my first name. That was the first cultural shock of my arrival, the informality of Americans. It made me a little uncomfortable, as the French are if one proceeds too quickly to the intimacy of *tu* instead of *vous*.

Unlike immigrants from the world's sundry tyrannies, I was not fleeing some hideous dictatorship. Canada was in some ways a more democratic and much freer country than the United States. This was, after all, only five months after Joseph McCarthy had been condemned by the Senate for what, in effect, was a reign of political terror.

Politics had nothing to do with my decision to move. It was mostly a matter of scope. When one's abilities and ambitions and yearnings had expanded to a certain size, one had no choice but to leave, which is why so many French Canadians have gone to France and English Canadians to England or the United States. The population of the United States is consistently ten times that of Canada, resulting in the southward drift of all sorts of Canadians of ability. The phenomenon is known in Canada as the brain drain: John Kenneth Galbraith, for example. Even old Bat Masterson was a Canadian. After his career as a gambler and lawman, associate of Wyatt Earp and Doc Holliday, he took up sports writing. He was hired as chief sports writer for the *New York Morning Telegraph* in 1901 and died at his desk there in 1921.

The flow of Canadians into the American automobile industry—such as Louis Chevrolet and the Dodge brothers—was critical to its evolution in Detroit. Actors and theater people went to Hollywood because there was *no* Canadian film industry, and they contributed beyond measure to the development of Hollywood: Mack Sennett, the Warner brothers, Louis B. Mayer, Mary Pickford, Glenn Ford, Douglas Dumbrille, Norma Shearer, Christopher Plummer, Jack Carson, Michael J. Fox, Norman Jewison, Arthur Hiller, Lorne Greene, Kate Nelligan, Walter Pidgeon, Yvonne De Carlo, Margot Kidder, John Candy, Dan Aykroyd, Colleen Dewhurst, Alexis Smith, Donald Sutherland, John Vernon, Mark Stevens, Genevieve Bujold, and even the archetypal "American" Indians Graham Greene, Jay Silverheels, and Chief Dan George. American television newscasting is permeated by Canadians—Peter Jennings, Arthur Kent, Thalia Assuras, Kevin Newman, Ray Pizzey, Morley Safer, Sheila McVicar, and more. You can sometimes spot them by their "out" and "about" and "house." Peter Jennings seems unable to get rid of

The author, Chicago, 1959 (Photo by Ted Williams)

that sound; I know I can't. But another clue is the word "dollar."
If someone pronounces it to rhyme with "polar" rather than "col-
lar," you've nailed one. And oh yes, if you ever hear someone say
"Yes eh?" or "No eh?" you know that person is not only Canadian
but from Montreal. It's comparable to the way Pittsburgh people

say "yuns" as a plural form of "you." Very regional stuff. Three of the most influential arrangers of our time were born in Toronto: Percy Faith, Robert Farnon, and Gil Evans. But all three left Canada, Bob Farnon for England, Percy and Gil for the United States.

Canada is larger than the continental United States or Brazil, and Quebec is bigger than Texas. But most of the population lives close to the American border. I like to say that it's a country five thousand miles long and about sixty miles wide, which is approximately true. From Westmount in Montreal, you can look down through the Eastern Townships of Quebec (where Bat Masterson was born) into the Green Mountains of Vermont. Thus it is that almost all the population of Canada can receive American radio and television stations. It amazes me that Canada has been able to maintain so strong an identity, given this constant inundation of American cultural influences. My heroes in childhood were all American, including Superman. The radio heroes, such as the Green Hornet, Jungle Jim, the Lone Ranger, and those in the comic strips and books, Red Ryder, Smilin' Jack, Dick Tracy, Batman, Flash Gordon, Buck Rogers, Captain Marvel, the Green Lantern, the Phantom, were Americans all. Tom Swift was an American, and so were Tom Sawyer and Huckleberry Finn. And of course all the heroes after whom we modeled ourselves in playing cowboys—Ken Maynard, Buck Jones, Tim McCoy, Tom Mix, John Wayne, the Three Mesquiteers—were American. Even the bad guys were Americans—John Dillinger, Baby Face Nelson, Al Capone, the James Boys, the Youngers. It is little wonder that so many of us grew up with an unexpressed feeling that nothing very interesting ever happened or ever could happen to a Canadian. This is the source of the notorious Canadian inferiority complex.

There was a parallel to this in the United States: a sense of inferiority toward European culture, particularly in the field of music. Earlier in the twentieth century, it was rare for an American symphony orchestra to have an American conductor. For that matter, most of the conductors of American orchestras still come from other countries, including one from India and another from Japan. Leonard Bernstein was one of the exceptions to this rule.

The reason for the American sense of inferiority about the country's own composers had a simple genesis: it was deliberately inculcated in the nineteenth century by music publishers. Since there was no copyright agreement between the United States and other nations, the music publishers could steal all the music they wanted from Europe; but royalties had to be paid on American music. And so the publishers perpetrated the myth of American musical inferiority. To this day, all too many "cultured" Americans do not appreciate the genius of Jerome Kern, George Gershwin, Harold Arlen, and others at the upper level of popular music, which very term they transcended. And in general Americans do not have anything approaching an adequate appreciation of the greatest contribution to world culture the United States has made: jazz. A Jamaican judge I met some years ago said, "Jazz is God's gift to America, and America's gift to the world."

I was listening to jazz before I knew its name. It came to us over the radio. The small city of St. Catharines in the Niagara Peninsula, where I grew up, is about ten miles from the American border. I heard the big bands from a time before I can remember, and when I was a little older I bought American records. When the first Capitol records came out during World War II, I would cross the border from Niagara Falls, Ontario, to Niagara Falls, New York, buy them in a favorite store, and smuggle them home under the seat of the bus.

One cannot claim there was no racism in Canada. But it was neither lethal nor legal. For one thing, Canada had no substantial background of slavery. The first American blacks arrived in Canada from Jamaica in 1791. England was the first European nation to outlaw slavery, but Ontario beat her to it. Slavery was outlawed by Act of Parliament in Upper Canada (now Ontario) in 1791. It continued for a time in Lower Canada (now Quebec), but one Emmanuel Allen, age thirty-three, was the last slave ever sold in Canada. He drew a price of thirty-six pounds in a Montreal auction on August 25, 1797. In 1804 there were 142 slaves in Montreal. The British order outlawing slavery throughout the empire passed on May 31, 1834, effectively ending it in Quebec, too.

The first important source of Canada's black population was the Underground Railway, on which escaped slaves traveled north to freedom. Some of their descendants are still there, although a great many returned to the United States after the Civil War. The railroads later recruited blacks from the United States to work as cooks, redcaps, and porters, and they soon monopolized these professions and resolutely resisted attempts by whites to penetrate their ranks. A substantial difference between the United States and Canada is that blacks were brought by force to the former and immigrated voluntarily to the latter, particularly from the U.S. and the Caribbean islands of the British Commonwealth.

In 1949, there were eighteen thousand blacks in a Canadian population of about thirteen million. There were approximately as many black Americans south of the border as there were white Canadians north of it. One American in 10 was black, compared with one Canadian in 722.

I claim no special virtue for Canadians: if there was little open prejudice against Negroes, it was because there were too few of them to inspire it. My father, who was English, as was my mother, made the point that there was no prejudice against blacks or any other group in England because there was almost no "minority" population. He said that racial bigotry arose only when the minority population was large enough to seem to pose a threat. He made the prediction that if England ever did have a large immigrant population, you would see racial prejudice arise. And with the postwar influx of blacks from the Caribbean, his prescience was fulfilled.

When I was growing up, I never met or talked to a black person. There was, however, a small lakeside amusement park in a little town called Port Dalhousie, a short distance north of St. Catharines on the shore of Lake Ontario. It had a modest dance pavilion and a carousel and clean sand. Every year, hundreds of black people, perhaps a few thousand, came up from the United States, probably from Buffalo, to celebrate something called Emancipation Day. No doubt they felt safe in Canadian parks, unharassed. Other than these annual visitors, I had never even seen such persons, except in the movies, where they were always portrayed as menial, lazy, and cowardly. Then, when I was about thirteen, I had a startling experience.

I was visiting my grandmother, as I did most weekends, in Niagara Falls. I used to take my grandfather's bicycle for long rides. Early one Saturday evening I saw crowds gathering outside the Niagara Falls arena. Curious, I left the bicycle (there was little worry about theft in those days) behind the building. I found an open exit door and slipped inside. People were assembling before a high bandstand, on which there were chairs and music stands. Musicians began to take their places—black musicians, or Negroes, to use the requisite polite term of the time. Before they made a sound, I was astonished by them. They wore tuxedos. There was all that black cloth and those black bow ties and crisp white shirt fronts and yellow brass instruments, which these men raised to their faces, and suddenly I was hit by a wall of sound. I must have asked someone in the crowd who these men were. I learned that this was the Duke Ellington orchestra. I stayed all evening, enthralled. And when I found that bands played the arena every Saturday night through the summer, I came back the following week to hear the Jimmie Lunceford band. I can still see them in my mind.

I began devouring *Down Beat* and *Metronome,* and soon my heroes included Count Basie, J. C. Higginbotham, Jo Jones, Cozy Cole, Edmond Hall, Coleman Hawkins, Lunceford and Ellington of course, Lucky Millinder, Ray Nance, Lionel Hampton, Sy Oliver, Benny Carter, and, hugely, Teddy Wilson. I was also partial to Artie Shaw, Woody Herman, and Bunny Berigan. Negro men were, to me, godlike, people from whom you shyly solicited autographs, and in the early days I did a lot of that. By fifteen, it had come to seem uncool. Before long my heroes included Nat Cole, whose Capitol records were among those I smuggled into Canada on the bus. I was very partial to the Cab Calloway band, because behind the show-biz Minnie the Moocher antics of the leader was a polished and swinging band. Its bass player was Milt Hinton, and one of the trumpet players was Dizzy Gillespie, of whom the whole world would soon hear more. Much more.

If I had any racial prejudice, it was this: I didn't think Canadians could play jazz; but then I wasn't sure they could do much of anything. Such is the power of prejudgment and the sense of one's own cultural inferiority that social circumstances may engender. If, later, I was able to glimpse into the mechanism that made black Americans feel inferior to whites, and why they would use creams and hair straighteners to try to look white, and why the Andy Razaf lyric to *Black and Blue* pleads, "I am white inside," and why younger blacks later would rebel against this sense of inferiority and even claim superiority, it was a result of its similarity to this overwhelming (and false) impression of Canadian inferiority toward Americans. And I was hardly alone. I have asked many Canadians about their experience of this process. When I toured Canada in 1989 to publicize the first edition of my biography of Oscar Peterson, I asked journalists across the country if things were still the same. The answer usually was that the Canadian sense of inferiority had probably weakened since my youth, but it had not disappeared.

The first black men I ever really knew or even spoke to were Oscar Peterson and Ray Brown. In the first week of May 1951, Peterson—already, as he is to this day, the most prominent jazz musician Canada ever produced—came to Hamilton, Ontario, the city where I was born. I was then a young reporter at the *Hamilton Spectator*. He and bassist Ray Brown were engaged for a week at a basement bar called the Hunting Room of the Fischer Hotel. Nearly forty years later, Ray told me what happened that May 3 and 4.

"In the South of the United States," Ray said, "you couldn't go into a white barber shop. And you weren't *comfortable* in a white barber shop in New York City. In Montreal, you could find a black barber. But not in Hamilton. There was very little black population. So I walked into a barber shop, picked up a newspaper, and sat there, and got into the first chair. The guy said, 'How do you want it?' I told him, and he cut my hair. That night Oscar said, 'Hey, you got a haircut.' I said, 'Yeah, and the guy didn't do too bad.' And I told him the shop. So he had to feel comfortable about walking in there, since my hair'd been cut."

When Oscar went there the next day, a barber refused to cut his hair. Oscar returned to the Fischer Hotel and called the police, who told him to go back to the shop, ask for a haircut, and should he be refused, to notify the Crown Attorney. Oscar did exactly that, and in the furor that followed, the shop's owner almost lost his license. Indeed, only Oscar's plea saved it. I was the reporter who covered that story.

One of my stories reported that Peterson was proud to be a Canadian, and that while on U.S. tours he boasted that "Jim Crow did not live in Canada—it was a great country." It quoted Ray Brown as saying, "He used to laugh at discrimination and say that you never got it in Canada." And Oscar said, "But when something like this happens to you, it almost makes you feel that you are not a man." That in itself is an insight into what racism does.

Oscar added, "I have three little girls. And it sort of makes me wonder what kind of world it will be when they grow up."

Years later, when I had come to know Oscar and Ray well, I learned that Ray had teased him unmercifully about the incident. And Oscar told him that at least, when this did happen, in *his* country the law was on his side. And I would add another point. Carried on the Canadian Press wire, my story made the newspapers across Canada. That in itself was an essential difference between Canada and the United States. Lynchings did not make the wire services in the United States; a barber's act of bias made headlines in Canada.

Long after this, Oscar's sister Daisy, a prominent piano teacher, told me of the subtle but damaging racism the family experienced in Montreal. Daisy said, "To be fair, can you name me a race that isn't racist? Racism exists among black people with black people. I was discriminated against because I was darker than other girls."

Oscar told me that Daisy was never appointed to teach piano at the Negro Community Center because she was dark. When we were discussing these experiences of their youth, tears welled in his eyes and he told me he found it hard to talk about these aspects of his early years in Montreal. He played in the Johnny Holmes band. When the band was booked into the Ritz Hotel, the manager told Johnny to "get that nigger out of the band." Johnny refused to do it. He had influence, and the manager had to back down. But Johnny never forgot it, and neither did Oscar.

I spent three years in Montreal, as a reporter for the *Montreal Star* some of the time, an editor at other periods. I covered labor (and rapidly learned that nothing would be printed in the paper that was against the interests of its owner or his friends), the waterfront, politics, and crime. I witnessed a lot of murder scenes and murder trials. I covered the crash of a Royal Canadian Air Force bomber in a forest and what I saw at that site left me with a permanent distaste for flying. I was a military correspondent, covering the air force in England, France, and Germany, and a foreign correspondent, reporting from Paris on the efforts of the French to extricate themselves from Algiers.

Naturally, I came to know all the jazz musicians of Montreal, including pianist Paul Bley and bassist Hal Gaylor, who was later with Chico Hamilton and Tony Bennett. Hal and I are still friends. And I met a young black pianist, cocktail-lounge singer, and aspiring songwriter named Cedric Phillips, born in Barbados and educated in Canada at Dalhousie University. We became quite close friends, and he taught me a lot about black history. He told me that one of the essential differences between the black experience in the United States and in the British Caribbean islands is that in the U.S. education was forbidden, and families were routinely shattered as fathers, mothers, and children were sold off separately. But in the British West Indies, he said, the policy was to encourage legal marriage among blacks and often to educate them, even sending promising administrators to England for schooling. Mostly, of course, Cedric and I talked about music. There were two important black nightclubs in Montreal, Rockhead's Paradise and the Cafe St. Michel. Cedric and I were among the regulars at both. I remember that when I acquired a ten-inch LP by Nat Cole called *Penthouse Serenade*, Cedric and I listened to it over and over, enraptured.

For all that, when I crossed into the United States that May afternoon in 1955, I was unprepared for the realities of American racism. Having been conditioned by my love of jazz to an admiration for black Americans, and knowing that I was not only going to move to the United States but to one of the southern states, I had been reading whatever I could get my hands on about the history of slavery, about the conditions of Negroes in the United States, biographies of boxers, anything. I read Ralph Ellison's *Invisible Man*. I read about Frederick Douglass. I read a biography of George Washington Carver.

Nothing prepared me for one simple symbol. As I left the Louisville & Nashville Railway train in Louisville, the first things I noticed in the station were the signs on two men's rooms. One bore a plaque saying White, the other a plaque saying Colored. I had heard about, read about, known about such signs. But to see them was another matter. They really did exist!

And Louisville, as I was to learn, was comparatively liberal among southern cities. Kentuckians would point out that the state was not the Deep South. It was a border state, in conflict with itself during the Civil War. The presidents of the Union and the Confederacy, Abraham Lincoln and Jefferson Davis, were both born in Kentucky, and Davis was largely educated there. While the case of *Brown v. Board of Education* was under consideration, the city of Louisville asked its attorneys to predict how the Supreme Court would rule. They advised that the Court would almost certainly strike down the doctrine of separate but equal and the schools of the South would have to be desegregated. And so Louisville had a well-considered plan for desegregation of its school system even before the ruling came down from Washington in 1954. That plan was being implemented when I arrived there in May 1955.

I had been hired by the *Louisville Times* as classical music critic, and I became friends with a number of the musicians in the Louisville Orchestra. The orchestra was involved in an extensive program of commissioning contemporary classical music. At the same time, I of course sought out the local jazz musicians, and, despite the indifference and even vague opposition of the paper I began reviewing jazz whenever I could get away with it.

There were actually two jazz communities in Louisville, one black, one white, and they didn't mix much. In those days, most cities had separate Negro and white locals of the musicians' union. In any event, for the most part the black musicians weren't in the union at all. One of the black musicians was a very good guitarist named John Woods. He was also a janitor at the newspaper. When he and I wanted to listen to records, I had to sneak him up the fire stairs of my apartment building. That's the way things were.

I soon had a fair number of black friends in Louisville, including members of the staff of a black radio station. One of the disc jockeys there had a rhythm-and-blues band that played dances in the black community. Sometimes I went with him to these events, where I would encounter curious stares but nothing you could call hostility. One woman asked me if I could explain something about white people. Why is it, she wanted to know, that we can cook their food and serve it to them at their tables, but we're not good enough to eat it with them? Did she think I, a baffled Canadian, had an answer to that one? Or any of the other questions I heard about white society?

Nonetheless, I was told repeatedly that things were better here than in other cities of the South, and these people thought of themselves as fortunate. Fortunate?

The *Louisville Times* was the sister paper of the more famous *Courier-Journal*. It was owned by the Bingham family, about whom at least two books have been written. The head of that family, Barry Bingham, was a Democrat and a close associate of Adlai Stevenson's. This in itself made him unusual. Newspapers are owned by the rich, and the rich almost always rationalize their wealth as something to which they are entitled due to unspecified virtues. This, in the United States, makes them Republicans. A liberal newspaper was an oddity then, and is now, despite the nonsense the right wing perpetrates about the liberal press. The purpose of a newspaper is to protect the interests of its owner and his or her friends. But Bingham's were the two best newspapers I had ever seen, and the *Times*—it was the afternoon paper—assuredly the best I ever worked for.

The two papers were in the forefront of what came to be

known as the civil rights movement, consistent champions of the cause of integration. But there were anomalies in the situation. For example, the black employees of the company, all of them in menial positions, were not allowed to eat in the company cafeteria. This annoyed those of us on the reportorial staffs, and infuriated one of them in particular. Bill Peeples constituted my first encounter with the impassioned southern liberal. I had not known such persons existed. Bill actually made rumblings about calling a strike to get the paper's black employees into the cafeteria. It is probably not a coincidence that Bill was a jazz lover. He might have been as liberal as he was purely by temperament, his great sense of fairness, but in my generation, an interest in jazz automatically set up a different view of "Negroes" than the commonality of white attitudes, for the simple reason that you became interested in the characters and lives of your heroes. Thus, in my opinion, jazz was a powerful if hidden force for civil rights.

Leontyne Price gave a recital in Louisville, and I reviewed it. It was presented by some Negro charity, and after the concert I was invited to the home of one of the sponsors. She was a wealthy woman, and through her I came to know some of the black upper class of the city. Theirs was a slavish copy of white society, which I found amazing and sad. They knew nothing of black culture, and weren't interested. I knew more about it than they did. They admired classical music only, and knew nothing of jazz, which they looked down on—an attitude, I learned over a period of time, that was common in black society. (As a student at Howard University, Benny Golson studied clarinet; he had to practice saxophone surreptitiously in a laundry room: it wasn't a "respectable" instrument.) Then the woman who had introduced me into that world of society blacks asked me to intercede on their behalf. She said that the society sections of the *Courier-Journal* and the *Times* never published any of their press releases about their events, never covered them, and didn't print photos they submitted. Would I speak to Barry Bingham about it? Would I ask him to give them coverage?

This put me in an awkward position: Who was I to question policy at the paper? But I did it. Barry Bingham was a friendly man, handsome and aristocratic in appearance, always beautifully dressed. He bore the air of noblesse oblige. So I approached him about the policy. Barry said that if the paper were to print photos of black people in the society pages, it would alienate the city's white society. The paper had to use its influence for more important aspects of the civil rights movement. The day would come when such pictures could be printed, but that day was not yet. It was a pretty lame explanation that I had to deliver to the woman who had asked me to be their legate.

I liked Barry Bingham. A lot. And I liked his wife, Mary Bingham, equally. She ran the *Courier*'s book page and would occasionally ask me to review books. But a joke went around at those two newspapers. The joke had Barry and Mary sitting in the garden of their palatial home, which was just beyond the edge of the city, near the Ohio River. Barry is scratching an itch and says, "These damn chiggers!"

And Mary says, "No, Barry! You must say Chegroes."

There may have been a point to that joke, one I didn't get. Years later, it was recounted in one of the books about the Binghams that their children invited the children of one of their black household employees for a swim in their pool. Mary said nothing. But afterward she had the pool drained and refilled.

But we can cook for them, handle their food . . .

I don't get it. I never will.

There are aphorisms along the way that form the vocabulary of your soul. I am partial to Rafael Sabatini's "He was born with a gift for laughter, and a sense that the world was mad."

The nineteenth-century linguist, author, traveler, and translator Richard Burton left us the unshakable: "Peace is the dream of the wise. War is the history of mankind."

But the most haunting, for me, is the line James Joyce assigns to his protagonist Stephen Dedalus, "History is a nightmare from which I am trying to awaken."

When I was very young, I did not find history credible. The Roman arena? Crucifixion? Henry VIII? Culloden? The auto-da-fé? Slavery? And even World War II, in which I was barely too young to participate: it was the stuff of American movies. I think history began to be real one day when I was nineteen, visiting Montreal for the first time. When I heard two small children speaking French on a streetcar, I knew—*knew*— that Wolfe's men really had scaled the ramparts at Quebec and defeated Montcalm's forces, after which the English took possession of the city. A few years later, in 1954, when I was assigned to write stories on the Royal Canadian Air Force in Europe, I was in an RCAF North Star, crossing the English Channel. I was, courtesy of the pilot, sitting in the copilot's seat, looking down. We crossed the coast of Normandy. The green face of the land just back of the beaches was covered with round yellow-brown marks, like the pitting of severe smallpox: the unhealed craters of the D-Day bombardment. Days later in Paris, I saw lines of chip-holes up the stone faces of buildings, the souvenir of machine-gun fire in the last days before the Liberation. And I came to understand that Paris was laid out in a series of spokes on the orders of Napoleon, ever the artilleryman, to facilitate command of the city by cannon. At last it became real to me that men really did from time to time dress all alike, go out and, on the orders of someone unseen, obediently kill each other.

But little that I encountered made our ghastly past real to

me as much as an interview I did not long after I arrived in Louisville.

Slavery remains one of the most difficult of all practices for me to come to grips with, even knowing that all races have practiced it, including Africans who enslaved other Africans and sold them to white men to take to lands west of the Atlantic Ocean. The Romans practiced it, the Greeks practiced it, the Aztecs practiced it, and, quiet as it's kept, it still is widely practiced. Girls from various countries are offered opportunities elsewhere and, on arriving, are forced into a prostitution from which, in many cases, only death frees them. I cannot believe men will do such things for profit. But slavery became very, very real to me one afternoon in Louisville.

I interviewed a woman, with her children and grandchildren and great-grandchildren around her, on her 104th birthday. She had been born a slave. She had, she said, been fortunate. She had a master who was kind and good. When she was seventeen or so, she fell in love with another slave, a boy of nineteen. Strange that I still remember their ages. The boy was apparently well regarded by the master, who had given him some education and put him in a position of responsibility. The two wished to marry. The master built them a small house and attended the wedding ceremony. Then one day he called them into his house. I remember the images her narrative conjured in my mind. They stood in his office. He was seated. He opened a small box on his desk and extracted some papers. He said something to this effect: "These are your freedom papers. I have signed them. There is going to be a terrible war. I don't want you to be caught in it. You must go north."

And she and her husband did, to Illinois, as I recall, probably landing in the vicinity of Chicago. They didn't like the climate, however, and after the Civil War they returned to Kentucky, where they raised their family and where, I would presume, some of the descendants I met still live.

One of my black acquaintances in Louisville, who played in a black nightclub I frequented on West Walnut Street (now Martin Luther King Boulevard) bore the nickname Pres, for his obvious admiration for and imitation of Lester Young. Whatever his real name was, he never told it to me, and I did not presume to ask. Sometimes at the end of his work night, we'd go back to my apartment and listen to records and talk about music.

On one of these occasions, he saw a spread of eight-by-ten photos of me that the newspaper had ordered taken for publicity purposes. By that point, I had my own column in the paper. Some of the photos were duplicates, and he asked if he might have one. I could hardly say no, and I gave it to him.

One Saturday night, we went back to my apartment to listen to records. As usual, we went up and later descended the fire stairs. I drove him home to Jeffersonville, Indiana. He gave me the directions to his house on an unpaved street in a dark neighborhood with meager street illumination.

When I went to my car in the morning, I saw his saxophone case on the back seat. I knew he needed his horn: he had mentioned that he had a job on Sunday afternoon. I had no way to telephone him. So I got into the car and tried to find his house, not even knowing his address, and for that matter his real name. This ramshackle neighborhood of old unpainted houses gray with weathering was different in the daylight. I drove around the streets, stopping to ask its black residents if they knew a saxophone player named Pres. You can imagine the looks I got. One elderly woman shook her head, but I somehow knew that she did know him. I pleaded with her. I said he had work today, and

I had his horn in my car and he needed it, and I showed it to her. Finally, still doubtful, uncertain, she pointed to a house and told me he lived there. Upstairs.

I mounted a flight of stairs so old and creaky they seemed about to collapse. At the top of the climb I knocked on a door. It opened. A young black woman answered. She was pregnant. She wore a shabby print dress. And in her face there was pure terror at seeing a white man at her door. Hastily I asked if Pres was there, and said I was a friend, and I had come to return his saxophone. She turned away and he came to the door and admitted me, almost eagerly. I remember everything as dark grey, the walls, the furniture, even the bed on which a small dark baby lay sleeping. Everything in that room bespoke an entire society's cruelty, denial of opportunity, denial of education, denial of one's very existence, indeed centuries of it. And pinned on one wall, unframed, was my photo. It was a proclamation, a statement.

It said: *I have a white friend.*

And for the first time in my life, I was ashamed of being white.

I lived in Louisville from 1955 through 1958, always impressed by the superb reporters who were my colleagues. Between the *Courier-Journal* and *Louisville Times,* we had some Nieman fellows, including Richard Harwood, later of *Washington Post* distinction, and a few Pulitzer Prize winners. The John Ogden Reid fellowship came up. Barry Bingham urged me to apply for it. He backed me and I got it.

It was a remarkably open fellowship. I went to Europe on it. I lived in Paris for a year, and attended almost every music, opera, drama, and film festival on the continent. That year was a superb education. I got a cable from the newspaper, and for a while I went back to work, covering the French negotiations to withdraw from Vietnam, and history (and Sir Richard Burton's dictum) became still more real to me. Later, when the Americans put forces on the ground there, I knew they were marching into disaster.

I returned to Louisville and the paper in the late winter of 1959. In March I was told by a friend, a publicist for the Disney studios who was visiting the city, that two jobs were open at *Down Beat* magazine, which was published in Chicago. The editor, Don Gold, had resigned, and the New York editor, Nat Hentoff, had also left. I wanted to move to New York, and so at my friend's urging (he actually placed the phone call), I spoke to Chuck Suber, the magazine's publisher. He asked me if I could come up to Chicago, at the magazine's expense, for a meeting. I made the trip, wanting that New York job. To my astonishment, I was offered the editor's chair.

I gave my notice at the *Louisville Times* and moved to Chicago. The first issue of the magazine I put out was that of April 16, and the first story I wrote for it was the obituary of Lester Young, yet another of my heroes, whose sufferings in the Army are part of the fabric of jazz—and racist—history.

In Louisville I was aware of the magnetic power of Chicago. When guitarist Jimmy Raney left Louisville, where he was born, he went not to New York but to Chicago. So did Lionel Hampton, although he went as a child with his parents. So too Jonah Jones, who was born in Louisville and played trumpet in local bands with names like Tinsley's Royal Aces and Perdue's Pirates. He moved up to Chicago to play with Stuff Smith.

I fell in love with Chicago the first time I saw it. It is visually the most striking city in America. Chicago surpasses New York in visual impact because of the way it is set up. It has not used up every square foot of ground for building. The edifices of its downtown section—the Loop, as it is known, for a now vanished streetcar line that made a loop there and for the elevated railroad that still does—are set amid plazas so that one can get a good look at them. Downtown Chicago is inspiring without being overwhelming. Chicago has grandeur, but it also has space.

Somewhere in its past its people did something not only smart but truly public-spirited. When everything in America from railway rights-of-way and mineral and lumbering rights to broadcasting licenses was being handed away wholesale to the robber barons by bought-and-paid-for politicians at all levels, Chicago somehow made a collective decision not to surrender its waterfront to what is known, not without irony, as free enterprise. Almost the entire frontage on Lake Michigan was reserved for public use, turned into what is in effect one huge spectacular park that runs almost from Evanston deep into the South Side. It takes on various names as it flows south, such as Lincoln Park, and it is interrupted briefly by a cluster of buildings in midtown, below which it becomes Grant Park and farther south Jackson and Washington Parks. And it is this huge swath of green, outlined on the west by tall buildings and on the east by beaches of pale sand, that lends the city its character, and a look that is a sort of cross between Nice and New York. No major city in America, perhaps in the world, has such an astonishing recreational resource. A gentle mood pervades this great lakefront green belt as young lovers and old ones walk hand-in-hand and joggers jog and mothers push baby carriages along its sidewalks and riders do their daily miles on its bicycle paths. Here and there boats snooze in the coves of its marinas, and out on that great blue fresh-water sea, tall sailboats go racing down the wind looking, in Malcolm Lowery's phrase, like white giraffes.

Modern high-rise building began in Chicago shortly after the great fire. It was in Chicago that the engineering genius William Le Baron Jenney invented the principle of skyscraper construction in 1873. The city's engineering innovations drew the brilliant architect Louis Sullivan to Chicago. He worked for Jenney, and when I arrived to live in Chicago, a number of his buildings were still around. They are disappearing now, cast bronze segments of their ornate facades being exhibited in museums and art galleries. It was Sullivan who first deplored the imitation of historical styles in building and called for an approach appropriate to the twentieth century. It was Sullivan who invented, and used in his writings and as the pivot of his philosophy, the phrase "form follows function." In 1887, Sullivan took on an eighteen-year-old assistant who became his passionate disciple and who always referred to Sullivan as "the Master." His name was Frank Lloyd Wright. With all due credit to Le Corbusier and Mies van der Rohe and the Saarinens and others, the principles that sent all those spires into the sky all over this planet were discovered by Jenney and applied by Sullivan. Crusty and uncompromising, Sullivan died, forgotten and in poverty, in Chicago in 1924. His relationship with Wright is echoed in Ayn Rand's *The Fountainhead*. Given the cumulative influence of that remarkable triumvirate, Jenney, Sullivan, and Wright, Chicago's importance in twentieth-century building exceeds that of any city and for that matter any country on earth.

Chicago has had its share of architectural frivolities, including the Wrigley building, which looks like a wedding cake, and the *Chicago Tribune* building, a goofy Gothic tower. Both buildings have, however, become so much a part of the Chicago cityscape that one would recoil in horror from any suggestion that they be removed.

The Chicago River, a two-branched stream of green water between stone walls, constantly plied by motorboats, flows in from the lake at the center of the city and then divides it into its north, south, and west sides. With its promenades and cafes, the river gives the downtown a little of the flavor of Paris. Downtown Chicago is a marvelous place in which to walk, and every corner you turn offers a discovery. The city has its share of urban blight and dangerous districts. But it also has sweet serene neighborhoods of old houses on polite streets thick with trees, and those parks, more than six thousand acres of them. My favorite is Lincoln Park, a riot of flowers all summer. Chicago has great stores, great hotels, and great museums, including the Art Institute of Chicago, the Field Museum, and the Museum of Science and Industry, and it is dense with universities and colleges.

And Chicago drips with story. "It's a gutsy city," says Audrey Morris, the singer and pianist, who for decades has been one of its fixtures. It is the city of the broad shoulders, as Carl Sandburg called it. It is the city of Sandburg, and Nelson Algren, and James Farrell, and Studs Terkel. It's the city of Al Capone (an adopted Chicagoan; he was from Brooklyn) and Machine Gun Jack McGurn and the St. Valentine's Day massacre, which happened only a few blocks from where I lived. So that bit of history too was real! A restaurant in the Rush Street area was named Elliot's Nesst. You can take a tour of the famous locations of the city's crooked past, including the movie theater where Melvin Purvis and fellow G-men gunned down John Dillinger. It's the city of the great fire caused, at least according to popular legend, by Mrs. O'Leary's cow; inevitably, there's a restaurant called Mrs. O'Leary's. The crenelated water tower on Michigan Avenue is the only building that remains from the fire.

Chicago has laughter. When a *New Yorker* writer called it the Second City and said it had a complex about its position relative to New York, Chicago just laughed—and some pioneering young actors started a company for improvised comedy called the Second City, whose influence on American drama in the past four decades has continued to spread. Chicago does not have a complex about New York; that's a New Yorker's conceit. Chicago is comfortable with itself, not smug like San Francisco or Toronto but unselfconsciously assured, and one of the reasons you have not heard of some of its best jazz players is that they won't leave. You can't pry them out of Chicago.

Although the importance of New Orleans in jazz history should not be slighted, it has been mythologized and oversimplified. Something like jazz was coming into being in various cities of the United States, in part as an aftermath of the popularity of ragtime, whose principal figure, Scott Joplin, was not from New Orleans but from Texas. As the late Bobby Scott wrote, when Louis Armstrong got to Chicago, he found a dialect of the music already there.

When I got to Chicago, it was aswarm with superior jazz musicians. Pittsburgh, Philadelphia, Detroit, have all nurtured great jazz players, but I don't think any city has produced anywhere near as many as Chicago.

The jazz people from Chicago and its immediate suburbs include Muhal Richard Abrams, Hayes Alvis, Albert Ammons, Gene Ammons, Vic Berton, Oscar Brashear, Ronnell Bright, Boyce Brown, Scoville Brown, Sid Catlett, Bob Cranshaw, Israel Crosby, Richard Davis, Jack DeJohnette, Dorothy Donegan, Joe Farrell, Bud Freeman, Russ Freeman, Von Freeman, John Frigo, Benny Goodman, Bennie Green, Lil Green, Johnny Griffin, Herbie Hancock, Eddie Harris, Johnny Hartman, Bill Henderson, Darnell Howard, Jimmy Jones, Jo Jones, Clifford Jordan, John Klemmer, Lee Konitz, Irene Kral, Roy Kral, Gene Krupa, Frankie Laine, Jim Lanigan, Ronny Lang, Lou Levy, Meade Lux Lewis, Abbey Lincoln, Ray Linn, Junior Mance, Joe Marsala, Marty Marsala, Dick Marx, Al McKibbon, Dick McPartland, Jimmy McPartland, Mezz Mezzrow, Johnny Mince, Ray Nance, Jack Noren, Hod O'Brien, Anita O'Day, Truck Parham, Ben Pollack, Julian Priester, Gil Rodin, Bill Russo, Muggsy Spanier, Victor Sproles, Joe Sullivan, Edmund Thigpen, Mel Tormé, Cy Touff, Dave Tough, Lennie Tristano, Wilbur Ware, Eugene Wright, Jimmy Yancey, and Denny Zeitlin.

That's only a partial list. Nor does it include all those people who, like Franz Jackson, Don Murray, Omer Simeon, George Wettling, and Joe Williams, were born elsewhere but grew up in and were shaped by Chicago. Eddie South was born in Missouri, but his parents moved to Chicago when he was three months old. Then there were all the players and singers who were drawn to Chicago from all the cities around it, people like Bix Beiderbecke from Davenport, Iowa, Woody Herman from Milwaukee, Wisconsin, Peggy Lee from Jamestown, North Dakota, and from farther away. The bassist John Levy was born in New Orleans but lived in Chicago from the time he was eight. So too Milt Hinton, born in Vicksburg, Mississippi, and Nat Cole, born in Montgomery, Alabama, but raised in Chicago.

I was quickly made aware of the significance in Chicago's musical life of two remarkable black music educators, strict disciplinarians with military backgrounds, both of whom insisted on being called by their military titles. Major N. Clark Smith taught at Wendell Phillips High School, named for the famous Boston abolitionist. When he left to take over the music department of a St. Louis high school, he was replaced by Captain Walter Dyett. Captain Dyett went from Wendell Phillips to DuSable High School, where he headed the orchestra and music program.

DuSable was named for the man who founded Chicago, a black man from Haiti. In 1779, Jean Baptist Point du Sable established a settlement at the mouth of the Chicago River, just east of the present Michigan Avenue Bridge. He was a man of taste, a carpenter, a cooper, a miller, and probably a distiller. He married an Indian woman, and the first election in Chicago history was held in his home.

Captain Dyett had played violin and banjo in Erskine Tate's Vendome Theater Orchestra, and conducted the all-black Eighth Regiment Army Band. He and Major N. Clark Smith were teaching jazz as a formal subject three decades before the high school and college jazz education movement arose in white colleges and high schools. His students included John Young, Gene Ammons, Johnny Griffin, Ray Nance, Von Freeman, Julian Priester, Joseph Jarman, Pat Patrick, Clifford Jordan, Eddie Harris, Bo Diddley (on violin), Wilbur Ware, Victor Sproles, Dorothy Donegan, Wilbur Campbell, Walter Perkins, Dinah Washington, Johnny Hartman, and Richard Davis, who said, "Maybe you weren't afraid of the cops, but you were afraid of Captain Dyett." Walter Dyett staged a Hi-Jinks Show every spring to buy instruments for the band because the school board declined to do so.

Only New Orleans, in the early days, compares to Chicago for the number of important jazz musicians it produced. What is more, the significance of Chicago in the gestation of jazz becomes all the more conspicuous when you consider those figures who were born in New Orleans but spent the largest part of their careers and died in Chicago: George Brunis, Lee Collins, Baby and Johnny Dodds, Freddie Keppard, John Lindsey, Paul Mares, and Fats Pichon among them. Though he was born ten miles out of New Orleans, and died in California, Jimmy Noone spent most of the 1920s and a good part of the '30s in Chicago, where he exerted a formative influence.

The reason for this flowering of jazz in Chicago is obvious: the speakeasies. When the Volstead Act was passed in 1919, Chicago made it perfectly clear that it had no intention of abiding by it, and the illegal sale of liquor built immense fortunes for gangsters and compromised the politics of the city. Chicago roared, in more ways than one, and the proliferating speakeasies created work for musicians playing "hot" music. When Chicago musicians like Sid Catlett, Jo Jones, Gene Krupa, and Dave Tough were in their adolescence in the 1920s, there were all sorts of places for them to play. With the repeal of Prohibition in 1933, the gangsters simply turned the speaks into nightclubs. So there were still places to work. And by then the Chicago musicians had changed the face of American music.

There was a dark side to this. The gangsters considered themselves the owners of the musicians, who were chained to their jobs, as on plantations. This was true of not only musicians but all entertainers who worked in the mob circuits, and not only black entertainers either. Singer Joe E. Lewis got his throat cut when he quit one job for another, and he became a standup comic afterward. Lucky Millinder (born in Alabama, raised in Chicago, alumnus of Wendell Phillips High), led a band for the Capones in their Cotton Club in Cicero, just outside Chicago. Ralph Capone told him, "My brother Al and I decided we're going to keep you boys working regularly, but you can't work for nobody but us." Roy Kral once had a band in a Capone-owned joint near Northwestern University.

When trumpeter and saxophonist George Dixon and two other musicians left the Earl Hines band at the Grand Terrace to join Don Redman in Detroit, they arrived only to be told by Redman's manager that the word had come down from the Purple Gang, which controlled Detroit, that they couldn't work for Redman. Dixon said later, "The three of us jumped into my little Ford and came back to Chicago. The mob, through intimidation and organization, had things so well-regulated we couldn't even change jobs."

Billy Eckstine, who sang at the Club DeLisa, told one of the three brothers who owned it that he wanted to join the Earl Hines band. "When the DeLisa brothers didn't want you to go," Eckstine told Dempsey Travis, who quotes the story in his book *The Autobiography of Black Jazz* (1983) "they would take you downstairs and walk you into the icebox and do a number on you." Since they didn't do that to him, he figured, "somebody up there with an iron fist in kidskin gloves was giving me an awful lot of help." He meant somebody with the Capone group, which had more muscle.

That bootleggers and killers should have contributed so much to the development of jazz is ironic; they hardly saw themselves as patrons of the arts. Yet they were de facto patrons of this one art, and nowhere in the country as much as in Chicago.

Artie Shaw, who at the age of sixteen made a pilgrimage to Chicago to hear Louis Armstrong, said, "If Louis had never lived, there would no doubt be something we would call jazz. But it would not be the same." If you consider what jazz has been throughout most of its history—a largely homophonic music dominated by great improvising soloists, each player in turn making his contribution to the music, rather than a polyphonic collective as exemplified by the Original Dixieland Jazz Band and Jelly Roll Morton's groups—then you have to give serious consideration to the idea that it was born in Chicago. For it was in Chicago that Armstrong developed this approach to it, influencing Coleman Hawkins and every other major jazz player who followed.

Bud Freeman is quoted in the Dempsey Travis book: "It's been said that New Orleans is the cradle of jazz. I say that's nonsense. Louis and Joe Oliver were the most talented men to come out of New Orleans, and they didn't really get their style together until they came into Chicago and started playing what we call show tunes. It was then that they developed a new style, and of course Louis had the creative genius to make this kind of music both palatable and jazzy."

Freeman was part of the so-called Austin High Gang, with Jimmy and Dick McPartland, Jim Lanigan, and Frank Teschemacher. Dave Tough played with their group, though he went to Oak Park High. Also growing up in Chicago at that time were Benny Goodman, who played on lake boats, and Gene Krupa, who went to Bowen High, Jo Jones, and all the others born in the early years of the twentieth century. All those young men were listening to Louis Armstrong and Bix Beiderbecke, who spent formative years in Chicago, and Benny Goodman was listening to Jimmie Noone. The development of Armstrong's solo style in Chicago, and the rapid dissemination of his influence through young men born in Chicago or drawn there by the magnet of his playing, give the city a significance to jazz that exceeds that of any other. Artie Shaw says the Chicago players learned not to rush, they figured out something about holding back, and he points to Gene Krupa as an example of that beautiful steady Chicago time.

The influence of Chicago musicians on jazz evolution was incalculable. Consider the career of Eddie South. A child prodigy on violin, he had extensive formal training in Chicago, and had the "classical" music world been open to black musicians in his time—and it still is not very open—it is almost certain that he would not have been a jazz musician. Even while he was studying at the Chicago Musical College, he was working with Erskine Tate's and other bands, and was musical director of Jimmy Wade's Syncopators in the mid-1920s at the Moulin Rouge in Chicago. He went overseas to study in Budapest and Paris. For all his travels, he always returned to Chicago, and had his own television series there in the 1950s. He was working at the DuSable Hotel until a few weeks before his death in 1962, at the age of fifty-eight. He was a lovely, sweet player, with a prodigious and very "legit" technique. And his influence spread far beyond Chicago: he is considered a major inspiration for the Django Reinhardt–Stephane Grappelli Quintet of the Hot Club of France. Listening to South's group with Everett Barksdale on guitar, you can hear why.

It is a further irony that racism actually contributed to the development of jazz. The exclusion from classical music of such violinists as South, Milt Hinton, and George Duvivier diverted their talents into jazz, in the case of Hinton and Duvivier, as bassists. I think it is possible that Hank Jones would have become a concert pianist had that road been open to him. James P. Johnson aspired to a life in classical music. Such musicians, with substantial training, enriched jazz.

The bassist with the Eddie South group for a long period in the 1930s was Milt Hinton. Hinton played violin in his Chicago high school orchestra. He says in his book *Bass Lines: The Stories and Photographs of Milt Hinton* (1988) that the orchestra played only "serious music, not jazz." He says that the "music was written out and there was no ad libbing whatsoever." Hinton switched to bass to make a living and, after his period with Eddie South, joined Cab Calloway. When the band played Chicago, he would study with Dmitri Shmulkovsky of the Civic Opera orchestra.

Jelly Roll Morton made his first trip to Chicago before World War I, then returned to the city in 1923 to make it the base of his travels and, of course, the center of his recording activities with his Red Hot Peppers.

Louis Armstrong arrived in Chicago to join King Oliver in the summer of 1922. Jazz did not go up the river to Chicago, as legend had it; Armstrong arrived by train. His records with Oliver, and later the crucially important series with his own Hot Five and Hot Seven, were made in Chicago. Artistically, Armstrong's period of residency in Chicago—recording, playing with his wife Lil's band and with Erskine Tate and Carroll Dickerson—was the most fertile of his life. The association with Earl Hines began in Chicago. Armstrong's influence on Hines during that period is another crucial factor in the development of the music.

Throughout the 1920s, Chicago was probably the most active jazz recording center in the country. It was also a major broadcasting center, more so at first than New York, presenting all manner of music. The prodigious pianist and composer Lee Sims, whose work was admired by Art Tatum, was heard regularly from

Chicago on radio in the early 1930s. His harmonic practice anticipated what Stan Kenton would do with a big band fifteen years
later. Zez Confrey, the pianist and composer who wrote *Kitten
on the Keys, Stumbling,* and *Dizzy Fingers,* was born in Peru,
Illinois, and educated at Chicago Musical College. His hundreds
of piano rolls, while not jazz, contributed greatly to America's
feeling for syncopated music. By the early 1930s there were regular nightly broadcasts by big bands from such Chicago locales as
the Grand Terrace, Trianon, and Aragon ballrooms, the Edgewater Beach hotel, the Panther Room of the Sherman Hotel, and
the Blackhawk restaurant. The effect on the country's musical
tastes is inestimable.

Chicago developed a school of tenor playing all its own, musicians whose work puts you in mind of Sandburg's term, big shoulders, and of Audrey Morris's word, gutsy. People like Gene Ammons and Johnny Griffin. Their playing is big, like the singing of
Joe Williams. The city thinks that way. Chicago is the end of the
East, the beginning of the West. Frank Harris's *Memoirs of My
Life as a Cowboy* starts in Chicago.

When I arrived in Chicago to live in April 1959, there were
jazz clubs everywhere. The city tended to be divided in two, the
North Side, whose population was white, and the South Side,
whose population was black. The division was the legacy of covenants put in place in the 1920s. At one time, as in other cities,
the musicians' union was divided into separate locals, black and
white, but that had broken down by the time I got there.

On the North Side, the clubs included the Bambu, the Continental, and Jazz Ltd., all of which catered to traditional jazz.
There you could hear the iron-lipped trombonist Georg Brunis
or Bob Scobey's band or Franz Jackson and his Jass All-Stars.
Mr. Kelly's featured singers, such as Ella Fitzgerald, Sarah
Vaughan, Betty Bennett, and Anita O'Day. The Cloister presented groups like the Miles Davis Quintet. In the Loop, at Clark

and Madison, was Frank Holzfiend's Blue Note of fond memory. The London House, at the windswept corner of Michigan Avenue and Wacker Drive, right on the river, featured jazz, including the groups of Oscar Peterson, Jack Teagarden, Kai Winding, and Earl Hines.

On the South Side, there were such places as the C and C Lounge, Lake Meadows, Budland, the Disc Jockey Lounge, McKee's, the Club DeLisa, the Coral Club, the Kitty Kat, the Trocadero, and the lounge of the Sutherland Hotel. And two South Side theaters presented jazz, the Tivoli and the Regal.

An agent in the Chicago office of Associated Booking, Joe Glaser's company, told me that there were at least a hundred clubs presenting jazz in greater Chicago, or Chicagoland as it was called by journalists.

There were countless musicians and singers who were hardly known outside Chicago, including the stupefyingly versatile trumpeter and saxophonist Ira Sullivan, master of any instrument he picked up, and the magnificent Lurlean Hunter, one of the best singers I've ever heard. Another of my first Chicago friends was the great tenor saxophonist Johnny Griffin, who told me: "The people in New York always seem surprised when musicians come in from Chicago and stand out so well when they're in sessions at Birdland and other places. But it's going on here all the time.

"Cats live and die right here and get no recognition. You have to go to New York to make it. And if you don't have any connections there, it's like starting all over. You have to get into certain little cliques. But I suppose in a way you can't fight New York. That's where everything is.

"San Francisco is the city in the situation most like Chicago's, I suppose. For the West Coast, that's it. San Francisco is all right. But it isn't like Chicago. They don't have the joints.

"Chicago is a city of joints and churches."

The late Leonard Feather, who began writing about jazz in the 1930s, knew personally almost every important jazz musician who had ever lived, because the founding figures were still active. Jelly Roll Morton lived until 1941. Sidney Bechet died only a few weeks after I joined *Down Beat*, and many of the major figures in this music were still going even then. If Leonard knew them all, I realize, I met most of them. I was more than a little awed to shake hands with Louis Armstrong. I came to know Duke Ellington moderately well, and Buddy Rich very well. I knew Jimmy McPartland, George Wettling, Art Hodes, Franz Jackson, and many more of their generation. I renewed my acquaintance with Oscar Peterson and Ray Brown, and the drummer in the Peterson trio of that time, Edmund Thigpen, became (and remains) one of my best friends. Horace Silver became a friend. And Woody Herman, in time, became like a father to me. Donald Byrd became a close friend.

Indeed, within a matter of months, I knew almost everyone in jazz, including many of the heroes of my adolescence, such as Count Basie and the members of the band, and I made most of the friendships that would last long after I left the magazine to move to New York, and indeed would last the rest of my life. Art Farmer, Paul Desmond, Gerry Mulligan, and Bill Evans soon were among my closest friends; I have lived to look around and find them no longer there.

This is how I came to know Miles Davis. He won the *Down Beat* readers' poll. I was to present him the plaque, an eighth note in brass mounted on a wooden shield, at the Regal Theater, a prominent vaudeville house on the South Side. I met him at the microphone and made some appropriately stupid little speech and handed him the plaque. The audience watching us was almost entirely black.

Unsmiling, Miles said, "Why didn't you make it black, like I *am?*" It was like a finger stabbing you in the chest.

I sensed something about Miles in that moment. If you backed down from him, you would remain perpetually off balance. I sucked in my breath and said, "Mr. Davis, I don't think they grow wood that dark."

The entire audience went up in laughter. And Miles broke into a smile, that devastating, melting smile of his. We were friends from then on.

That Miles had angers should surprise no one. Born not only to comfort but to wealth, he was in as much danger in his travels in this country as any other black American. He was given to provocative remarks, such as the one he made to me when I proffered that plaque. Artie Shaw was disturbed by something Miles once said, which was widely quoted: "I want to kill one white man before I die."

I laughed when I heard that, wondering which white man he'd said it to, and what the man had done to provoke it. For in another incident, when a black rhythm-and-blues producer presumed intimacy on the basis of color with Miles—an incredible folly—Miles growled, "You're the right color, but you're still a stupid motherfucker."

And once Miles said to me, actually hurt and baffled, "Gene, why do they call me a racist when my manager is Jack Whittemore and my best friend is Gil Evans?"

My immediate boss at *Down Beat* was Charles Suber, with whom I became good friends. His title was publisher. Above him was Lou Didier, whose title was president. But the man who retained tight control was the owner, John Maher, a wealthy former printer who had taken over the magazine when the previous owners had failed to pay their printing bill. He had no knowledge of jazz and certainly no interest in it. The West Coast editor was John Tynan, called Jack or Jake, a fine journalist who had been trained at the Hearst newspapers. Maher once said to him, "A Jew can't let a dollar pass through his hands without keeping ten cents of it." He knew full well that Jack's wife was Jewish.

After I had been at the magazine about a year, Lou Didier came into my office and said, "Mr. Maher says to tell you: no more Negroes on the cover." Aside from ethical considerations, the order was patently stupid: most of the magazine's poll winners were black, and to bar them from the cover was to exclude precisely those artists who were most popular with readers and thus likely to generate newsstand sales.

I told Didier, "You can give Mr. Maher a message from me: I quit."

Didier, flustered, went to Chuck Suber's office and told him he would have to speak to me: I was going to quit.

"Why?" Chuck asked.

Didier told him.

Chuck said, "Give Mr. Maher a message from me: I quit too."

The order was quietly withdrawn.

No white person can even begin to understand the black experience in the United States. One can only try, and in the process imagine a life of constant insult and rejection and punishment, and danger from the police. Perhaps there is a clue in Kafka's *The Trial*, in which a man is tried for a crime unspecified. He cannot defend himself because he does not know the charge. As Andy Razaf wrote in a famous lyric, "What did I do, to be so black and blue?" I told one black friend in Louisville, "Had I been born Negro in this country, I'd have probably killed somebody before I was twenty."

"No you wouldn't," he said. "You'd have learned to live with it, as we do."

Maybe. And maybe that suppression is the reason for the incidence of hypertension and cardiac problems and a whole range of ailments in black American men. In many ways I find the anger of Spike Lee easier to comprehend than the broad humanity of Nat Cole, Dizzy Gillespie, Clark Terry, and Milton Hinton, among others.

All four men were among my heroes. I met Dizzy and Clark in Chicago, during those first months at *Down Beat*.

Birks and His Works

The week after Dizzy Gillespie's death in January 1993, a note-worthy obituary appeared in *Newsweek*. It was exceptional if only because the magazine devoted a full page to him; departed jazz musicians are rarely accorded such respect in the lay press. Written by David Gates, it took the measure of the man and the artist with precision and perception.

"You didn't need to know anything about Dizzy Gillespie's paradoxical career," Gates wrote, "or his more paradoxical personality to discern that he was a lively mix of contradictions—you only had to hear him play. His trumpet solos often sounded like duets. He'd catfoot around, toying subversively with the chord structure and the rhythm: that was the wryly self-mocking Dizzy who, when asked if his trademark goatee was an affectation, said, 'No, it's a fetish.' Then he'd shift into musical warp drive, a streak of notes blazing across the tune's inner sky; that was the Dizzy who saw himself, proudly and accurately, as jazz's last hero trumpeter. 'I'm on a direct line from Buddy Bolden,' he once said. 'After Bolden there was King Oliver, Louis Armstrong, . . . Roy Eldridge, and me.' Gillespie was an artist and an entertainer, an avant-gardist and a throwback. Small wonder that when he talked about his Baha'i faith, what seemed important to him was its doctrine of unity. 'They say the prophets are one; if I believe that, I also believe that music is one and that Louis Armstrong and I are one and the same.'"

I met Dizzy shortly after I joined *Down Beat* in 1959, and I was enchanted by the man. Everyone I ever met who knew him was similarly captivated. He was not only one of the greatest musicians of our time, he was brilliantly insightful, shrewdly observant, and—when he wasn't discussing something seriously—unfailingly funny. I not only remember the moment of meeting him, I have a picture of it. I had gone with my photographer friend Ted Williams to get a picture of him at a nightclub in the Loop called the Preview, where he was appearing. He immediately asked if I could play chess, to which I had to answer, "No."

"What? You can't? I'll teach you." And he tried. The chess lesson was a failure; the friendship was not.

As I got to know him in that period of his life, I sensed a hurt that he was being treated by the press as a secondary figure in the evolution of jazz during the 1940s, while his late friend Charlie Parker (who had been dead four years at this point) had been elevated to a higher plane, held in almost religious reverence.

Jazz criticism has from the earliest days been plagued by puritanism. Much of the writing about it has come from what is known, often imprecisely, as the political left.

Puritanism, as H. L. Mencken defined it, is "the haunting fear that someone, somewhere, may be happy." To those who succumb to it, it is hard to perceive anything as having value only because it is beautiful or exciting, or merely diverting. This leads

Birks, Chicago, 1960 (Photo by Ted Williams)

to the belief that all art is propaganda. Abbey Lincoln said this in an interview. Whether she meant that it was, since it inevitably expressed *somebody*'s vision, or should be, I cannot say. But I do know that as an underlying assumption, it leads to the view that art should be *doing* something, accomplishing something, and more specifically the reform and improvement and advancement of society. It is art seen as utility.

Stravinsky asserted that music is about music. But that doesn't sit well with some people, and those who fulfill Mencken's dictum often resent success. In jazz, particularly, this has led to attacks on those who attain it, such as Dave Brubeck and the late Cannonball Adderley. Jazz admirers pride themselves on the superiority, and indeed exclusivity, of their taste. And for all the breast-beating that goes on in the panel discussions at those bizarre periodic conferences of jazz critics and editors and educators and producers and others who circle about the art—reiterating year after year that "We've got to do something about the state of jazz!"—the fact is that all too many of its fans don't really *want* it to be widely accepted, for popularity would end its talismanic emanations as proof of rarefied taste and exalted sensitivity. In other words, nothing would displease the stone jazz fan more than for the music to become truly, massively popular. What the public likes is usually bad. Ergo, anything the public likes is bad; which does not truly follow. What the public *doesn't* like is necessarily good, which also doesn't follow. But these are often the tacit assumptions.

There are exceptions to these generalizations. An artist who is widely admired *may* be worthy of consideration *if* he or she has suffered a miserable life. This gets a lot of drunks and junkies into the pantheon on a pass. Some of them, to be sure, deserve to be there, but the right artist may be elected for the wrong reason. Bill Evans almost certainly would not have received the immense reverence his memory evokes (and deserves) had he been in his personal life as stable and prosperous as, say, Dave Brubeck or John Lewis. Much of the mystique surrounding Bix Beiderbecke grows out of his short and tragic alcoholic life, rather than from his gifts as an artist. Lenny Bruce is celebrated as much for his crucifixion by the "authorities" as for the brilliance of his insights. There is an implicit condescension in this process: I can admire him because I feel sorry for him, affirming my own superiority. Condescension to brilliance is the ultimate arrogance. America, land of ambition and success, has, paradoxically, an ongoing love affair with failure and premature death.

Dizzy Gillespie made some mistakes, but despite a miserable childhood, he achieved happiness, a stable marriage, and a status as an almost regal ambassador of his music and his country. His life was an unrolling carpet of laughter and achievement.

Alyn Shipton, the English musician, commentator, and BBC broadcaster, is the author of *Groovin' High: The Life of Dizzy Gillespie* (1999), the first biography to be published after Dizzy's death. Shipton contends: "Perhaps because of Dizzy's longevity compared to bebop's other principal character, Charlie Parker, who burned out at the age of thirty-four in 1955, and perhaps also because of his cheerful demeanor and obvious talents as a showman and entertainer, his contribution to jazz's major revolutionary movement has been consistently underrated. Yet in many ways he was a far more wide-ranging, original, and innovative musician than Parker, possessed of a similarly miraculous instrumental talent, but with a ruthless determination to achieve and, for much of his life, a clear sense of direction."

At another point, Shipton writes: "Jazz is a music full of thrilling sounds. It can also span the full breadth of human emotion from exhilaration to profound sadness, from love to alienation, from celebration to commiseration. . . . Dizzy Gillespie's music has managed to inhabit all of them, while simultaneously conveying more of the sheer joy and excitement of jazz than that of any other musician."

Farther on, he says, "Dizzy was always modest about his own contribution to bebop. Partly in deference to the memory of Charlie Parker, he always stressed Parker's input at the expense of his own. . . . By being the one who organized the principal ideas of the beboppers into an intellectual framework, Dizzy was the key figure who allowed the music to progress beyond a small and restricted circle of after-hours enthusiasts. . . . Modern jazz might have happened without Dizzy, but it would not have had so clearly articulated a set of harmonic and rhythmic precepts, nor so dramatic a set of recorded examples of these being put into practice."

I remember Nat Adderley coming out of a corridor backstage at some jazz festival in the 1960s, grinning so broadly that I asked him, "What are you so happy about?"

Nat said, "Dizzy just showed me some shit on the horn that I don't *believe!*"

I mentioned this to Nat two or three years before he died, asking if he remembered the incident. "Yeah!" he said. "I not only remember it, I still remember what he *showed* me!"

A few months after the Preview engagement, Dizzy played in Milwaukee, which was a comfortable drive north of Chicago. Ted Williams wanted to get more pictures of him, and we spent a few days with him there.

The press seemed to be passing him by. Miles Davis was the new "man." Yet Miles told me, "I got it all from Dizzy," which was something of a hyperbole, since he got some of "it" from Freddie Webster, and some from Bix Beiderbecke, including the spaced, airy approach to phrasing. When I asked Miles if he had listened to Bix, he said, "No, but I listened to Bobby Hackett, and *he* listened to Bix." But there is no question that his major inspiration was Dizzy. Interestingly, Hackett was friends with both Dizzy and Miles. In the summer of 1960, Dizzy was only forty-two, nine years older than Miles.

About the time I met him, at least one critic—British—was talking of Dizzy's better days, as if it could be taken for granted that the best was in the past. I thought he was playing better than he ever had in his life. But, as he put it simply: "I just don't see my name in the magazines any more."

As for the comparisons to Miles, Dizzy said, "I'm a Miles Davis fan myself." A black journalist, noted for being a signifying monkey always attempting to start feuds among black artists, tried to goad him into criticizing Miles. This infuriated Dizzy. His geniality vanished. He told the man, "How do I know why Miles walks off the stage? Why don't you ask him? And besides, maybe we'd all like to be like Miles, and just haven't got the guts."

In 1961, Dizzy told me this story of how he got his famous uptilted trumpet: "It was four or five years ago, at my wife's birthday party. I had to do a disc jockey show and left it on the stand. And everybody was having a ball while I was gone. Stump and Stumpy"—a well-known comic team—"were on the stage, kidding around. And someone pushed over my horn.

"So Illinois Jacquet, he left! *Immediately*. He said he didn't want to be there when I got back.

"I was mad. Then I play it a little bit and I say, 'Oh my goodness! Isn't this something?' But next day I had it straightened back. After about three weeks, I wrote to the Martin company and asked if they could make me one like this.

"I've had several of them since then—five at one time, when we toured the Middle East. It looked good. It sounded nice, too.

"Guys play down into the music stands and you don't get the full value with ordinary horns. And trumpet is a piercing instrument. It'll bust your ear drums if you're up close and there are four or five of them coming at you at one time. But if it gets a chance to spread first . . .

"And besides, you can hear yourself play better with this horn."

Alyn Shipton suggests that another factor may have influenced Dizzy's adoption of the new horn. Shipton says that there was in one of the English orchestras a trumpet player who had eyesight problems. He had a horn built with the bell tilted upward, so that it was out of the line of vision when he was reading music. Dizzy met that man. He may have filed that image in his head and eventually had a horn built to similar specifications. I remember one of his early bent horns: the bell was detachable for packing away, and it attached to the horn with a little thumb screw. Later Dizzy had horns built in his preferred configuration and had a trumpet case made to accommodate the odd shape.

Ray Brown was playing bass with the Luis Russell band. It was working in Miami, Ray recalled. "Three other guys and I began plotting to get to New York and try our luck," Ray told me. "But the night before we were to go, everybody chickened out, leaving me with my bags all packed. So I said, 'The hell with it,' and went.

"I got to New York, took my bags to my aunt's place, and the very same night had my nephew take me down to show me where Fifty-second Street was.

"That night, I saw Erroll Garner, Art Tatum, Billie Holiday, Billy Daniels, Coleman Hawkins, and Hank Jones. I'd known Hank before. While we were talking, he said, 'Dizzy Gillespie just came in.' I said, 'Where? Introduce me! I want to meet him!'

"So Hank introduced us. Hank said to Dizzy, 'This is Ray Brown, a friend of mine, and a very good bass player.'

"Dizzy said, 'You want a gig?' I almost had a heart attack! Dizzy said, 'Be at my house for rehearsal at seven o'clock tomorrow.'

"I went up there next night, and got the fright of my life. The band consisted of Dizzy, Bud Powell, Max Roach, Charlie Parker—and *me!* Two weeks later, we picked up Milt Jackson, who was my roommate for two years. We were inseparable. They called us the twins. Milt and I did some *starving* to death together at times. Milt introduced me to my wife, Cecille. They'd been kids together.

"After I'd been with Dizzy about a month and figured I had everything down, I cornered him after the gig and said, 'Diz, how'm I doin'?' He said, 'Oh—fine. Except you're playing the wrong notes.'

"That did it. I started delving into everything we did, the notes, the chords, everything. And I'd sing the lines as I was playing them."

Dizzy told me: "Ray Brown's always been that type of guy, very, very inquisitive. On *I'm Through with Love*, we get to one place where the words go, *for I mean to care*— Right there, that word *care*." (Freddy Cole, Nat Cole's brother, once pointed out to me that all the older musicians knew all the lyrics.) Continuing, Dizzy explained, "The melody went up to an E-flat, B-natural, and G-flat, and that sounds like an A-flat minor seventh chord. *Sounds* like it. So I told Ray, 'Now, Ray, you're making A-flat there. Your ears are good. Make a D there.' He say, 'But you're making A-flat minor seventh.' I say, 'No, I'm not.' He say, 'Show me.' So I take him to the piano and play D and there's the same note up there in the D. And he say, 'Ah-*hah!* But I had to show him. He'd have done it anyway, because I'm the one playing the solo. But Ray wanted to know why."

One morning in 1989, I was riding in a taxi with Benny Golson. "Dizzy was talking about Art Farmer last night," Benny told me. "Dizzy said, 'Did you hear Art's recording of *U.M.M.G.*?'" He referred to Billy Strayhorn's *Upper Manhattan Medical Group*. "The first recording of it I heard was Dizzy's, that he did with Duke. He just happened to come by the studio that day, when they were recording, and he just happened to have his horn. Duke said, 'Take your horn out.' He didn't quite understand the tune, and so Swee'pea, Billy Strayhorn, said, 'Well look, this is the way it goes.' And he played and it was fantastic."

So I told Benny and Art a story about that recording. Dizzy was talking to me one day about critics and how wrong they could be about a performance. Playing devil's advocate, I defended them, saying, "And listen, Birks, haven't you ever been wrong about one of your own performances?"

He thought for a minute. "Yes," he answered, and told me

about the *Upper Manhattan Medical Group* session. He thought he played badly because he had just looked at the tune for the first time. A short time later, Duke called to ask him to sign a contract form so he could be paid for the session. Dizzy said, "You're not going to put that *out*, are you?"

Ellington insisted that it was a good recording. Dizzy signed the paper and forgot about it.

Some time later, he continued, "I was driving along in my car. I turned on the radio, and got this cat playing trumpet. I listened and said, 'Hey, he's stealing my shit! And he's *good* at it.' And I kept getting more bugged, and then I realized it was me, on *Upper Manhattan Medical Group.*"

Art and Benny laughed, and then Benny told us: "Dizzy and I talked about an hour on the phone last night. I called him in Atlanta. I told him that many people can follow those who are already taking the lead. But when he came along, he was stepping out into dark places, at some personal risk, I guess—risk of being ridiculed. Louis Armstrong said something like, 'They play like they're playing with a mouthful of hot rice.' Where's the melody? The bass drum is dropping too many bombs. There were all kinds of derogatory things said about them. And now today, it's the standard.

"When John Coltrane and I—we were together every day during that time—went to the Academy of Music in Philadelphia to hear Dizzy in 1945, and they started to play, we almost fell off the balcony. Because we had been playing with local bands. And we all were used to playing—" He sang an example of swing era riffing. "And all of a sudden, Dizzy was playing other things, things we had never heard, and you can't imagine the impact it had on me. I told Dizzy last night that that moment changed my whole life, and I've spent the rest of my life trying to comprehend what it's all about. It's so limitless. It's perpetual. Of course, Dizzy is so modest, I could hear the embarrassment coming through the phone.

"He was always didactic. Really. He was a teacher without even intending to be."

"And he makes no claims whatsoever for himself," I said.

"He gets embarrassed," Benny said. "Like a little boy."

I told him that Bobby Scott had argued that the rhythm sections were ten years behind Bird and Dizzy.

"That's true," Benny said. "They were playing boom-chank boom-chank."

Not long after that, I told Dizzy, "Everybody I've ever talked to, Phil Woods, Benny Golson, Art Farmer, said you have always been the great teacher. I remember Nat Adderley saying, 'Dizzy's the greatest teacher in the world if you don't let him know he's doing it.'"

"Is that true? I don't know about that," he said. "But what little I do know, I'll give it, any time. So I guess it's not actually someone with a whole lot of knowledge giving it out to people. But anything I learned, I'll tell somebody else. So that's what they mean by that. I will tell anything that I've learned."

Dizzy hired pianist Junior Mance as casually as he did Ray Brown, and began teaching him. Junior had been working with Cannonball Adderley, but the group broke up. Dizzy encountered him on the street in New York and asked what he was doing. "Nothing," Junior shrugged.

"The rehearsal is at my house," Dizzy said, and handed him a card with his address on it.

"That's how it started," Junior said. "In the three years I played with Dizzy, I think I learned more musically than in all the years I studied with teachers and in music schools. Besides his being a hell of a nice guy.

"We lived near each other in Long Island. He lived in Corona and I lived in East Elmhurst. Two villages, you might say, right next to each other. I was, like, a five-minute walk away from his house.

"You never knew what he was going to do. I used to try to play at tennis. And so did he. He'd say, 'Let's go play tennis.' I figured we're going to a court or something. We'd go out and find an open field in Queens and just hit the ball back and forth.

"It was always exciting. I remember when the band was in Pittsburgh once. One day he took a walk. He saw a firehouse. Some of the firemen were playing chess. He sat down and wiped them all out. They told him to come back the next day. And he did. He was always relaxed and nonchalant about everything. He was a man who could converse with anybody on any subject. It really amazed me. He could meet people in other walks of life, far removed from music, and hold the most brilliant conversation. He had a picture in his house of him and former chief justice of the Supreme Court Earl Warren, playing chess on a plane. They had the board on a support between the seats.

"I used to spend time with him in his basement, where he had his own private little studio. He would show me things on the piano. But he never forced you to play any way you weren't comfortable. I got the impression that he knew how you played before he hired you. And by listening to him, I would think you would have to get better. It's like Miles Davis said, any trumpet player who played in Dizzy's big band and didn't improve didn't have it to begin with.

"Everybody who played with him improved. Especially drummers. He made so many guys who were just average drummers into fantastic drummers. I didn't hear Charlie Persip before he played with Dizzy, but somebody told me he was just another drummer. After a while with Dizzy's big band, he was one of the most fantastic big-band drummers, *and* small-group drummers, around.

"Dizzy had such a great sense of rhythm. He could teach you any kind of rhythm. It was almost as though he'd invented the rhythms. Rhythms you might think you'd been playing right for years, and one little thing he injected would change the whole thing.

"Dizzy was a master of programming. He'd fit the situation, it was like tailor-made for each room. He'd use the same tunes, but maybe in a different way each time. That's one of the things I learned from him, how to program things. So many of the young cats now, they'll get up there, they'll play one tune after another the same tempo, they'll play all they know each tune. They're good musicians, but you can't get an audience that way. Dizzy would mix it up, he knew how to do it. I do it myself. I'll do it in a different way. I'll start with one rhythm or one tempo, and a ballad, then maybe throw a blues in there. But it's all stuff that I like. And this is what I noticed about Dizzy. He wasn't Tomming, or bending over backwards to get anybody's attention—even when we played *School Days*. After a while, *we* began to like *School Days*, too, because that shuffle rhythm will get you every time. I like shuffle rhythm. And Dizzy, being Dizzy, when he put that horn up, it worked, and I said, 'Wow, yeah!'"

Junior left to form his own group with Dizzy's firm support and permanent friendship. Like pianist Mike Longo and others, Junior became part of Dizzy's reserve army of musicians who would go anywhere, do anything, for him. Junior played with him for a week at the Blue Note on the last gig of Dizzy's life.

Dizzy always gave a gift to his fellows: knowledge. And his was immense, unfathomable.

He was born John Birks Gillespie in Cheraw, South Carolina, on October 21, 1917, the youngest of nine children, seven of whom survived. Dizzy told friends and interviewers that he was terrified of his father, James Gillespie, a bricklayer and weekend piano player who beat him and his brothers every Sunday morning, whether they had done anything wrong during the week or not. This didn't break the boy's spirit; on the contrary, it made him into a prankster and a fighter. Taught by a neighbor, a former schoolteacher, John Birks could read and do his numbers before he went to kindergarten. Dizzy's brother, James Penhold Gillespie, ran away from home because of their father's cruelty.

There was an angry streak in Dizzy, and it could flare suddenly. It would come like a sudden storm and pass as quickly. He was the most benign of men, although I always felt Dizzy could carry a long grudge toward anyone who did him wrong, such as cheating him and his band on money, which happened on more than one occasion.

Dizzy learned to play trombone in school. Then a friend next door was given a trumpet at Christmas. It fascinated him.

James Gillespie forced all his children to take piano lessons, though only John Birks became truly interested in music. Dizzy retained a deep interest in the piano. Dizzy and Milt Jackson, in later years, would take turns playing piano to back each other up.

Thus Dizzy was almost entirely self-taught. They are treacherous terms, "self-taught" and "self-educated," often carrying a connotation of *untaught* or *uneducated*. The terms mean no such thing. One of the values of formal education, at least in the arts, is that a good teacher can shorten your search time, guiding what is in the end self-education. You can learn to draw only by the repeated doing of it, until the coordination between eye and brain and hand is reflexive and unconsidered. Thus it is with musical education, for in the last analysis, in learning an instrument you are training muscle memory. It may indeed be the great virtue of the older jazz musicians that they *were* self-taught, each of them working out his individual problems in his own way.

In any case, Dizzy was far from being the only "self-taught" musician. But his self-education left John Birks with certain idiosyncrasies. He was never restrained from letting his cheeks bulge out, which is by all theory supposed to cripple a trumpet player's technique. But Dizzy did it, and so did (and does) Maynard Ferguson, and no one ever accused either of them of lack of technique. Miles, on the other hand, with good classical training on trumpet, never had the fluid technique that Dizzy had, nor the command of the horn of Maynard Ferguson, nor the chops of Harry James. Dizzy did not himself understand why and how his cheeks bulged out: he said they fascinated his dentist. And, Dizzy said, he had been written up in dental literature, the phenomenon being known (and he sounded a little proud of it) as "Gillespie pouches."

Dizzy worked for a time in the 1930s picking cotton. Then he had another stroke of luck. One of the few high schools for blacks in the area was the Laurinburg Institute, about thirty miles away in Laurinburg, North Carolina. It had a scholarship program for the poor. Dizzy and his cousin Norman Powe, a trombone player, were both admitted without fees. He worked on the school farm to pay for clothes and other necessities, and claimed in later life that he was a master farmer. He practiced trumpet and piano incessantly. Norman Powe recalled, according to Shipton, that they studied classical music. One wonders what they heard. In 1935, Debussy had been dead seventeen years, Ravel had only two years left to live, and Stravinsky's *Firebird* was nearly twenty-five years old. In later years, Dizzy would refer to listening to classical music as "going to church." So one is justified in wondering how much (given his incredible ears) he was picking up from that source. Certainly much of what he and Charlie Parker did was adapted, not invented, the flabbergasted response of later critics with no knowledge of classical music to the contrary notwithstanding.

Early in 1935, Gillespie's mother moved to Philadelphia, and in May, when he failed physics in his final year at Laurinburg, he left Cheraw to join her. Years later, when he was a famous musician, Dizzy stopped in Laurinburg. The head of the school said, "Here's something you forgot," handing him his high school diploma and his football letter.

Living in South Philadelphia, John Birks formed friendships with organist Bill Doggett and worked in a band led by Frankie Fairfax. During one rehearsal, a trumpet player looked over at the chair where John Birks was supposed to be and asked, "Where's Dizzy?" Dizzy was at the piano. The name stuck. Though Dizzy did not object to the nickname in the press or publicity, he did not want it used by his friends. His friends for the most part seemed to call him Birks. I must have picked it up by osmosis, but certainly that's what I always called him.

Dizzy's leap into the big time came in 1937 when he joined the band of Lucky Millinder, a product of the same Chicago high school that produced Lionel Hampton, Nat Cole, and Milt Hinton. Dizzy told me that Millinder was not himself a musician, but he was a great bandleader with big ears and an instinct for talent. Also in the band was Charlie Shavers, who would be an important mentor to Dizzy. Living by then in New York, Dizzy made friendships with Kenny Clarke and trumpeters Benny Harris, Bobby Moore, and Mario Bauza. And he sat in a lot at the Savoy Ballroom, where he met Teddy Hill. Dizzy signed on with Hill's band for a tour of Europe. The band sailed for Paris in May 1937. Just before their departure—on May 17—the band went into the studio to record. The testimony of musicians who heard him at that time indicates that Gillespie already had a formidable range, playing effortlessly two octaves above middle C.

On Jelly Roll Morton's *King Porter Stomp,* Dizzy played his first recorded solo; it can be found on *Dizzy Gillespie: The Complete RCA Victor Recordings.* One already hears the emergence of the "real" Dizzy Gillespie. The playing is fierce, and focused with a kind of acetylene flame that was always characteristic of his work. This two-CD set gives a good chronicle of Gillespie's work from that session with Hill through to July 6, 1949, when he recorded Lester Young's *Jumpin' with Symphony Sid* and three other tracks. By then he was fully developed as an artist, master of his medium. The rest of his life would be devoted to refinement and dissemination.

John Chilton, the English musician and writer, discussing Gillespie's skilled use of the microphone, said: "If you heard him without a microphone he had a noticeably thin tone." Dizzy's tone was thin, knifelike, penetrating, when he wanted it to be. It could also be, with or without microphone, quite fat, particularly in the low register. One thing that struck me as I listened again to recordings through his career was the range of tonal shadings he commanded.

Birks had become enamored of a young dancer named Gussie Lorraine Willis, usually called just Lorraine. His lovely ballad *Lorraine* is named for her. Dizzy courted her by mail while she worked at the Apollo Theater. She seemed unattainable, a strong and disciplined woman who was unimpressed by his role as a musician. At the same time, she helped him with money while he was waiting out his New York City union card. She would remain the great stabilizing constant of his life.

The next plateau of his career was the period with Cab Calloway, which began in 1939. Like Lucky Millinder, Calloway was not a musician. But Millinder made his own judgments. Dizzy told an English interviewer: "Cab didn't know anything about music, he was a performer and a singer. He knew very little about what was going on, but he did have a good band. He relied on other people to tell him how good a guy was . . . and these guys were at the top of their profession. It was the best job in New York City at the time."

Calloway's was one of the most successful of commercial big bands, and one of the most tasteful. In his drape-shaped white zoot suits, Calloway made himself a figure of comedy, cavorting about the stage, singing his Hi-de-ho, and displaying a snowplow mouth of white teeth. As a kid, encountering him in movies, I felt an embarrassed discomfort at his monkeyshines, as surely as I did the grovelings of Stepin Fetchit and Mantan Moreland. To me it was the same thing, disguised as hip, or hep, as they called it in those days. Louis Armstrong similarly embarrassed me, so much so that at first his image blocked my perception of his musical importance. What I did not see (and neither did some of the militant young black musicians of later years) is that this was the way of show business. I think I understood it at last when I saw Guy Lombardo swooping and scooping about a stage in front of what, as both Armstrong and Gerry Mulligan recognized, was a very good 1920s dance band.

Furthermore, early in the century, not only the blacks were patronized and mocked in show business. So were the Irish, the Jews, and the Germans, the latter by what were called Dutch comics. Ethnic insult songs were common. One of my favorite politically incorrect titles came out in World War I, as the United States tried to achieve some sort of unity of its disparate peoples: *When Tony Goes Over the Top (Keep Your Eye on that Fighting Wop)*.

So the self-mockeries of Armstrong and Calloway have to be seen in perspective: they were in show business, and jazz had not yet been defined as an art form. John Birks Gillespie, an incredible natural humorist, never loaded the music with that burden, and for that he has been often misunderstood.

The Calloway band was one of the best of the era, and one of the most successful. If Cab in movies embarrassed me, some of the band's instrumental records, such as *A Smooth One*, rather than *Minnie the Moocher*, were key elements of my collection when I was about thirteen.

The Calloway band was moving forward, partly due to the impetus of Milt Hinton, guitarist Danny Barker, and drummer Cozy Cole in the rhythm section. Dizzy's Cuban friend Mario Bauza joined the band just before Dizzy. He was to be a powerful influence, deepening Gillespie's interest in Latin rhythms generally and Cuban rhythms particularly, which of course led back to Africa, and in jazz led to the term Afro-Cuban. Composer Chico O'Farrill told me that back in the mountains of Cuba when he was a boy, local percussionists played more authentic African rhythm than one could find in Africa, because of their long insulation from European music; the situation would be parallel to the preservation in pure form of Elizabethan song in the Appalachians. In each case, isolation preserved authenticity. Chico told me this was coming to an end with Fidel Castro's drive for universal literacy. Radio made its incursions, too. In 1962, in a jungle village far up a small tributary to the Demerara River in what was then British Guiana, I considered with fascination the thatched homes of the autochthonous people, and observed uneasily a young man with a small radio, listening to rock-and-roll.

Dizzy said in 1979 that his style had cohered by the time he joined Calloway. Shipton corroborates this, writing that "by 1939–40 his bop vocabulary was largely in place, and when he cut his 1939 records, he had not heard Charlie Parker or felt his influence." And Dizzy was already the great teacher. Milt Hinton, in a 1990 conversation with me, recalled: "Dizzy came into the band while we were at the Cotton Club. Doc Cheatham got sick, and Dizzy took his place. Dizzy had just got back from Europe with Teddy Hill. Dizzy and I got to be very tight. I was young, and he was younger than I." (He was seven years younger than Milt.) "He had a mouthpiece that was so damn brass it was eating through his lip. I gave him five dollars to go and get it plated.

"Dizzy was harmonically miles ahead of me, and everybody else at that time. He'd show me things. At intermission, instead of hanging around and getting drunk, we'd go up on the roof of the Cotton Club and jam. Every night, Dizzy and I would be on the roof, just he and I. There was an old fire escape, winding stairs. He'd help me get my bass up there, and we'd rehearse on the roof. Dizzy would show me some new changes. The flatted fifth, which nobody was using in 1939, altered tenths and thirteenths. We'd rehearse until it was time for the show to go on, and we'd come back down.

"When Benny Goodman started the quartet with Gene Krupa and Teddy Wilson, Cab tried to follow suit. He named his quartet the Cab Jivers. He got the four biggest names in his band, Chu Berry, Cozy Cole, Danny Barker, and myself.

"The drummer in the band had been Leroy Maxey. He'd been with the band since it was the Missourians. When Gene Krupa started playing all them drum solos, Cab wanted drum solos. Maxey was a great show drummer, but he didn't know how to take drum solos. Cab got him to take a solo one night, and he got so hung up in it, he stood up and sang the rest of it. Cab fired him, and got Cozy Cole, who was with Stuff Smith and was a hot drummer around New York.

"So now we're doing this thing as the Cab Jivers. Slam Stewart was very big now. Slim and Slim had *Flat Foot Floogie* going.

"We had a piece to play, *Girl of My Dreams*. Dizzy said, 'Let me show you a solo on that. Play it like Slam Stewart, use the bow.' Dizzy sang it to me, and played it on his horn, and I used my bow. It goes to a flatted fifth. And I couldn't hear that damn thing. Every night I would play it on the air, and I would look back at Dizzy. If I would get it right, he'd nod, and if I missed it, he'd say, 'Jesus Christ, you stink.'

"This went on and on.

"Dizzy's chops weren't right yet, not like they got to be later. He would start things he couldn't finish. In the band, we didn't mind that he was even *attempting* it." Milt sang a typical Gillespie line and screwed it up. "We'd say, 'That was a great try.' Cab would turn around and say, 'What the hell you got to play that damn Chinese music for?' He was always on Dizzy. And Dizzy would do all kinds of crazy things.

"Cab would be singing a ballad." Milt sang: *I've got you under my skin* . . . "Dizzy would look out at the audience like he saw someone he knew, and wave. And the people would start laughing. Cab would turn around to see what's happening, and Dizzy sat there like he was in church.

"Tyree Glenn came into the band. And Cab would be singing a beautiful ballad, and Dizzy would act like he was throwing a football. And Tyree would act like he caught it. Just as he'd catch it, Cozy Cole would hit the bass drum, *doom!* And the people in the audience were falling *out*. It drove Cab *crazy*. And he keeps trying to find out who in the hell is doing it.

"We get to Hartford, Connecticut. Sunday afternoon. The band is all set to play. And then comes the spot for the Cab Jivers. We go out front. They drop the lights down on the band. Cab introduces us and goes off in his white suit. He's got two pretty ladies in the wings, waiting for him back there. It's my turn to play the solo on *Girl of My Dreams* and I missed it a mile. I look back at Diz and Diz says, 'You stink!' And Cab is in the wings and sees this. Just then somebody threw a wad of paper up in the air and it landed on the stage in the spotlight, right beside me.

"When the curtain closed, the show was over, the band walked off, I got to put my bass back up on the stand. Cab walks away from these two chicks, and walks over to Diz and says, 'You stupid son of a bitch, these men are out there entertaining the people, and you're playing like you're a kid in school throwing spitballs!'

"Dizzy hadn't done anything. The guys called Cab 'Fess.' Dizzy said, 'Fess, I didn't do that.' Cab says, 'You're a damn liar. I'm looking right at you.' Now Dizzy gets kind of mad about this, because he's right this time. He says, 'You're another liar, I didn't do it.'

"Now Cab can't have the youngest cat in the band talking to him like that when he's got these fine chicks standing over there on the side. He's the leader. Cab said, 'Get away from me, or I'll slap the hell out of you.' And Dizzy said, 'I didn't do nothin'.'

"Cab turned around and slapped his hand upside his face.

"I'm ambidextrous. We used to play with knives when we were kids, like cap guns. Not switchblades, case knives that you throw. I taught Dizzy to do this either hand. If you know how to do it, the blade opens right up. And Dizzy came up with this knife and went right for Cab's stomach. If I hadn't been standing there, Cab would have been dead twice.

"Dizzy was always bigger'n me, and strong. I just hit his hand and deflected the knife. Cab grabbed Dizzy. Cab was a strong guy, and a street fighter, a tough dude. He was one of those Baltimore alley cats. He grabbed Dizzy's wrist, and they had this big scuffle. The musicians were in the band room, and they hear the scuffling, and they rush back out. Chu Berry and Benny Payne, two big guys, pull them apart and push Cab into his dressing room. Dizzy went to the band room. By the time Cab gets into the dressing room, his white suit is red, all the way down his leg. The knife went into his leg when I deflected it.

"Dizzy was scratched on the wrist from the scuffle. Cab walked into the dressing room. My wife Mona was there and Dizzy's wife, Lorraine, was there. Cab said, 'I guess you cats know, this cat cut me.' And he said to Dizzy, 'Get your horn and get out of here.' Dizzy packed up his horn. Lorraine was standing in the door. And they left. And it was quiet.

"The guy who did the spitball did not mention it.

"We finished the engagement that night and went back to New York. The bus always went to the Theresa Hotel at 125th Street and Seventh Avenue. That was home base in New York. Cab always had the first seat on the bus.

"When we get to the curb, Cab stepped off the bus. Dizzy was waiting. He said, 'Fess, I didn't do that.' Cab just hit him on the hand and walked away. The newspapers and *Down Beat* made it up like it was a big fight.

"It made 'em both famous."

"Did they ever get over it?" I asked.

"Absolutely. When there was a big reunion of the Cab Calloway band, everybody was there. Tyree Glenn, Budd Johnson, Illinois Jacquet. Dizzy was there. Dizzy started some of his antics, and one of the guys said, 'Don't start!' Dizzy went out and played his solo and turned around to the band and said, 'Who threw the spitball?' And the whole band yelled, *'Not me!'* And Cab grabbed Dizzy and hugged him and said, 'I know you didn't do it.'

"Later, we were all in Nice, France, and Cab pulled his pants down and pulled Dizzy over and said, 'Feel here,' and put Dizzy's hand on his leg. The scar was still there.

"Dizzy always sent Cab a Christmas card. He loved Cab."

If Milt Hinton was open to Dizzy's explorations, not all the musicians were. Yet he was assigned most of the trumpet solos until Calloway got Jonah Jones into the band. It was in fact, Milt Hinton told me, Jonah Jones who threw the paper wad.

Dizzy found the arrangements ordinary, and he was increasingly restless. But new arrangers were constantly presenting new charts, and I would think that this honed Dizzy's reading skills, which became almost awesome. And during this time, he was at every opportunity sitting in at Minton's, meanwhile explaining his harmonic thinking to Milt Hinton and guitarist Barker. Shipton concludes from the evidence that Dizzy met Charlie Parker on June 24, 1940, when the Calloway band played Kansas City. One of the things I noticed about Dizzy over the years is that he rarely referred to Parker as Bird. He usually called him Yard, contracted from Yardbird.

Dizzy was astounded by Parker when he heard him play. "The things Yard was doing, the ideas that were flowing . . . I couldn't believe it. He'd be playing one song and he'd throw in another, but it was perfect."

This is what Dizzy told me in 1959 of that first encounter: "It seems to me that I always knew him, as far back as I can recall, though it isn't true, of course.

"In South Carolina, we heard none of the Kansas City bands. They didn't come through our part of the country. We heard only the bands from the east coast. But I knew little Buddy Anderson, the trumpet player. Later, he developed tuberculosis and had to quit playing, but he was a fine trumpet player.

"When I joined Cab Calloway's band, we went to Kansas City. This was in 1939." According to Shipton, it had to be somewhat later. Dizzy went on: "Now Buddy Anderson was the only trumpet player I knew who had the idea of exploring the instrument through piano. I played piano, too, and sometimes we'd spend the day at the piano together, never touching a trumpet. And he kept telling me about this Charlie Parker.

"One day while we were in Kansas City with Cab, Buddy brought Charlie Parker over to the Booker T. Washington Hotel and introduced us. We understood each other right away.

"Yard had brought his horn with him. The three of us played together, in the hotel room, all that day. Just the three of us. You didn't find many musicians who could show you on the piano what they were doing. But Charlie Parker could, even then. He was only a kid. We were both only kids.

"The method and music impressed me, the more I heard him play. Because it was so much the way that I thought music should go. His style! The style was perfect for our music. I was playing like Roy Eldridge at the time. In about a month's time, I was playing like Charlie Parker, maybe adding a little here and there. But Charlie Parker was the most fantastic . . . I don't know. You know, he used to do tunes inside of tunes. He'd be playing something and all of a sudden you'd hear *I'm in the Mood for Love* for four bars. Or two bars. Lorraine told me one time, 'Why don't you play like Charlie Parker?' I said, 'Well that's Charlie Parker's style. And I'm not a copyist of someone else's music.' But he was the most fantastic musician."

After that encounter, Dizzy returned to New York. Parker joined Jay McShann's band and also came to New York.

"In 1941, I left Cab," Dizzy remembered. "I played two weeks with Ella Fitzgerald and then with Benny Carter, at Kelly's Stable. In the band was Charlie Drayton on bass, Sonny White on piano, Kenny Clarke, drums, and Al Gibbons on tenor. Nat Cole and Art Tatum were playing opposite us. Did we hear some piano playing!"

He had known Ella Fitzgerald probably for four years at the time. He met her at the Savoy Ballroom. He was one of her most important mentors, she told me. Two or three years before her death, and his, I had lunch with her at her home in Beverly Hills. She was always an extremely shy woman, but that day she talked about many things, including Dizzy. "Dizzy was with the Teddy Hill band and I was with Chick Webb," she recalled. "We used to get off the stage at the Savoy Ballroom and start dancing. We'd jump off and start Lindy hopping." That was probably in 1937, when Ella was twenty, as was Dizzy.

By the time of the shows at Kelly's Stable with Ella, Dizzy was married: he and Lorraine Willis were wed on May 9, just before he met Parker. To the end of his days, he credited her with the stability of his life, saying that without her he might have got involved with drugs and alcohol. He meant heroin, of course; everyone who knew him is aware that Dizzy, like Basie, was not, shall we say, averse to a little pot.

After the Kelly's Stable engagement with Ella Fitzgerald, and his leaving Calloway following the spitball incident in September 1941, Dizzy told me, "I went out with Charlie Barnet for three weeks in Toronto, then rejoined Benny Carter, then went with Coleman Hawkins. This was getting on toward 1942 or 1943. I worked with Earl Hines, and with Billy Eckstine in 1944. Oscar Pettiford and I formed a group, as co-leaders. And we immediately sent Charlie Parker a telegram asking him to join us.

"By the time we heard from Yardbird, we'd been in there for several weeks. Don Byas had come in to work as a single, and Oscar and I had broken up the group. In fact, I was co-leader across the street from the Onyx with Budd Johnson, and Bird still hadn't showed up. Budd and I were there six weeks. By then, Charlie Parker was just getting into town—and I no longer had a group for him to work *with*.

"But Yard was in New York, and that was the main thing, and a number of us were experimenting with a different way of playing jazz."

As for *who* invented bebop, he said, "It depends on your viewpoint and on what you consider were the important contributing factors. If you consider that Charlie Parker was the prime mover, then bebop started at Clark Monroe's Uptown House, because that was where Yard used to go to jam. If you consider that Thelonious Monk was the prime mover, then it was Minton's, where Monk was playing after hours with Joe Guy, Nick Fenton, and Kermit Scott. I was in an odd position: I was jamming at both places, and ducking the union man at both."

With characteristic modesty, he claimed nothing for himself. But in that simple statement about jamming at both places, he implicitly acknowledges that he was the unifying force. As for who was the most important, he said, "What is the most important ingredient of spaghetti sauce?"

"But it is true that we used to play unusual substitute chords to throw some of the other musicians who came up to sit in. That did have a lot to do with it.

"I can remember when nobody except us played the chord progression A-minor seventh to D-seventh to D-flat. That was one of the chord progressions I showed Monk. But Monk was the first to use E-minor seventh with a flatted fifth, or as some call it an E half-diminished. Monk just called it a G-minor sixth with an E in the bass."

Legend accrued that the purpose of these exercises was to keep the "white boys" off the bandstand. This is ridiculous. Parker and Gillespie were both men of great intellect, and they would never invest that kind of thought and study and practice for the mere purpose of racial exclusion. Although Dizzy had angers, he was far above a simplistic racism. Furthermore, he and Parker never excluded whites from their company or their groups. Al Haig, Red Rodney, Gerry Mulligan, Phil Woods, Lalo Schifrin, and Mike Longo, among others, would come into their orbit and fellowship, and Dizzy, ever the compulsive teacher, went to considerable lengths to show them what he was doing. And anyway, a skilled arranger could analyze what was going on at Minton's.

Shipton says that hints of the bebop to come are heard in some of the Calloway recordings. Moonlighting (with Milt Hinton and Cozy Cole) from Calloway, Dizzy recorded several sides, as they called the songs put down on 78s in those days, with Lionel Hampton. One of them was *Hot Mallets*, of which Hampton would later say, "The first time bebop was played on trumpet was when Dizzy played on *Hot Mallets*." But about all you hear of Dizzy (the track is in the RCA two-CD collection) is some brief cup-muted solo work at the start, and it isn't very boppish to me. What I find notable about the record is that Benny Carter plays alto on it, and did the chart; he and Dizzy would always be friends.

Milt Hinton recalled, "We would go to Minton's and jam every night. A lot of kids would come in, because they know the name guys are gonna be there. These kids got their horns out, they want to get up on the bandstand and jam. There was no room for us to get up there and do *our* thing. So Dizzy said, 'Okay, we're gonna change these changes all around.' The kids are all standing around, and they say, 'Whatchall gonna play?' We say, '*I Got Rhythm*,' and we'd play these other changes, then they'd have to get off the bandstand. Black kids and white kids both. They just didn't want no beginners up there."

In short, the key figures did not welcome fools gladly. One fool who would jump up on the bandstand and, despite a spectacular lack of talent, have the temerity to play with Parker and Gillespie, was a black tenor player Dizzy nicknamed Demon. I'd heard the story, and asked Dizzy about him.

"Demon," Dizzy remembered in sly reflection. "He was the original freedom player: freedom from melody, freedom from harmony, and freedom from rhythm."

One of the participants in the sessions was Ella Fitzgerald. "I learned a lot from those musicians," Ella said, "and I'm very grateful for it. When they used to have the after-hours jam sessions at Minton's, and Monroe's Uptown House, I used to sneak in with them. And I feel that I learned what little bop I do have by following Dizzy around these different places. I feel that that was my education. He is a wonderful teacher, and I am very grateful to him. I probably never would have tried to bop, but I wanted to do what he was doing. We used to go in there and jam all night, and sometimes we'd go down to Fifty-second Street to the Three Deuces and we'd listen to Lady Day.

"I don't know how I got it, but I think I owe it mostly to musicians. By being around them, I learned by ear."

According to some, Fitzgerald may have originated the term bebop or, as it was at first also known, rebop. It is said that she used these syllables in a characteristic phrase when she was scatting with the musicians. Whether or not she really did invent the phrase, she was the first singer in on the experimentation and innovation that would lead to bebop.

Another of the significant locales for the ongoing experimentation was the apartment at 2040 Seventh Avenue that Dizzy and Lorraine took after their marriage. Dizzy told me that Lorraine disapproved of Charlie Parker, because of his chaotic way of life, probably fearful that he would influence Dizzy. Dizzy recalled that he would be sitting at his upright piano, writing down whatever he and Parker were working out. Lorraine would come home and tell Parker to leave. "Yard" would walk to the door, still playing his horn, Lorraine would shut the door behind him, and he would stand in the hall, still blowing, as Dizzy wrote out the material. How often this happened, I don't know; I remember only how I laughed at the images when Dizzy told me the story.

There is a hiatus in the recorded history of bebop's evolution, due to the recording ban imposed by James Caesar Petrillo, head of the American Federation of Musicians. It lasted more than a year, creating an illusion that jazz (not just bebop) moved forward in one great leap. This seems to have happened to the Woody Herman band as well. When it went back to recording, it reflected some of the innovations of Parker and Gillespie, including an exuberant wildness with band members shouting encouragement to each other and behaving in a goofy manner. Dizzy had written for Woody and even played with the band as a sub for a time in early 1942. Dizzy wrote three charts for the band, including *Down Under*, which Woody recorded in July of that year, *Swing Shift*, and *Woody 'n' You*. The latter two were not recorded. *Down Under* is startlingly ahead of its time, and Woody was so impressed by Gillespie's writing that he encouraged him to give up playing to devote himself to it. "I'm glad he ignored me," Woody told me.

After writing for Woody, Dizzy spent a short period with the Les Hite band and then a second stint with Lucky Millinder, who—musicians testified he would fire a man for no other reason than sudden whim—dropped him, then tried to rehire him. But Dizzy was working steadily in Philadelphia and commuting to New York to sit in with, among others, Charlie Parker at Kelly's Stable. Ira Gitler noted that Dizzy paid a six-dollar train fare to play a ten-dollar job.

Dizzy was further revealing his complete lack of color bias. In Philadelphia, he worked with Stan Levey. Dizzy took up a pair of drumsticks to teach the young drummer some of the ideas he and Kenny Clarke had developed, once again illustrating that generosity with knowledge that was one of his most admirable characteristics. This must be seen against the pattern of selfishness in early jazz musicians; some trumpeters played with a kerchief over their right hand to prevent others from "stealing" their stuff.

Early in 1943, Dizzy joined the Earl Hines band. He told me: "I was the first one to join Earl Hines, though Yard came with the band right after. Lucky Millinder fired me in Philadelphia in 1942. I worked a club there for a while, then joined Hines in '43. We all asked Earl to hire Bird. Unfortunately, there were already two alto players in the band. That didn't stop us. Billy Eckstine said, 'Let's get him anyway. He can play tenor.' So Yard joined the band right after that, on tenor. He played superbly with that band. I remember Sarah Vaughan would sing *This Is My First*

Love, and Bird would play sixteen bars on it. The whole band would turn to look at him. *Nobody* was playing like that."

The band was a greenhouse in the evolution of bebop, in spite of the fact that Earl Hines didn't much care for what Parker and Gillespie were doing, even though he had himself been a radical innovator and, further irony, directly influenced two of the major players in the emerging musical movement: Bud Powell and Al Haig.

"By this time," Dizzy told me, "Bird and I were very close friends. He was a very sensitive person, in the way that creative people are. Everything made a profound impression on him. He also was very loyal, and had a terrific sense of humor.

"I remember one incident that illustrated all these characteristics. It was after the period of Minton's and Monroe's Uptown House. We were with the Earl Hines band. I was sitting at the piano one night in Pine Bluff, Arkansas, and some white guy came up and threw a quarter on the bandstand to me and said, 'Hey, boy! Play *Darktown Strutters' Ball.*' I paid him no mind and kept playing.

"When the dance was over, I went to the men's room. As I came out, this guy hit me on the side of the head with a bottle. Blood was spurting, and I grabbed for a bottle myself. Some people grabbed me, before I could crown him with a bottle of Seltzer.

"They took me off to the hospital. I remember as they were taking me out, Charlie Parker—he wasn't very big—was wagging his finger in the man's face. I'll always remember his words. He said: 'You cur! You took advantage of my friend!'"

A few years ago, I had a conversation with the late Mel Powell, who during the period when Dizzy was doing his deepest experimenting, was writing and playing piano for Benny Goodman.

"Now," I said, "all those guys were aware of the movements in modern music in the 1920s. William Grant Still was studying with Varèse by 1927. The harmony in dance bands became more adventurous through the 1930s until you got Boyd Raeburn in the '40s, and Bob Graettinger's *City of Glass* for Kenton, which sounded radical to me at the time but no longer does. I can't believe that the arrangers were not aware of all that was going on with the extension of harmony in European music. Bill Challis was starting to use some of that stuff when he was writing for Goldkette. Is there an answer to this question: were the writers waiting for the public to catch up?"

"I think I'll surprise you," Mel answered. "They were waiting for the bandleaders to catch up. The bandleaders were much more aware of what a negotiable commodity was." He chuckled. "When an arrangement would be brought in and rejected because 'That's too fancy,' that was a signal that I was no longer welcome. So I meant exactly what I said. If the arrangers were waiting for anything, they were waiting for the bandleaders."

Goodman was one of the bandleaders who hated bebop. And what did they hate? They hated its harmonic practices, including the use of extensions that had been common in European classical music for more than half a century: jazz has always played harmonic catch-up to classical music.

But this was not the only thing about bebop that was disconcerting. Parker and Gillespie "evened out" the eighth notes, which is to say they did away with the strong stress of doo-BAH-doo-BAH-doo-BAH; and to the ears of a John Hammond, this didn't swing. To younger ears, unburdened by preconception, it swung more. But beyond that, Parker and Gillespie developed some really odd uses of stress points, and started and stopped phrases in unexpected places. To anyone used to Bach, this presented nothing really unsettling—laden with surprises, to be sure, but exciting for just that reason—but it disoriented many older (and even some younger) listeners and musicians. Others perceived and admired what they were doing, among them Benny Carter and Coleman Hawkins. Hawkins, after his *Body and Soul* record, and with his penchant for exploring the harmonic contents of a song, was a sort of proto-bopper, as was Mel Powell. Aware of and interested in new developments in classical music as well as jazz (and in graphic art; he haunted museums), Hawkins welcomed the innovators, and in February 1944 he recorded with a band that included Dizzy, Oscar Pettiford, Max Roach, and Budd Johnson.

In the Earl Hines band, Parker and Gillespie continued their explorations, refining *Salt Peanuts*, which Dizzy and Kenny Clarke had developed earlier, and polishing *A Night in Tunisia*, which had begun life with the title *Interlude*. Dizzy also wrote the arrangement of *East of the Sun* that Sarah Vaughan recorded with the band. And Hines, whatever his misgivings, allowed Gillespie and Parker to use his band as a laboratory for their ideas, with Dizzy of course doing the writing.

In August 1943, the Hines band's singer Billy Eckstine left the group, and nine of the musicians went with him, including Dizzy. Eckstine planned to form his own band with these men as the core of it, but that band did not immediately materialize, and Dizzy went back to freelancing in New York. Billy Taylor, yet another of the musicians to whom Gillespie became a mentor, said, "Of all the people who were taking part in this bebop revolution, Dizzy was the one who really intellectualized it." In the last months of 1943 and into 1944, Dizzy and bassist Oscar Pettiford led their group at the Onyx Club on Fifty-second Street. Their pianist was a young man born in Sicily named Giacinto Figlia, who changed it to George Wallington, wrote some bebop anthems, including *Godchild* and *Lemon Drop*, then walked away from music to go into his family's air-conditioning business.

Early in 1944, Eckstine was able to launch his band. Its personnel at various times included Sarah Vaughan, Charlie Parker, Tadd Dameron, Fats Navarro, Charlie Rouse, Gene Ammons, Lucky Thompson, Miles Davis, Dexter Gordon, Sonny Stitt, and Art Blakey. Dizzy was its musical director and chief arranger, a role he took up at the behest of Billy Shaw, head of the Shaw booking agency, who promised that if he did the job well, the agency would back him in his own big band.

The Eckstine band, Dizzy said, "was a radical band. It was the forerunner of all the big modern bands. But a lot of ballroom operators didn't dig it. They thought it was just weird. But it was a very fine band, very advanced."

Its legacy on records is thin; it was poorly recorded on the independent Deluxe label. Art Blakey remembered it, in a radio interview with the British writer Charles Fox, as a really crazy band, with Gillespie and Parker the chief clowns and Sarah Vaughan their willing foil. Blakey was shocked by the profanity in use; Eckstine told him he'd better get used to it, and in later years Blakey marveled in memory at the magnificent spirit and dedication of the band. The band survived until 1947, but Dizzy left it early in 1945.

He told me: "I can't remember whether Charlie Parker and I left the band together. We must have, because from the band, we went into the Three Deuces. The group was in my name, and the members included Stan Levey, Al Haig, Curley Russell, and Bird. We were there for several months."

Among the more ardent listeners were members of the Woody Herman trumpet section, including Neal Hefti, Shorty Rogers—both of whom were contributing arrangements to the Herman band—and Pete Candoli. On February 26, 1945, Woody took the band into the studio to record for Columbia Records one of its biggest hits, *Caldonia*, which Woody picked up from the Louis Jordan record of the tune, as Dizzy picked up *School Days* from a Jordan record. They were all friends. Rumor spread among the more serious young fans of the Herman band that the unison trumpet passage on *Caldonia* was a transcribed Gillespie solo.

Not so, according to Neal Hefti. Soloists in bands would polish their solos in advance for the three-minute recordings of the era. That trumpet passage was a solo Neal had worked out for *Woodchopper's Ball*, and the rest of the trumpets picked it up and played it in unison with him. On the *Caldonia* session, Woody decided to use it.

"So it wasn't a Dizzy Gillespie solo," Neal said. "But it was certainly Dizzy Gillespie inspired. He was my hero from way before that."

But one passage on a Herman record was indeed transcribed from a solo. Ralph Burns, who was the band's principal arranger and at that time was playing piano with it, said, "On *I've Got News for You,* I took a passage note for note off a Charlie Parker record and harmonized it for the saxes. When I did a thing for Ray Charles, he asked me to write the same sax chorus."

In mid-January 1945, Dizzy joined the highly experimental Boyd Raeburn band, both on trumpet and as arranger. The band included Oscar Pettiford, Benny Harris, Al Cohn, Serge Chaloff, Shelly Manne, and Johnny Mandel. Dizzy was also freelancing as a writer. In January he was voted "new trumpet star" in the *Esquire* poll, putting the lie to the theory of general public and critical rejection of bebop, and took part in a network broadcast from Carnegie Hall set up to publicize the winners. In May 1945, he and Charlie Parker performed together at Town Hall with Al Haig, Curley Russell, and Max Roach.

By now the message of bop had spread. *The Bebop Revolution* (Bluebird CD 2177-2-RB) chronicles some of that expansion. A group called the Fifty-second Street All-Stars, in a Denzil Best tune titled *Allen's Alley,* features Pete Brown (a favorite of Paul

Desmond's) and Allen Eager on tenor. The music hangs between swing and bop. It was recorded February 27, 1946. Six months later, on September 5, a group billed as Kenny Clarke and his Fifty-second Street Boys recorded *Epistrophy* (by Monk and Clarke), *52nd Street Theme* (by Monk), *Oop-Bop-Sh-Bam* (by Dizzy and Gil Fuller), and Clarke's own *Royal Roost*. Clarke was an incomparable drummer, and one of the innovators in the new idiom. There is some marvelous Bud Powell on these tracks. The influence of Gillespie on Fats Navarro and Kenny Dorham is inescapable, but even more obvious is that of Parker on the late Sonny Stitt's alto work. Dizzy told me: "The closest to Yard I have heard is Sonny Stitt. When I hear a record sometimes, I won't be sure at first whether it's Sonny or Yard. Sonny gets down into all the little things of Charlie Parker's playing. The others just play his music; Sonny plays his life."

As for Dizzy during this period, Whitney Balliett wrote in the *New Yorker*: "Few trumpeters have ever been blessed with so much technique. Gillespie never merely started a solo, he erupted into it. A good many bebop solos begin with four- and eight-bar breaks, and Gillespie, taking full advantage of this approach . . . would hurl himself into the break, after a split second pause, with a couple of hundred notes that corkscrewed through several octaves, sometimes in triple time, and were carried, usually in one breath, past the end of the break and well into the solo itself. Gillespie's style at the time gave the impression—with its sharp, slightly acid tone, its cleavered phrase endings, its efflorescence of notes, and its brandishings in the upper register— of being constantly on the verge of flying apart. However, his playing was held together by his extraordinary rhythmic sense."

Given the ultimate impossibility of describing music in words, Balliett's description comes as close as one can imagine to capturing Dizzy. And he is quite right about Dizzy's uncanny coherence, the rhythmic equivalent of absolute pitch. One musician maintained that Dizzy played like a drummer, with the notes in pitch. I don't think jazz has ever known anyone with Dizzy's infallible rhythmic sense, and he influenced generations of drummers.

The qualities described by Balliett are all evident in a date Dizzy led in February 1946, found in the RCA two-CD package previously mentioned. The personnel included Gillespie, Don Byas on tenor, Milt Jackson on vibes, Al Haig on piano, Bill DeArango, guitar, Ray Brown, bass, and J. C. Heard, drums. The tunes are Monk's *52nd Street Theme, A Night in Tunisia,* by Dizzy and Frank Paparelli, *Ol' Man Rebop,* by Leonard Feather, and *Anthropology,* by Parker and Gillespie. Dizzy's flying gyrations are amazing, and deeply exciting. His powers of invention and execution were awesome. Years later, listening to him in clubs, I used to marvel at not only his thinking but the coordination of mind and neurotransmitters and muscle that permitted such instantaneous flowing realization of his imaginings.

After a series of successful appearances with Charlie Parker, Dizzy, creature of the big-band era, assembled an eighteen-piece unit to go on the road. In July 1945, after a rehearsal of quintet material expanded to full band and some new material from Gil Fuller, they began a tour that featured the Nicholas Brothers, under the title "Hep-sations of 1945." They toured the South, sleeping in the homes of black families forming a sort of circuit for traveling blacks, who could not get into the hotels in those days. White audiences weren't interested in the band, and black audiences were baffled by bebop. It was not, they said, music they could dance to, and Dizzy, according to Alyn Shipton, was not comfortable onstage during this tour. By late September, Dizzy put aside his ambitions to have a big band, and he returned to small-group work in New York.

By now, Miles Davis was with Charlie Parker's quintet. But Parker and Gillespie were reunited for a famous sojourn at Billy

Berg's Club in Los Angeles. Dizzy hired Ray Brown on bass, Milt Jackson on vibes, Al Haig on piano, and Stan Levey on drums. The booking called for only five men. Dizzy explained: "I wasn't always sure that Bird would show up, and that's why I hired Milt Jackson. With Bags we were sure to have at least five men on the stand whether Bird showed up or not. Later, Billy Berg said we needed more body! And he had us hire Lucky Thompson on tenor. That gave us up to seven pieces."

Patronage for the engagement came heavily from musicians, who had heard elements of bop from, among others, Howard McGhee. One of those who came by was Art Tatum; another was Ernie Royal. "We stayed there eight weeks," Dizzy told me in 1961. "Ah, it would be nice to work eight weeks in one club again. The musicians out there were all over us. We had a ball, but we didn't do too well as far as the public was concerned."

Parker, deep in his addiction to heroin, behaved erratically, as Dizzy had feared he might, and when the band returned to New York on February 9, Parker missed the flight. He remained behind and was eventually admitted to the Camarillo State Hospital, where he stayed from August 1946 until January 1947.

Dizzy was losing patience with Bird. For all he admired Parker, Dizzy could not tolerate his personal and professional instability. "But by now," Dizzy said, "bebop was well established. Fats Navarro, Howard McGhee, Wardell Gray, Freddie Webster, and, if memory serves me, Miles Davis, were all on Fifty-second Street in New York when we returned from California. Bebop was getting plenty of publicity. There had even been articles in *Life* magazine."

The articles, unfortunately, made humor of it, and of Dizzy, concentrating on his antics rather than the musical advances that were being made.

The Three Deuces, Birks recounted, wanted his group. But

Clark Monroe, owner of the Uptown House, also wanted them for his new Spotlite Club. "He offered us a deal," Dizzy said. "If we didn't go into the Three Deuces, we could come into the Spotlite for eight weeks with a small band and then eight weeks with a big band. He said we could build it from his club.

"At one time, for a one-week date in the Bronx, I had Yardbird, Miles, and Freddie Webster in that band. That was only temporary, of course. While I had the big band, Bird had his quintet. He had such people as Miles, Max Roach, and Duke Jordan with him.

"I didn't know it, but the job in Hollywood had been the last time Bird and I were ever to work together in a permanent group."

At the Spotlite, Dizzy's group included Milt Jackson, Ray Brown, Stan Levey, and Al Haig. For the big band he was building, Gil Fuller was to be the arranger. Dizzy recruited Kenny Dorham, Sonny Stitt, Kenny Clarke and, in due course, Thelonious Monk. Monk's own unpredictability disturbed Dizzy as much as Bird's, and when, after a month, Kenny Clarke introduced Dizzy to John Lewis, whom Clarke had known in the Army, Dizzy inducted him into the band. Along with playing piano in it, Lewis wrote for it.

Because the Gil Fuller charts were hard to play, particularly for the brass section, Dizzy suggested that the rhythm section and Jackson perform as a quartet for fifteen-minute periods, to give the band a rest. And they did: Milt Jackson, Ray Brown, John Lewis, and Kenny Clarke. These interludes became integral to the performances, and eventually the four musicians stepped out to play other gigs, first as The Atomics of Modern Music, a tacky nom de guerre that gave way to the Milt Jackson Quartet. They kept the initials when they changed the name later to the Modern Jazz Quartet, with John Lewis as musical director.

Brown and Clarke left, to be replaced by Percy Heath and Connie Kay, and this quartet lasted longer without a personnel change than any group in jazz history.

John Lewis wrote full charts, not sketches, for the Gillespie band, augmenting the book being built by Gil Fuller with contributions by Tadd Dameron, Dizzy, and Ray Brown.

Probably from the beginning of the big-band era, the audiences in ballrooms tended to divide into two parts: the dancers who went in for some (at times) astonishingly gymnastic dancing alternating with close and seductive movement during the ballads, and the conscientious listeners who crowded close to the bandstand to pay attention to the soloists, stars in their own right, and, probably to a lesser extent, to the writing. These dedicated listeners were, one sees in retrospect, the core of what would become a concert audience in the years after the war, when the dancers dropped away. The Gillespie group was essentially a concert band. Dizzy expressed puzzlement that audiences couldn't dance to this music. He maintained that he could; but then Dizzy was an exceptional dancer, as Ella Fitzgerald always said.

Dizzy's interest in more complex rhythms than the straight four of jazz grew during that edition of his big bands. Had his big bands been called Herds, like those of Woody Herman, this would have been billed as the Second.

He had been using Latin rhythms for some time. He once told me that most of his own compositions used Latin rhythms—*Con Alma,* for example—and when I thought about it, I realized this was so. His friend Mario Bauza pulled his coat to the remarkable Cuban percussionist Chano Pozo, whose full name was Luciano Pozo y Gonzales. He joined the band and inspired its off-the-wall chanting, seeming to evoke moods and images of Africa, whatever the syllables meant (if anything). Chano Pozo collaborated with Dizzy on a piece titled *Cubana Be–Cubana Bop,* which George Russell arranged for the band.

Chano Pozo enriched Dizzy's feeling for and knowledge of Latin polyrhythms (ultimately African rooted, even more purely so than jazz) and led to such pieces as *Manteca, Guachi-Guaro,* and many more in later times.

It was the beginning of Afro-Cuban jazz. It would be imitated by other bands, and Stan Kenton had already recorded *Cuban Carnival,* but no one could equal the energy and passion it produced in the Gillespie band.

Meanwhile, Billy Shaw kept the focus of publicity on Dizzy's ostensible eccentricities. *Life* magazine ran photos of Dizzy and Benny Carter exchanging a "bebop greeting." If memory serves me it was a gesture with the fingers making what was supposed to be the sign of the flatted fifth.

Dizzy began to emerge as a public figure, but above all as that of a clown. It is difficult at this distance to know why he allowed this image of himself to be sent forth. But various factors suggest themselves.

Perhaps since so many persons were viewing bebop as a joke, Dizzy decided, consciously or otherwise, to give them what they expected. Much was made of his horn-rimmed glasses and beret, though neither was particularly unusual, let alone outrageous, and his little goatee. The beret was always a practical item of headgear, as witness all the world's military units that have worn it, not to mention the French. And many trumpet players avoid shaving the lower lip.

In any case, Dizzy came out of show business, with all its attendant horseplay. One of the masters of onstage clowning and funny singing was Louis Jordan. Dizzy had known him since 1937, when Chick Webb would invite Dizzy to sit in with his band at the Savoy Ballroom. Alto saxophonist Jordan was in the band, and he was being featured as a vocalist. Ultimately, with his Tympani Five, he would have a series of hit records, all of them comic and using an infectious basic beat. The group is often cited as a precursor of rock-and-roll.

Later, in the Cab Calloway band, Dizzy observed night after night the way a flamboyant showman controlled an audience.

A significant issue arises here. Most of the early trumpet players, including Louis Armstrong and Henry Red Allen, and even later ones, such as Clark Terry, Jack Sheldon, and Conte Candoli, did a certain amount of comic singing. There is a reason for it. (Excepting Chet Baker, they largely eschewed singing ballads.)

A symphony trumpeter plays a comparatively few measures of music in the course of an evening, none of it in the *altissimo* register common among jazz trumpeters. And the jazz trumpeter played hard music all evening long. One of the ways you get high notes on a trumpet is to jam the mouthpiece into your lip, which in many cases cuts it up badly, leaving white scars on the mouth. Dizzy, curiously, didn't have much scarring. (Once, when the three of us were doing guest appearances on the Steve Allen TV show, I shared a dressing room with Dizzy and Doc Severinsen. I anticipated some interesting conversation. Mostly they talked about lip unguents.) So Dizzy, singing *Swing Low Sweet Cadillac, School Days,* and *The Umbrella Man,* was resting his chops while amusing the audience and making it more open to his music.

In any case, Dizzy had a natural proclivity for clowning. It was just born in him. He had Jack Benny's kind of slow timing and powerful presence, the ability to make people laugh while doing hardly anything. Dizzy loved to laugh, and to make others laugh. But jazz was in the phase of being discovered as a Serious Art Form, and the antics of Dizzy didn't seem to be helping the cause. Bird, dark, doomed, and remote, made a better icon for idolaters. This too, without question, contributed to the diminished perception of Gillespie's importance.

Dizzy once told me, "If by making people laugh, I can make them more receptive to my music, I'm going to do it." And, he added, he didn't give a damn what the critics said.

As for his seriousness about his music, let there be no doubt. When Grover Sales did a retrospective on Dizzy's career at San Francisco State University, with Dizzy in the audience, a student asked a question about jazz and "serious" music. Dizzy called him on it. "Men have died for this music," he shot back. "You can't get no more serious than that."

But the press concentrated on his shenanigans, and a famous and very funny photo from the period shows him in a long-lapeled, chalk-striped gray flannel suit, standing with his trumpet in his arms and his legs crossed at the ankles, staring into the camera with a demure schoolgirl smile. That and other photos of him set off fads among his fans. It seemed that every young man who dug Dizzy had a pair of those horn-rimmed glasses, whether he needed them or not, and a beret.

By this time, the quail were rising from the tall grasses. The attacks on bop, Bird, and Dizzy were shrill and even vicious. The supposedly perspicacious John Hammond, self-advertised always as the great discoverer and perpetrator of jazz, asserted, "Bop is a series of nauseating clichés, repeated ad infinitum."

Critic George Frazier wrote, "Bop is incredible stuff for a grown man to be playing." In 1947, Ralph de Toledano wrote, "Bebop music is usually based on a repeated phrase or series of phrases with 'modernist' pretensions. To watch earnest collegians discussing 'bebop' with the seriousness which Stiedry brings to a Bach fugue is a gruesome experience."

But the most abysmal writings about bebop came from the late Philip Larkin, England's poet laureate, who wrote articles on jazz for the *Daily Telegraph* in London.

"It wasn't," he wrote, "like listening to a kind of jazz I didn't care for—Art Tatum, shall I say, or Jelly Roll Morton's Red Hot

Peppers. It wasn't like listening to jazz at all. Nearly every characteristic of the music had been neatly inverted: for instance, the
jazz tone, distinguished from 'straight' practice by an almost-
human vibrato, had entirely given way to utter flaccidity."

Dizzy's tone? Flaccid? Parker's?

"Had the most original feature of jazz been its use of collective
improvisation? Banish it: let the first and last choruses be identi-
cal exercises in low-temperature unison. Was jazz instrumentation based on hock-shop trumpets, trombones and clarinets of
the returned Civil War regiments? Brace yourself for flutes, harp-
sichords, electronically-amplified bassoons.

"Had jazz been essentially a popular art, full of tunes you could
whistle? Something fundamentally awful had taken place to en-
sure that there should be no more tunes."

One wonders if Larkin ever heard such gorgeous Gillespie
tunes as *Lorraine* and *Con Alma*, Tadd Dameron's ballad *If
You Could See Me Now*, and Gil Fuller and Chano Pozo's *Tin
Tin Deo*.

Larkin continues: "Had the wonderful thing about [jazz] been
its happy, cake-walky syncopation that set feet tapping and shoulders jerking? Any such feelings were now regularly dispelled by
random explosions ('dropping bombs'), and the use of non-jazz
tempos, 3/4, 5/8, 11/4."

This poet apparently did not know the difference between a
tempo and a time signature. And of course in his book of rules,
only a simple 4/4 rhythm was comprehensible. In other cultures,
such as the Greek and Armenian, complex time figures are common in popular music. Dave Brubeck recalls hearing a group in
Turkey improvising collectively in 9/8, with the division being
one-two one-two one-two one-two-three. He said to himself,
"Why can't we do that?" He returned to America and wrote *Blue
Rondo à la Turk*, which he recorded along with Paul Desmond's

Take Five for the album *Time Out*. The album was made up entirely of time signatures other than 4/4. It became one of the best-selling albums in jazz history. In 1962, in Guyana (still British Guiana at the time), I saw couples dancing effortlessly to *Take Five*.

"Above all," Larkin fumes, "was jazz the music of the American Negro? Then fill it full of conga drums and sambas and all the tawdry trappings of South America, the racket of Middle East bazaars, the cobra-coaxing cacophonies of Calcutta."

What this critic finally reveals is an authentic British neo-imperialist, a racist condescending to all cultures, and an admirer of jazz so long as its happy singin' and dancin' darkies keep it simple so he can tap his feet and shake his shoulders.

Larkin may have been preposterous, but he expressed the prejudices of those who so ardently attacked Parker and Gillespie and Monk and Clarke and their brilliant advances in the music. Charlie Parker, asked what it was he and his colleagues were rebelling against, denied that they were rebelling against anything. He said they merely thought it was the way the music ought to go. And surely it was time for it to advance as far as, say, the harmonic practices already in place in the popular music of, among others, Jerome Kern, Harold Arlen, and Cole Porter.

Critics were not alone out there on that limb. Some musicians, as the French say, put their foot in the plate. In a *Down Beat* magazine "Blindfold Test," when Leonard Feather played him a piece by Dizzy and Monk, Sy Oliver grumbled, "It's one of those bop records in the sense that I detest it. No stars."

As late as 1953, Buck Clayton protested, "Bebop is not, never was, and never will be true jazz if it has a beat or not." Tommy Dorsey charged, "Bebop has set jazz back twenty years." Back to what? The harmonic practices of the mid-1920s? He did not foresee that those bands and small groups that embraced or at least tolerated bebop, such as Herman's and Basie's, were the ones that would survive; those that didn't were the ones that died, Dorsey's among them.

Even Charlie Barnet fired a shot at bebop, though he liked it, saying, "Outside of the top exponents of the music like Charlie Parker and Dizzy Gillespie and a few others, the boppers were a bunch of fumblers who were obviously incapable of handling the new idiom. . . . This effectively delivered the death blow to the big bands as we had known them."

But not all the bands embraced the new idiom. And the public had the right to ignore the bands that incorporated it and patronize those that did not. This is not what happened. But that mindlessly reiterated argument that "bebop killed the big bands" is an echo of the schism that was opened up by journalists like Barry Ulanov. The causes of the death of the era were social and economic.

The jazz press wallowed in all this. Ulanov produced two battles-of-the-band on radio, with Charlie Parker and Dizzy in combat with a traditionalist band put together by Rudi Blesh, and these polarized positions were described in a piece in the November 1947 *Metronome* by Ulanov, a critic with an imperious confidence in his own proclamations. This fomented hostility between the Moderns and the Moldy Figs, as the lovers of older jazz were termed. Shipton rightly observes that Ulanov's articles and "similar pieces from Blesh's side of the critical divide contributed to a schism in public taste and critical opinion from which jazz has never fully recovered."

There is no question that Dizzy's onstage antics did him harm, contributing to the elevation of Parker to the role of bebop's almost sole creator. Parker's hagiographer Ross Russell, in a book titled *Bird Lives: The Life and Hard Times of Charlie "Yardbird" Parker* (1973), abetted the idea that Parker was *the* force in bebop, Gillespie the disciple. The very title of the book suggests that it was Parker's private torments that enraptured Russell.

Jon Faddis, a superb trumpet player who has come about as close to capturing the Gillespie style as anyone ever has, told the *New York Times*, after viewing the widely excoriated Ken Burns documentary *Jazz*, that it gave him "the anger that comes from hearing the philosophy of Wynton Marsalis, Stanley Crouch, and others presented as fact, rather than opinion or interpretation. A glaring example: the assertion that Charlie Parker was the sole genius of the bebop era."

The problem of evaluation is compounded by Dizzy's self-effacement and his deep devotion to Parker's memory. No one really is as qualified as Dizzy was to evaluate Parker's contribution to music. In 1961 he told me: "Bird's contribution to all the jazz that came after involved every phase of it. He sure wasn't the beginning, and he wasn't the end—but that middle was *bulging!* But even he had his influences.

"Charlie Parker had a Buster Smith background. And, of course, there was Old Yard—an old alto man—in Kansas City. He had that same feeling. Charlie came up under the aegis of Lester Young and Buster Smith. Regardless of what anyone says, there's so much music out there in the air, all you have to do is get a little bit of it. Nobody can get more than a little bit, but some guys get more than others. Charlie Parker bit off a big chunk—I'll tell you! Still he had influences—Lester Young and those others. But he added to it.

"One thing he added was accent—the way of stressing certain notes. And a different way of building melodies.

"When he was playing a B chord, he was playing in the *key* of B.

"Another thing was rapidity with sense—not rapidity just for the sake of rapidity but *melody* rapidity. He was so versed in chord changes and substitute chords that he was never lost for melody. He could play a blues and sound just like a blues singer, just like he was talking.

"I saw something remarkable one time. He didn't show up for a dance he was supposed to play in Detroit. I was in town, and they asked me to play instead. I went up there, and we started playing. Then I heard this big roar, and Charlie Parker had come in and started playing. He'd play a phrase, and people might never have heard it before. But he'd start it, and the people would finish it with him, humming. It would be so lyrical and simple that it just seemed the most natural thing to play. That's another important thing about Charlie Parker—his simplicity.

"And Charlie Parker was an accompanist. He could accompany singers like they never had been accompanied. He'd fill in behind them and make little runs. He could make a run and it would end right where it should. This is very hard to do. What a mathematical mind he had.

"I remember one record date for Continental especially. It was with Rubberlegs Williams, a blues singer. Somebody had this date—Clyde Hart, I believe. He got Charlie Parker, me, Oscar Pettiford, Don Byas, Trummy Young, and I don't remember the drummer's name. The music didn't work up quite right at first. Now at that time we used to break inhalers open and put the stuff into coffee or Coca Cola; it was a kick then. During a break at this record date, Charlie dropped some into Rubberlegs' coffee. Rubberlegs didn't drink or smoke or anything. So we went on with the record date. Rubberlegs began moaning and crying as he was singing. You should hear *those* records!"

Parker liked sitting in with big bands. Whenever he could, he would do so with Dizzy's band or that of Woody Herman.

"He'd never heard the arrangements before," Birks said. "But you'd think he'd written them. The brass would play something and cut off, and bang! Charlie Parker was there, coming in right where he was supposed to. It's a shame that when he was making those records with strings that the music wasn't up to his standards. There should have been a whole symphony behind him.

"I doubt whether he knew *everything* he was playing. I'll bet that seventy-five percent of his playing he thought of and the other twenty-five percent just fell in place, fell under his fingers. But what he did was enormous. You hear his music everywhere now.

"You hear so much about him that I don't like to hear—about his addiction, and all sorts of irrelevant nonsense.

"It's still hard for me to talk about him—not because he's dead, because he's not really gone to me, but because it's hard for me to think where my life ends and his begins. They were so intertwined."

It is impossible in our time to perceive how Beethoven's music was perceived in his. This is true of artists generally. We can deduce it from the outrage visited on them by critics—Nicolas Slonimsky's *Lexicon of Musical Invective* is a fascinating compendium of such writings—but we can never actually feel the original impact.

Even knowing how original Louis Armstrong was, we can never perceive him the way the thunderstruck young musicians of his early days did. By the time many of us became aware of him, we had already been steeped in the work of those he had inspired, such as Roy Eldridge and Harry James, which further veiled the fact of his originality.

Bill Evans put a high value on personal discovery, as opposed to imposed methodology. What you learn for yourself is idiosyncratically yours, and since there were no schools of jazz in its first decades, musicians had to find their own approaches to their instruments and the music itself, leading to the "wrong" fingering of Bix Beiderbecke and the "wrong" embouchure and special fingerings of John Birks Gillespie. All this private exploration led to the personal and identifiable sounds and styles of earlier jazz musicians. The teaching methods of the jazz education movement have led to codified procedures and because of them a leveling. There is a widespread competence in young players, but they are often as interchangeable as the parts on a GM pickup. They may be accomplished at the technical level, but too many are no more individual than Rich Little doing impressions.

The flatted fifth chord and the minor-seventh-flat-five chord were not new in Western music, but as composer Hale Smith points out, they were probably, for Monk and other jazz musicians, discoveries, and thus became personal vocabulary.

As composers explored what we call Western music over the past centuries, they expanded the vocabulary but they did not invent, or reinvent, it. However, this expansion, particularly in the Romantic music of the nineteenth century, appeared to be invention. Thus too with jazz, when Parker and Gillespie entered with such éclat on the scene. The nineteenth century led to the illusion that to be original, one must invent a new language rather than use the existing lexicon with personal powers of invention. It can be argued that those who use known vocabulary to say new things are more creative than those who affect the invention of a language. For the personal use of existing materials, we need look only to Earl Hines, Art Tatum, Errol Garner, John Guarnieri, Dave Brubeck, Teddy Wilson, Mel Powell, Bud Powell, Fats Waller, Phineas Newborn, Oscar Peterson, Tommy Flanagan, John Lewis, Roger Kellaway, Horace Silver, Thelonious Monk, McCoy Tyner, Jimmy Rowles, Milt Buckner, Nat Cole, Bill Evans—all of them inventing within the same broad vocabulary of Western music, all of them strongly personal, even instantly recognizable, and all of them producing their own tone qualities on an instrument on which, it has been argued from a scientific standpoint, individual tone is not even possible. *That* is originality.

There is nothing original in jazz as such. Improvisation is not original; it has been with us for millennia. Collective improvisation is not original: it is found in flamenco, mariachi, Irish instrumental folk tradition, and other musics, including even the simple but stirring music of Paraguayan harp bands whose players have minimal conscious knowledge of what they're doing. Specific "swinging" rhythm is not original; again, we can look to flamenco, and all the regional musical styles of Brazil and Cuba. This is why a universally acceptable definition of jazz has never been elucidated. Jazz is a combination of many things used in a fresh way, and something may be jazz (such as some of the fixed solos of Armstrong and Tatum) even when it is not improvised.

The theme-and-variations form is old and elemental. But it makes possible most of what we call jazz, for there is no other way to set up a comprehensible framework within which the musician can make his statement. It is, however, the implicit limitation of jazz, and many a musician has writhed in its confines. Yet throw it out, embrace "free jazz," and you abandon the lingua franca audiences can comprehend and thus lose financial support the artist must have to continue developing. Abandon that and get in line for the doles of fellowships and grants and other supports for hothouse art unable to withstand the touch of even the most benign natural breeze. Art that does not communicate isn't art at all, for the act is completed only in the reception and response of an "audience." All else is mirror-gazing.

It is rational to say, as Phil Woods and George Russell effectually do, that this is what I do and I hope enough people like it to permit me to live from it. But it is what I do. It is another matter to say, "Society owes me and must give me grants to permit my endless explorations." This has led to a proliferation of the indecipherable on the "artistic" end of the spectrum in a pathological symbiosis with the explosion of meretricious trash at the commercial end of it.

But fresh art, truly fresh art, is always startling, even when expressed with conventional materials, and Parker and Gillespie were nothing if not surprising.

Dizzy Gillespie did not come out of a tradition of art; he grew up in the world of entertainment. All high art is ultimately rooted in folklore, but Dizzy was never far from it. His was the tradition of Armstrong and Eldridge and Ray Nance and Woody Herman, with roots in or recent descent from vaudeville and minstrelsy; it was the critics, partly in celebration of their own perceptions, who saw it (rightly so, to be sure) as art. I suspect that Dizzy loved the attention, the giddy journalism, that attended bebop.

In August and December 1947, Dizzy and a big band recorded a group of sides for RCA, rushing to get them done before the onset in January of the second AFM recording ban. Then he took the band to Europe on a tour that was a commercial fiasco due to mismanagement, not to mention theft, by some of the business people involved, but a public, critical, and aesthetic triumph. Once, in Paris, the audience was so stunned by the music that at the end of the first number, it forgot to applaud. That tour affected jazz in Europe ever afterward, and Kenny Clarke took residence in Paris, to become a fixture of the European musical world, and eventually co-leader with Francy Boland of the Clarke-Boland Big Band, one of the best big bands in the history of the music.

Dizzy broke up his band on returning to New York, then reorganized it and kept it together through 1948 and '49. That band is heard to advantage in an album titled *Dizzy Gillespie in Concert* (Crescendo CD GNPD 23), recorded by broadcaster and impresario Gene Norman when he presented it in concert on July 19,

1948, at the Pasadena Civic Auditorium in California. The band's dadaesque high spirits are evident throughout. It was made when Dizzy was thirty.

The band had everything: laughter and swing and invention and vitality, an incredible fire and an exquisite balance of abandon and control. It is almost beyond belief that "traditionalists" could have found this music nihilistic or antisocial or sullen or nervous; it is filled with joy and exuberance. The antics in the album indicate that the whole band had taken the cue from its leader. There are sudden unison vocal outbursts, even in a ballad such as *Round About Midnight*.

Though other bands had been influenced by bebop, Dizzy's was the only flat-out all-bop big band. It played for listeners, not dancers. Every man in the band was a disciple, including James Moody on tenor saxophone, Ernie Henry on alto, and Cecil Payne on baritone. The surprising thing is how many musicians had by 1949 assimilated the Parker-Gillespie approach and vocabulary, enough that Dizzy was able to put together this band.

Its personnel included Chano Pozo, who was murdered in New York not long after this concert. (Gene Norman believes this was his last recorded performance.) Here again we see the breadth of Dizzy's vision, his role in the Afro-Cuban infusion into jazz and, later, his part in importing Brazilian samba.

A way to catch a sideways glance at Dizzy's brilliance is found on this album in the scat vocal track *Ool-Ya-Koo*. Yes, it's funny, yes it's clownish. But just as his musical invention is luxuriant, so is his abstraction of language. In a perfect onomatopoeic evocation of his own playing, he flings out sounds and syllables unknown to English or any other language, free of inhibition or any trace of desire to have them make sense, except musically, and again you find yourself wondering how that mind works, how his neuromuscular system has been put into such responsive touch with the incorporeal inner self.

His singing and playing are *ecstatic,* the root of which, as Rollo May points out in *The Courage to Create* (1975), is "ex-stasis"— to stand out from, to be, as May puts it, "freed from the usual split between subject and object which is a perpetual dichotomy in most human activity."

He says: "*Ecstasy* is the accurate term for the intensity of conscious that occurs in the creative act. But it is not to be thought of merely as a Bacchic 'letting go'; it involves the total person, with the subconscious and unconscious acting in unity with the conscious. It is not, thus, *irrational;* it is, rather, suprarational. It brings intellectual, volitional, and emotional functions into play altogether."

And there you have Dizzy's playing on that stage in Pasadena a little over fifty years ago, and its spirit infuses the entire band.

But the big-band era was over, and it was impossible to maintain a touring band of such size. In early 1950, Dizzy surrendered to the ultimatum of his wife and broke it up. He went back to a small group and toured with Jazz at the Philharmonic.

"The period 1950 until 1953 was to be an artistic low point in Dizzy's career," Alyn Shipton writes, "redeemed by a few examples of his technically brilliant playing on record or in concert and with a few glimpses of the future direction he was to take."

By then Miles Davis had made the nonet recordings with Gerry Mulligan, Gil Evans, John Lewis, and others, the so-called Birth of the Cool recordings. The relationship between Miles and Dizzy, Shipton says, "has always been hard to pin down." He maintains that a master-and-pupil relationship, begun in the Eckstine band, continued into the 1950s. But Miles was critical of Dizzy's behavior before an audience, saying, "As much as I love Dizzy and loved Louis 'Satchmo' Armstrong, I always hated the way they used to laugh and grin for the audiences. I knew *why* they did it—to make money and because they were entertainers as well as trumpet players."

That Miles's seemingly sullen stance was fully as theatrical as Dizzy's clowning, and just as effective in commanding an audience, should be obvious. But I must admit that a slight uneasiness over Dizzy's antics for a long time clouded my own perception of his art. Later I came to understand his use of so-called showmanship and eventually to know just how purposive his clowning could be.

I never told him that in the early days, his laughter, his clowning, had deceived me, as it had others, impairing my vision of the brilliance of the music. Why did he take such apparent delight in putting people on?

"Oh," he told me in 1960 in Milwaukee, "that's just a characteristic of the human race. Everybody wants to put people on, I think. And get away with it! That's the thing about it: put people on and *get away with it*." His eyes twinkled. "That's a science in itself."

But hadn't it cost him status in the world of jazz?

"It's a possibility, all right," he said. "Especially among people who are so *serious* about this.

"Now to come into the serious part of this music, that's something else. Serious as far as the *music* is concerned. But as far as your actions are concerned, that has nothing to do with your seriousness about jazz. Because I'm extremely serious about the music. I don't put music on.

"But a lot of people can't tell the difference. I get a lot of write-ups saying, 'If only he wouldn't do such-and-such a thing, if he wouldn't make people laugh.' I read a lot of articles like that, here and in Europe.

"But I think I have a definite commitment to do things and let people feel good, and put them in the right vein as to the music. The music is extremely important. But other things are also important—developing a rapport between the audience and yourself. You want them to try to understand what you're doing.

"But sometimes you read all the articles in the magazines, and you don't see your articles, and naturally you feel something. Sometimes, you know? I don't ever hear anybody come out and say I sound *bad.* You know, some people come up to me and say, 'Damn, you would have been so nice if you hadn't been funny.' So I say, 'Be specific about it. What didn't I do just now that I did ten years ago?' And they never come up with an answer.

"Sometimes I read in the Sunday section of the *New York Times* about jazz, and I don't see my name. Now I have nothing against people because they have their own views about who contributed what. A lot of guys who contribute don't know what they've done. But I'm in a different position. I know *exactly* what I've done. Now these guys who've set themselves up as critics, they're supposed to know what's been done . . .

"You can listen to the records and tell the stature of a musician—but with many records, not one record. You take them chronologically, and you can get a pretty good picture.

"Of course, it's very seldom that you hear a guy at his best on records, but you can tell where his mind is going. Sometimes it gets on records, and then there's a masterpiece.

"I've never played my best on records. And I've only played my best four or five times in my whole career, and I know records wasn't one of them, one of those times when everything was clicking. You never know where it's going to happen.

"The musicians I'm working with inspire me, rhythm sections inspire me, and then soloists. Charlie Parker used to give me tremendous inspiration. He'd always play before me. We had it arranged.

"But I hear my music all over, even in Frank Sinatra's arrangements, and it really doesn't matter to me, because it will all come out in the wash, baby. History avenges itself, and this is history, the history of music. Whether I get the recognition now, it will all come out. Because the records are out and the records are . . . well, a matter of record.

"Why do they ignore me?" Dizzy said that day. "Only because I'm funny. Do I intend to stop being funny? Hell no! If the music goes, I can always go on the stage as a comedian!"

And then this dark musing: "Maybe I should go on and die."

But that cloud quickly passed. I pointed out to him that many musicians thought he was playing better than he ever had. He said, "Barring physical things that happen to you—your chops and things—you're *supposed* to get better as you get older. As you get more experience, you know more what to do. So naturally you must, in the greatest part of cases, get better.

"A lot of things you become cognizant of. The most important is *taste*. The *most*. The same thing that you play here, it's a bitch. You play it someplace else, it's nothing. It's not how you play it, it's where you put it.

"Of course your playing is *never* fulfilled. But I think I'm doing a lot of things now I couldn't do ten years ago. I could name a hundred things. You have more confidence in the way you do it."

Then he said something that startled me: "I have to fight tension constantly." Within weeks I heard Miles Davis say the same thing, and Miles added: "And it gets worse every year."

"*You* get nervous?" I said to Dizzy.

He said, "Yes I do. Sometimes when I'm playing I listen to myself and say, 'Hey, wait a minute!' And then another time, it'll just settle down. And that has something to do with your own personal thing, how you feel.

"What I want to do now is extend what I've done. When an architect builds a building, y'know, and decides he wants to put on some new wings, it's still the same building. That's what I want to do. He keeps on until it's finished, and when he dies, somebody else can do it.

"I want to extend what I've done, and make the money. I don't mean that money means that much to me. I just don't want anybody doing benefits for me after I'm dead. And I want my wife, if she lives longer, to live just like I was here."

He had thirty-two more years ahead of him.

On May 15, 1953, Dizzy took part in a performance at Toronto's Massey Hall with Charlie Parker, Bud Powell, Charles Mingus, and Max Roach. That program is available on Debut (originally Mingus's own company and now one of the labels belonging to the Fantasy group) under the title *The Quintet* (OJC-044). Among that concert's other virtues, Parker plays superbly, and Bud Powell, whose unstable mental condition had vitiated many of his performances, was brilliant. When he was off his game, his time could be flakey. It isn't here. In Shipton's view, "No better example survives of the intrinsic difference between Bird's spontaneous ability to conjure endless variations in a jam-session environment and Dizzy's to construct architecturally thought-through choruses in which his stock phrases are carefully integrated."

He concludes: "The Massey Hall concert has become one of the most celebrated events in jazz history and is especially valuable because of the relative scarcity of collaborations between Dizzy and Bird after 1946."

The middle 1950s saw Dizzy traveling with Norman Granz's Jazz at the Philharmonic package, and recording such albums with small group as *Have Trumpet, Will Excite* and *The Ebullient Mr. Gillespie* for Granz's Verve label. But Dizzy, like others who had grown up on, and through, the big bands (Gerry Mulligan among them) retained the yearning to have one, and he was at it again whenever he could keep one floating.

The opportunity came when he was asked to go on one of the

State Department's cultural exchange tours, this one of the Middle East. The tour took place in early 1956, with Dizzy fronting the first big band he'd had since 1950. It was such a success that the State Department asked him to tour South America. Dizzy asked his friend Dave Usher from Detroit (who had run Dizzy's short-lived Dee Gee record label) to come along. Dizzy had purchased an Ampex 600 tape recorder, and Usher recorded the band. Volumes 1 and 2 of *Dizzy in South America* are available on CD by mail order from Consolidated Artists Productions, the cooperative organized by Mike Longo, one of Dizzy's favorite pianists.

Usher said, "In every hotel, people were always waiting in the lobby, day and night, to meet Dizzy, or even just get a glimpse of him. Somehow a few of them would always get upstairs. They would be waiting in the hall outside Dizzy's room."

Dizzy's comedic sense served him well. His peculiar ability simply to stand there and inspire a smile or laughter, his little dance steps, his uncanny capacity to communicate, sailed through whatever barriers of language there might be.

In São Paulo, Brazil, Dizzy and Usher went to a school sponsored by the U.S. government, Casa Roosevelt, to teach English. Usher said: "It was an open-air, backyard kind of thing. There were a great many kids, junior high and high school students, who were asking Dizzy questions. They wanted to come to the evening performance, but they didn't have the money. We found out that our secondary sponsor, the American National Theater Academy, was charging admission. We told the kids to present their IDs and they'd get in. Dizzy refused to play until the kids were allowed in. He said, 'We're doing this for the people.'"

The albums derived from the Usher tapes, despite some shortcomings in sound, are fantastic. If ever anyone should ask what jazz is all about, you could play the *Cool Breeze* track on Volume 1. Dizzy plays an extended ballistic solo that is truly awesome—one of the great solos in jazz history. There are, in addition, some superb solos by Benny Golson and Phil Woods, among others.

Phil Woods was widely considered one of the most promising saxophonists inspired by Charlie Parker, a promise that has long since been richly fulfilled. At that time he was married to Parker's widow, Chan. (They later divorced.) Today Phil plays with unmistakable individuality, but in those days, obviously, he lacked confidence. After the South American tour, he left the Gillespie band. One night, as he recalls the incident, "I was in Birdland, stoned, as I often was in those days. Dizzy and Art Blakey kidnapped me. Took me home to Dizzy's and sat me down and said, 'What are you moaning about? Why don't you get your own band?'

"I tearfully asked them if they thought I was good enough, and one of them said, 'Yeah! If you stop behaving like an asshole!'

"I asked them if if a white guy could make it, considering the music was a black invention. I was getting a lot of flak about stealing not only Bird's music but his wife and family as well, especially from Mingus. Miles was always nice to me, very supportive, as was and remains Max Roach. And Dizzy said, 'You can't steal a gift. Bird gave the world his music, and if you can hear it you can have it.'

"Wow. They thought I could play, and that was enough for them."

Trombonist Al Grey, who played in the bands of Benny Carter, Lucky Millinder, Jimmie Lunceford, Duke Ellington, Count Basie, and Lionel Hampton, remembered that period with Gillespie as a pinnacle of his life. "What a band!" Al said to me several years ago. "Come on! We'd come to work twenty minutes before time, warming up getting ready to hit. The trumpet section had Lee Morgan, Bama Warwick, Lammar Wright. The trombone

section was Melba Liston, Chuck Connors, Rod Levitt, and me.
The rhythm section was Wynton Kelly, Paul West, and Charlie
Persip. The reed section was Benny Golson, Billy Mitchell, Ernie
Henry, Jimmy Powell, and Billy Root on baritone, who came
from Stan Kenton's band. For a while we had Phil Woods. This
is what I admired about Diz. And Lucky Millinder. They didn't
care what color anybody was.

"But Dizzy was losing so much money. To play in that band
we all had to take a *drop* in fees. We all got $135 a week, and
you had to pay your hotel and all your expenses out of that."

Norman Granz also recorded Dizzy with the big band (there
had been personnel changes after South America), on July 6,
1957, for *Dizzy Gillespie at Newport* (Verve CD 314 513 754-
2). An excellent studio collection is the two-CD *Birks' Works:
The Verve Big-Band Sessions* (Verve 314 527 900-2). So Dizzy's
big-band work in the mid-1950s is well documented on recordings.

A good three-CD package called *Dizzy's Diamonds* (Verve 314
513 875-2) documents Gillespie's work with Granz. The material
was selected and sequenced by drummer and scholar Kenny
Washington. For liner notes he interviewed Jon Faddis, whose
work on trumpet probably comes closer to Dizzy's than anyone's.
Faddis told Washington: "When he has a big band behind him,
it pushes him in different directions and that's when I think Dizzy
is actually at his best."

Dizzy was known for the casual way he would hire sidemen, as
he did with Ray Brown and Junior Mance. Composer Hale Smith
got a call when he was a student at the Cleveland Institute of
Music. The voice on the phone said, "This is Dizzy Gillespie."
Hale thought, Oh yeah, sure it is. But in a moment he realized
it was indeed Dizzy Gillespie. Dizzy had heard from Sahib Shi-

hab, who was playing saxophone in his group, that Hale was a pretty good pianist. He said, "Do you want a gig?" So Hale went to a job that night. He asked for the charts. There weren't any.

"Fortunately, I knew most of the tunes from the records," Hale said. And he eared his way through the rest. At the end of the night, Dizzy asked if he wanted to work with him another night. And then for a time he became Dizzy's pianist, when he could get away from his studies. They remained lifelong friends. Years later, Dizzy told him the directors of the Hartford Symphony had asked him to perform the Haydn *Trumpet Concerto*. Dizzy asked Hale if he would run through the piece with him. Hale played it from a piano reduction score; Dizzy sight-read it flawlessly, and then said at the end of it that he thought he wouldn't play it. He said it wasn't really his cup of tea.

Dizzy met Lalo Schifrin in Buenos Aires during the South American tour. Dizzy played with him briefly and urged him to come to New York. Lalo detoured through the Paris Conservatory and composition studies with, among other teachers, Olivier Messiaen. When at last he came to New York, playing with Latin bands to eke out a living, he finally, hesitantly, called Dizzy. Dizzy told him to write something for him. Lalo sketched the *Gillespiana Suite*. He showed it to Dizzy, who said he would perform it. At the moment, he had no pianist for his small group. Who was he planning to get? "I sort of had you in mind," Dizzy said. And so Lalo joined him on piano and as resident composer. It changed the course of his life.

Lalo told me many stories of Dizzy from that period. Once he and Dizzy were in a hotel room with a friend who was putting golf balls into a glass. Dizzy asked if he could try it. And, repeatedly, he putted the ball into the glass. The man asked if he had played a lot of golf. He'd never touched a golf club before. Then how was he doing this?

"I just think I'm the ball and I want to be in the cup," Dizzy said. That is a form of zen, and I think Dizzy approached playing the horn in the same way. How else to account for the liquid direct contact with the instrument and the music it was emitting?

Lalo told me funny stories, too, stories of Dizzy's humor. In Scotland, Dizzy would approach someone on the street and say, in his most formal enunciation, "Pardon me, my name is Gillespie, and I'm looking for my relatives." He did of course have white relatives, and in his later years, he told me, when he went home to Cheraw, some of them recognized and welcomed him.

Lalo also played Berlin with him. When the bellboy showed them to their rooms, Dizzy said to him, "Would you mind trying out the shower?"

"*Wass?*" the man said.

"You Germans have some funny ideas about showers," Dizzy said.

That was about as close to malicious as I think he could get— although he did carry that knife. But even that could be a tool of humor. Mike Longo recalled an occasion when he and Dizzy and other members of the group were playing cards backstage. Dizzy pulled out his blade and, with a grand gesture and an ominous glower, stabbed it into the table top. "What's that for?" Mike said.

"That's in case any of you motherfuckers mess with me."

Mike took out a dime and dropped it on the table. "What's that?" Dizzy said.

Mike said, "That's a dime to call the Mafia in case any of you motherfuckers mess with *me*."

Dizzy experimented with large-orchestra formats. He became deeply impressed by the orchestral writing of the young Clare Fischer, and commissioned him to write an album for him. They decided to do Ellington material. According to Shipton, "It is one of the least successful of Dizzy's big band ventures, lacking the authentic stamp of Ellington's own personality."

I don't think it was meant to reflect Ellington as much as the broader instrumental palette that Gil Evans had explored. If, as Shipton suggests, Dizzy wanted a setting comparable to that Miles Davis had found with Gil Evans in *Porgy and Bess* and *Miles Ahead*, he had found the right arranger. But when Fischer arrived in New York from California, charts completed, he found that Dizzy, with the out-to-lunch carelessness of which he was capable, hadn't bothered to book an orchestra. Fischer had to do it at the last minute. Most of the best jazz players in New York were already engaged, and Fischer had to fill in the instrumentation with symphony players. They didn't grasp the idiom, and the album is stiff. In a word, it just doesn't swing. But the writing in that album is gorgeous; its failure is Dizzy's fault.

Lalo Schifrin presented Dizzy with the *Gillespiana Suite*, recorded in New York on November 14 and 15, 1960. It is an interesting album. It uses French horns and tuba instead of a saxophone section. One of the things it has over the Clare Fischer album is a beautifully booked band of some of the best players available in New York at the time, including John Frosk, Ernie Royal, Clark Terry, and Joe Wilder on trumpets, Urbie Green, Frank Rehak, Britt Woodman, and Paul Faulise on trombones.

An album in this genre that I like is *Gil Fuller and The Monterey Jazz Orchestra*, recorded in Los Angeles in 1967 after Dizzy's early-autumn appearance at Monterey and available on a Blue Note CD, alas now out of print. As in *Gillespiana*, four French horns are used, but no tuba, and there is a sax section. Fuller gets top billing, and his writing is delicious, both in his own compositions and arrangements of two of Dizzy's pieces, *Groovin' High* and *Things Are Here*.

Something had occurred at the Monterey Jazz Festival the year of its inception, indeed in the first moments of its existence, in

1958. No one wanted to "open," the protocol of show business holding that the opening is a demeaning slot. Grover Sales, who was the festival's publicist in its early years, witnessed what happened next. Dizzy said, "Shoot, I'll open," and went onstage and played *The Star Spangled Banner*. Then Louis Armstrong came onstage. Dizzy got down on one knee and kissed his hand. "A lot of people said Dizzy was clowning," Grover recalls. "He wasn't clowning. There is a photo of that. Louis looks pleased and surprised.

"Some time after that, I played an Armstrong record for Dizzy. He said, very quietly, 'Louis Armstrong was a miracle. Imagine anyone playing that in 1930.' " And, Dizzy said of Armstrong, "No him, no me."

As the 1960s progressed, Dizzy moved deeper and deeper into an inner spiritualism, of which the incident with the golf balls is perhaps an expression. He embraced the Baha'i faith, although he never talked about it, he never proselytized. Nat Hentoff said: "I knew Dizzy for some forty years, and he did evolve into a spiritual person. That's a phrase I almost never use, because many of the people who call themselves spiritual would kill for their faith. But Dizzy reached an inner strength and discipline that total pacifists call 'soul force.' He always had a vivid presence. Like they used to say of Fats Waller, whenever Dizzy came into a room he filled it. He made people feel good, and he was the sound of surprise, even when his horn was in its case."

I had always found Dizzy an accessible man, and as the years went on he became only more so, even as part of him withdrew into an inner peace. I suppose it was comforting to him to know that he was revered by musicians everywhere.

I remember going to hear him at a matinee at the Regal Theater in Chicago, taking my son, who was then probably three, with me. Backstage, Dizzy got down on his knees with him, put his trumpet mouthpiece to the tip of his nose, and buzzed his lips in a tune. My son giggled delightedly; how he got the joke, I don't know. But Dizzy could reach any audience, of any age and apparently any nationality, and those who derogated his showmanship just didn't get it. It was always at the service of his art.

I saw this one night in Ottawa, probably in 1969. Peter Shaw, a producer for the Canadian Broadcasting Corporation's radio division, stationed in Ottawa, asked me to come up from New York and sing a group of my songs for broadcast. In those days the CBC still generated a lot of original music. He said I could use a fair-sized orchestra. When he asked who I wanted for an arranger, I said, "Chico O'Farrill." Chico was my friend, neighbor, and Saturday-night drinking companion. Chico and I went to Ottawa and recorded that hour of radio.

Later, Peter asked us to come up again and do a concert at a place called Camp Fortune, an outdoor amphitheater across the Ottawa River in the beautiful Gatineau Hills of Quebec. Then Peter called and asked if Chico would consider performing the *Aztec Suite,* which he had composed for Art Farmer. They had recorded it in an album for United Artists.

We tried to reach Art, but he had moved to Vienna and was working mostly in Europe. Chico looked at me and said, "How about Dizzy?"

Why not? So Chico called Dizzy, who said he'd love to do it.

Back to Ottawa Chico and I went. When the day of the first rehearsal arrived, no Dizzy. His flight had been grounded by extreme storms in the St. Louis area. Chico rehearsed the orchestra. Dizzy phoned to tell us the weather was clearing and he would be there next day for the dress rehearsal and the performance.

Living in Ottawa at that time was a fine saxophonist from Brooklyn named Russ Thomas. He had a Russian wife, an exceptional seamstress who had made him several dashikis, not in the exquisite cottons of Africa but in wool, suitable for the weather of Ottawa winters. Russ wore one to the dress rehearsal and brought another for me. They were in beige and dark earth tones. Dizzy loved them on sight. Russ and I were wearing them when Dizzy walked in, and all the musicians stood up in obeisance. I said, "Now see here, Mr. Gillespie, I hope you realize you're now on our territory."

"*Damn!*" he said, ignoring the remark. "Where'd you get that?"

I introduced him to Russ and told him Russ's wife had made it.

"I want to wear that in the concert!" Dizzy said.

I took it off and gave it to him.

Then he rehearsed, reading the *Aztec Suite* flawlessly at sight. Forget his genius: this was his *musicianship*.

Even before the concert, on the phone from New York, I had told Peter Shaw that there was absolutely no way I was going to follow Dizzy Gillespie onto a stage, even if in theory this was "my" concert. I'm not crazy, I said.

But if I opened, it would create an imbalance. Chico and I came up with a solution. We would write a new piece, which Dizzy, Chico, and I could do together to close the concert.

I did the first half of the concert. I said I was pleased to be able, for the first time, to do my songs in the country where I was born. Followed by: "And now, may I introduce my friend Mr. John Birks Gillespie."

Dizzy came onstage in that glorious dashiki, toting his tilted horn, took the mike in his hand as I walked off, and looked around (as was his wont) as if surprised to find there were people there. And there were indeed, perhaps five thousand of them, spread up the grassy slope of a natural amphitheater. He had them smiling before he uttered a word, and then, when he said, "Damn! I'm glad I'm a Canadian!" they roared. He had them, without playing a note.

And oh did he play. Magnificently, soaringly. When the suite came to its end, the audience stood, screaming. But we had prepared no more material. And at this point I was to walk out and do the song, a ballad, with him and Chico. My God! I could never walk out into that inferno of applause. That audience had forgotten I existed, and with good reason.

Dizzy, acting as if he didn't hear them, got out the music for his part in the song we were to do. It was through-composed, and his music was in a long accordion-fold strip. Somewhat formally, still ignoring the applause, he pretended to put it on his music stand, but dropped it. It spilled on the stage. The audience laughed, and the applause died down a little.

He gathered it up, his horn under his arm, and then went through gestures of putting it back together, like a man who can't quite figure out how to refold a road map. At last he succeeded, and, with an air of ostentatious triumph, put the music up a second time. And it fell again.

This time he stood his horn on its bell, its body tilted at that odd forty-five-degree angle. He got down on his knees, put the music together yet again, and had the audience helpless with laughter. He stood up, and put the music back. This time it stayed in place. He held up a hand for quiet, then said into the microphone, "Ladies and gentleman, Gene Lees."

And he and Chico and I did the song. He had calculatedly broken the mood of his own success, changed the ambience entirely through laughter, and then handed me the audience as a gift. It was incredibly clever, not to say deeply generous, and ever afterward I understood the meaning of the comedy in the midst of his great and serious art. Shakespeare knew how to use light moments to set up the serious material to follow. So did Sibelius.

So did Stravinsky. Indeed, you cannot write tragedy without a sense of humor, for without it, everything is dirge and darkness and boredom. Whether Dizzy had ever given this a conscious thought, I shall never know; but he certainly understood the principle.

Afterward there was a small party at Peter Shaw's home, the upper floor of a duplex. I remember Dizzy's graciousness to my mother and my sister. My mother knew nothing of jazz, and never understood my fascination, and my sister's, with it. But Dizzy held her enthralled.

For part of the evening, some of us, including Dizzy, were out on Peter's balcony, overlooking the leafy parkland along the Rideau Canal, the glow of street lamps casting shadows through the trees. More and more, as the years had gone on, I'd found Dizzy's purported rejoinders to Armstrong at the time of bebop's burgeoning hard to credit. I asked him about this, out on that balcony. He said, in a voice as soft as the evening, "Oh no. I'd never say anything like that about Pops."

He was very serious about his Baha'i faith. He once told pianist, songwriter, and author Ben Sidran, "Jazz musicians are just naturally peaceful people, because there's so much on their minds trying to figure this music out that they don't have time to be evil."

And once, when he was appearing as a guest with the Phil Woods Quintet, he said, "I am so lucky to be a musician."

Dizzy's work in the later years is often seen as a turning away from the revolutionism (although he and Parker denied that it was a revolution) of bebop, a surrender to conservatism. I don't see it that way. I once asked him what he looked for in a tune.

He said, "Simple changes." Perceiving my surprise—he didn't miss much—he added, "If they're too complicated, it won't swing."

I don't think he became conservative. He abandoned the excesses of bebop. And, in the exuberance of youth, there were excesses. Some of the music of that time now seems cute and coy. Also, Dizzy embraced lyricism in later years, playing ballads with an ardor that isn't there in the early stuff. In any event, it is a pattern for great minds to define their innovations early— and great innovations always do come from the young, which is well known in the sciences—and spend the later years exploring, refining, and teaching the revelations of the early years.

To expect Dizzy to continue revolutionism is unreasonable. And, melodically and harmonically, he and Bird and Bud Powell pushed jazz about as far as it could go without abandoning completely the vocabulary of Western music. It seems that a lay audience—and one can hardly expect to survive on a professional audience—can follow art only so far into obscurity. Bill Evans and some others refined what Dizzy and his colleagues had achieved, adding a little more derived from European concert music, and it is questionable whether some of what Bill and others did should be called jazz at all. Brilliant, yes, marvelous and moving, but it escapes the bounds of jazz. There is something else he achieved. Sonny Rollins, quoted in Ira Gitler's *Swing to Bop* (1985), said it:

"Jazz has always been a music of integration. In other words, there were definitely lines where blacks would be and where whites would begin to mix a little. I mean, jazz was not just a music; it was a social force in this country, and it was talking about freedom and people enjoying things for what they are and not having to worry about whether they were supposed to be white, black, and all this stuff. Jazz has always been the music that had this kind of spirit. Now I believe for that reason, the people that could push jazz have *not* pushed jazz because that's what jazz means. A lot of times, jazz means no barriers. Long before sports broke down its racial walls, jazz was bringing people together on both sides of the bandstand. Fifty-second Street, for all its shortcomings, was a place in which black and white musicians could interact in a way that led to natural bonds of friendship. The audience, or at least part of it, took a cue from this, leading to an unpretentious flow of social intercourse."

Dizzy took all his pain, all his resentment—he once said to me, "Jazz is too good for the United States," but I saw this as a passing anger, and it was—and by whatever mysterious process inverted it all, making himself into the fabulous creature and creation that he was, not only one of the greatest musicians of his century, but also this, especially this: a great healer. That is an achievement even beyond his music; indeed, the music is an expression of it, along with his laughter. All this makes the present induced polarization of jazz a searing insult to the great heart, great soul, great mind, great art, and great life of John Birks Gillespie.

When Creed Taylor was producing the album *Rhythmstick* at Rudy Van Gelder's studio in New Jersey, he asked me to go to Newark airport to pick up Dizzy, who was flying in from Washington for the date. Dizzy came off the plane carrying that rhythm stick, a broom handle (I suppose) with pop-bottle caps nailed to it. Shaking it, tapping it against his shoe sole, he could produce the most astonishingly complex rhythms. Phil Woods said that when he traveled with Dizzy (whom he called Sky King, because he was always flying somewhere), that thing would set off metal detectors in every airport they passed through. And you always knew where Dizzy was in the airport; you could hear it.

I hadn't seen him for a while, and when we got into the car I said impetuously, "Gee, Birks, I'm glad to see you."

He tapped his forefinger on his sternum and said, earnestly, warmly, "Me too." I never felt more honored.

My friend Sahib Shihab fell ill with a cancer we all knew was terminal. I called Dizzy, told him, and gave him the hospital number. There was nothing humorous in *that* conversation. He telephoned Sahib almost daily until Sahib died.

Jon Faddis, James Moody, and a few more of his friends were at Dizzy's bedside on January 6, 1993, when he died peacefully in his sleep, of pancreatic cancer. The CD *Dizzy's Diamonds* was playing quietly in the room.

It is my privilege that I can say I knew him. And, oh yes, this too: once, just once, I sang a song with him.

You Gotta Sing

One evening in 1981, at the Monterey Jazz Festival, I was sitting with Clark Terry and saxophonist Plas Johnson listening to Dizzy Gillespie. Clark smiled and shook his head in wonder, and announced: "He's still the master."

But Clark himself is one of the masters. If one reflects on the classical trumpet literature, on the use of the instrument in all sorts of pre-jazz music, and ponders his astounding flexibility and effortless expressivity, the inevitable conclusion is that he too is one of the greatest trumpet players in history. He and Dizzy may be the pinnacles of the instrument. Not just in jazz history, in all history. He is so individual that one can identify him not just in two or three bars but in two or three notes. Sometimes in one note.

Clark does a circus turn whose complexity is not always appreciated. He'll play trumpet with one hand, fluegelhorn with the other, in duets with himself. He does so with a joy and exuberance that is incredibly infectious, as indeed is all of his music.

It must be remembered that his fingering is ambidextrous. But more to the point, he seems to be partitioning his mind. It may be fun to watch and hear; it is deeper than it looks, and it tells us something about the remarkable brain and neurological organization of Clark Terry.

In the 1960s, when jazz musicians made their New York headquarters in a bar called Jim and Andy's on the south side of Forty-eighth Street, just east of Sixth Avenue, Clark Terry was working in the NBC *Tonight Show* band, at first under the leadership of Skitch Henderson, later of Doc Severinsen. I did not know then that he and Doc were especially close friends.

Rockefeller Center, where the show was taped, is one block up Sixth Avenue from where Jim and Andy's stood. J and A's, as we called it, which might have been named the Institute of Osmotic Learning, has long since been effaced, replaced by one of those undistinguished glass-and-steel verticalities that have stripped the character out of central Manhattan. Doc was often in there. So was Clark. I used to talk with him almost daily. The exchanges in Jim and Andy's were endless, and insights burgeoned and blossomed in one's mind. Many of mine came from Clark.

He was always busy, with the *Tonight Show* band, with the quintet he and Bob Brookmeyer led in the early 1960s, with the Gerry Mulligan Concert Jazz Band (his recorded duet with Mulligan on *Blueport*, naming various cities through quoted song titles, is one of the wittiest bits of music I know), with guest appearances on the recordings of an enormous number of musicians, and with studio engagements of all kinds, up to (or down to) performances on the kazoo. And always there was sunshine when Clark entered the Gymnasium, as the late Gary McFarland called J and A's.

Roger Kellaway played piano in the Terry-Brookmeyer quintet for two and a half years, starting in 1962, made two albums with

Clark Terry with the author, Chicago, 1961 (Photo by Ted Williams)

Clark, and did a good deal of studio work with him, back in the era when jazz musicians could pay the rent, even very high rent, by such engagements. In Roger's estimation, "Clark Terry is consistently one of the most up, positive human beings I have ever known. I can't remember a negative conversation, ever. He is always a joy to be around.

"And the music! Delightful, inventive, lyrical, and full of Clark's sense of humor. I have always looked forward to playing with him. It is one of those can't-wait-to-do-it situations."

When I see Clark at all now, it is for a few minutes between sets somewhere. We share as a greeting a whispered obscenity, a private joke that I will not tell you. But a couple or three years back, Clark played on a cruise of the S.S. *Norway*. We both had the flu, and we spent a lot of time together, if only in commiseration. Most of the conversations that follow occurred then on that ship, mostly in Clark's stateroom.

Whence this incredible flexibility? Is it a consequence of his having begun his career by playing a garden hose?

Clark Terry was born in St. Louis, Missouri, on December 14, 1920, the son of a laborer at Laclede Gas and Light Company, the seventh of eleven children, seven of them girls. Before Clark's birth, one girl died. Clark's brothers never escaped the destiny of their father. Clark alone did.

In the history of music you encounter families in which music is the accepted and even expected profession: the two Johann Strausses, the Bach family (whose tradition may still be going on), Leopold and Wolfgang Amadeus Mozart, the Casadesus family, the Brubecks, and many more. Then there are those in whom the imperative for an art seems to emerge from a genetic umbra, an atavism, boon perhaps of an unknown ancestor. Debussy, for example.

I'd known about the garden hose for years. "I must have been ten, eleven years old," as Clark remembers it. "Twelve, maybe. My older sister's husband, Cy McField, played tuba in the Dewey Jackson band—Dewey Jackson's Musical Ambassadors—at a place called Sauter's Park in Carondolet in South St. Louis. That's where I was born.

"The park was all Caucasian. We were not allowed to go in there. Us kids, we'd walk down there, about three miles. Walk down to the end of Broadway, the county line. We'd stand up on something behind the bandstand and we'd listen to the band that way.

"I remember one cat who played in Dewey Jackson's band,

Mr. Latimore. He was a big, huge guy, played lead trumpet. He used to like me and my brother-in-law used to take me to all the rehearsals. He'd say, 'Son, you can watch my horn.' And I'd say, 'Oh thank you,' and I'd literally sit there and watch his horn. After so many rehearsals, I became very very close to him. He owned a candy store, and he always kept a pocket full of caramels and mary janes, and he'd give me a couple of caramels and a couple of mary janes and sometimes a couple of pennies. He was the greatest cat in the world, so I wanted to play the horn he played. I'm glad he wasn't a banjo player!

"So one time they went on a break. He said, 'You watch my horn.' I said, 'Okay, Mr. Latimore,' and by the time they came back, I had been magnetically drawn to this horn, huffin' and puffin' away, trying to make a sound. And he walked in. He said, 'Ah, son, you're gonna be a trumpet player.' And I've always said, 'And I was stupid enough to believe him.'

"That, plus the fact that on the corner called Iron Street and Broadway, near where I lived, there was a sanctified church. We used to sit on the curb and let those rhythms be instilled in us." Banging a beat with his hands, he sang against it a strong churchy passage. "You know, with the tambourines, and the people dancin' and jiggin' and all that. That was as much as you needed to be instilled with the whole thing.

"We had this little band. We used to play on the corner. My first thing was a comb and tissue paper. The paper vibrates. Then I came across a kazoo, which is the same principle. Later on in my life, we had to have kazoos as standard equipment in the studio. Sometimes we would have to do little things when you were recording for different commercial products.

"We had a guy named Charlie Jones—we called him Bones— who used to play an old discarded vacuum hose, wound around his neck like a tuba, into a beer mug." Clark sang a buzzy bass line in imitation, mostly roots and fifths. "It was a better sound than the jug." The jug of course was the old earthenware jug used in country music and jazz.

"We had a cat who played the jug, too. With the two of them, we had a good solid foundation. My brother Ed played—we called him Shorts, he was a little short cat—played the drums. He took the rungs out of some old chairs for sticks. In those days we didn't have refrigeration, we had ice boxes, and when the water pan wore out, started leaking and got rusty, it would sound just like a snare. They had those tall bushel baskets in those days, I haven't seen one in a long time. He'd turn one of those upside down and hang the old discarded ice pan on the side and take the chair rungs and keep a rhythm like that. He got an old wash-tub and fixed it so he could beat it." Clark laughed that delicious and slightly conspiratorial laugh of his as he pounded a beat.

"He sounds like some kind of a genius," I noted.

"Yeah!" Clark said. "He was. Well, I got an old piece of a hose one day and coiled it up and got some wire and tied it so that it stuck up in three places so it would look like valves. I took a discarded kerosene funnel and that was my bell. I got a little piece of lead pipe—we didn't realize in those days that there was lead poisoning—and that was my mouthpiece."

It struck me that Clark had invented a primitive bugle, on which he could presumably play the overtones. "Yeah!" he said again. "By the time I got into the drum and bugle corps, I had already figured out the system like the Mexican mariachi players use. They were taught back in those days to play the mouthpiece first."

He did a rhythmic tonguing like a mariachi player, then pressed his lips together and buzzed. "After a while I figured out how to change the pitch." Pursing his lips, he did a glissando, up one octave and down, flawlessly. "And then they could do that with the mouthpiece. After you got the mouthpiece under control, and you got a bugle, you could play notes. You could make all the notes that went from one harmonic to the other."

Never having seen Clark teach, I realized what makes him such an incredible—and so he is reputed—pedagogue, and why young people who study with him worship him. And all of it is communicated with laughter and a sense of adventure.

I told Clark of a conversation I had in the early 1960s with Jack Teagarden. Teagarden's group was playing the London House in Chicago. Jack and I were sitting in one of the booths, with conversations going on all around us. It was legend that Jack could play all sorts of notes in "false" positions on the trombone because, as a child with short arms, he could make them no other way. As we discussed this, Jack, very softly, played a major scale with the slide in closed position. "You should be able to play any note in any position," Jack told me. "All the slide does is make it easier."

"Yeah, I agree," Clark said, laughing. "I'll never forget when I met Sweets Edison in the Basie band. Well, I knew him before that around St. Louis. That was before he really got known. He had an old Reynolds trumpet. It was an old, old, old brand. I don't think there's even one on the scene today. It was jammed, and you couldn't tune it. But Sweets could play the damn thing in tune! It was just his chops.

"This proves the important thing is the mastery of the embouchure. Like Jack proved to you."

"You've never gone in front of the audience with a stern look and challenged the audience to like your music," I observed to Clark. "Neither did Dizzy. That doesn't mean one isn't serious about the music itself."

"Not at all!" Clark said vigorously. "Who was more serious about playing than Dizzy was? Nobody!"

"When did you begin to think of jazz as art, rather than merely entertainment?"

"Well, I think from the very beginning," he answered. "I wasn't aware of how much it was attuned to art until later years. But from the very beginning I knew that it was an entertaining thing, and you had to get involved if you were going to have a certain amount of success. My older sister's husband, Cy McField, played tuba in that Dewey Jackson band, as I mentioned. He used to do a little bit about a preacher. I was just a kid, and used to enjoy the music, and I found it very entertaining. Made you want to move, you know, and it made you laugh. People like to hear things that make them forget about their worries. People had a lot of worries in those days. It was the Depression. So jazz was in a sense born out of that, too. People wanted to forget about their inhibitions, and their problems, and where the next meal was coming from. They wanted to sing and dance and play instruments. In New Orleans, the pawn shops were loaded with ostracized instruments. These cats got hold of them, and played them by hook or crook. We always show this in clinics. How they played here, or over there or over there."

With a mouthpiece he demonstrated aberrant and off-center embouchures, which you saw fairly often in the old days among older players. "They were never taught properly. They just grabbed the instrument and played it however they thought they should. Maybe they saw somebody else do that. Most of them had very bad tone. But a lot of things came out of that. They had bad habits. But somebody had the ingenuity to figure out how to make his sound more acceptable to those who were considered legitimate players. This cat figured out how to hum and play at the same time."

Clark demonstrated the burry sound that this produces. "All those cats, all the way up to Vic Dickenson, knew how to play and hum. It was known as a buzz. It made the sound seem bigger.

This was, in a sense, a by-product of ignorance. And people would say, 'You don't want to listen to this cat. He sounds puny. He sounds like a monkey pissing on a shovel.'

"Things in the Italian vocabulary for music, we can't use a lot of them. You wouldn't get on the bandstand and say, 'Let's play some largo blues.' You'd sound like an educated fool. You want to say funky, greazy, slimey, ass-kicking, or whatever. The jazz cats figured out ways to communicate without knowing all that vocabulary. There was no way for them to get to that. There were no schools they could go to."

He imitated the kind of big, pushed sound that Ben Webster, among others, obtained. "There was no vocabulary for it," Clark explained. "It's from the abdomen. We called it 'body huffs.' *Hoo! Hoo! Hah! Hoo, hah, ho!* The reason Duke Ellington's band sounded so different was because the guys would use things like body huffs." He sang, remarkably reproducing the feeling of the Ellington sax section, an eighth-note pickup, the quarter notes anticipated by an eighth: *Huh-hoo, hoh, hoh!* "Any section," he went on, "that tries to phrase like that, if they don't know how to do the body huffs, it ain't comin' through." He sang it again, without that pushed body sound, reproducing an effect in which the time was academically the same, but the feeling wasn't there.

"It's from the abdomen," Clark repeated. "Like, for instance, when Prez played—" He sang in a completely different manner, the phrases light and airy. "We called it the *lull* sound, *lu, lu lu-lah.*" Then he made another sound, *Thuh, thuh, thuh.* "You produced the sound from between the teeth. You stop it with the tongue and the air continues around it." He sang some more, beginning the notes with the unvoiced *th* sound and ending it with the longer, voiced, buzzy *th.* "This is the kind of thing you ain't gonna find in no Italian dictionary. Ain't gonna find it in no classical players, and if they know, they're not gonna condone it because *they* didn't figure it out.

"We had an occasion with Duke to play with the Buffalo Philharmonic. At the end of the piece, I'll never forget the phrasing." He sang it. "That was the figure he wrote. They passed it out to the strings." And he sang the fixed classical phrasing of the same passage. "So Duke said, 'Let's take a break.' And he rewrote it in triplets. They came back and they played it. It came off. Tom Whaley, who did the copy work—he was with the band for years and years and years, and he died in complete obscurity two or three years ago—and Strays were there, and they got it. It took about an hour. But Duke made it swing." "Strays" was Bill Strayhorn.

"Now, getting back to your garden hose and your bugle . . ."

"I heard other notes," Clark said. "I was able to get those open tones on the bugle." He sang the racetrack bugle call.

"Were you able to get those in-between tones on that garden hose?"

"Not really. But it was a device that satisfied my yen for a trumpet, which I couldn't afford. I didn't have to use it too long because luckily the neighbors got tired of hearing me make sounds on that hose and—you won't believe this, Gene—they chipped in and bought me an old C. G. Conn trumpet from the pawnshop for twelve dollars and fifty cents."

"That's a sweet, dear thing, to give such encouragement and an instrument to a kid."

"Yeah it is," Clark agreed, "and I don't forget it. I've bought tons of instruments and given them to kids. I got a lot of kids started."

"How old were when you got that real trumpet?"

"I'd say roughly fifteen years old. I was at Vashon High School in St. Louis. Our director was Mr. Clarence Haydn Wilson. He was head of the music department. He issued the instruments for band. I wanted a trumpet, but there were no trumpets available. There was a valve trombone. He said, 'Take this, it's the same fingering. You can make more noise with it than you can with a trumpet.'"

"Was it in concert?" I asked him.

"I don't know. Wait, come to think of it, I think it was in B-flat. Same as trumpet. So, when I finally got hold of a trumpet the next semester, Mr. Wilson assigned me to a guy named Leonard Smalls to teach me the scales. Up till then I was just making noise on it. Old timey stuff." He sang a couple of riffs of the period. "We'd sometimes play on the streetcar, on our way to or from school. When the people from the neighborhood bought me this Conn, I didn't know from nothing, and Mr. Smalls taught me the fingering. I think by then I had lucked up on the right embouchure. From watching people, and asking questions."

"Did you also start boxing during that period?"

"Yeah. I learned it in St. Louis," Clark said. "Archie Moore and I were friends. Archie used to go with my sister, and we were pretty good buddies. He said in his book that I could have become a champion boxer if I'd wanted to. I was pretty good. There was a guy named Kid Carter, he used to teach all us kids. He'd walk up and hit you in the belly, and say, 'You gotta learn how to take it, boy.' He gathered us up and taught us the art of self-defense. He taught us how to punch and how to shift and recoil and all that. We got some pretty good little boxers out of there."

"Miles boxed too," I pointed out.

"Yeah, but Miles learned to box after he got to New York. He was a fan. I started early."

"Miles talked in his book about coming to hear you and play for you."

Specifically, in *Miles: The Autobiography* (1989), Davis describes his studies with Elwood Buchanan, who taught at Lincoln High School, where Miles played in the school band. Other than his father, he cites Buchanan as the greatest influence in his life. Then, the book continues: "One of the most important things that happened for me in high school—besides studying under Mr. Buchanan—was when I met Clark Terry. . . . He became my idol on the instrument. . . . He was older than me." (Miles was born May 26, 1926, so Clark was five or six years his senior.) "Anyway, we went down there to Carbondale to play and I saw this dude and walked right up to him and asked him if he was a trumpet player. He turned and asked me how I knew he was a trumpet player. I told him I could tell by his embouchure. I had on my school band uniform and Clark had on this hip coat and this bad, beautiful scarf around his neck. He was wearing hip butcher boy shoes and a bad hat cocked ace-deuce. I told him I could also tell he was a trumpet player by the hip shit he was wearing.

"He kind of smiled at me and said something that I have forgotten. Then, when I asked him some things about playing trumpet, he sort of shined me on by telling me that he didn't want to 'talk about no trumpet with all them pretty girls bouncing around out there.' Clark was really into the girls at that time, and I wasn't. So what he said to me really hurt me. . . . But I never forgot that first time me and Clark met, how he was. I decided then I was going to be that hip, even hipper, when I got my shit together."

Clark's memory of their first encounter differs somewhat, although it's conceivable that both stories are true. Clark's version goes: "His teacher, Elwood Buchanan, was a good buddy of mine. We used to hang out in the beer joints and drink beer together. He said"—and Clark went into almost a Louis Armstrong growl—"'Man, you gotta come over to school and hear this Miles Dewey Davis, this little Miles Dewey Davis is *bad*.' Miles was from East St. Louis. So I went over one day to hear this little cat. He was very, very thin, a timid little cat, man. He couldn't look you in the eye. He'd hold his head down. He was so skinny that if he'd turned sideways, they'd have marked his ass 'absent.' And he played. And he played his ass off even then. Just a little kid.

"Buch"—his friend, Buchanan (Clark pronounced it "Buke," as in the second syllable of *rebuke*)—"had a long ruler with some tape on one end of it. He said, 'He's got only one problem. Every time he shakes them notes, I have to hit him with the ruler.' Miles liked to play like Harry James. He loved Harry James. Buch said to Miles, 'Stop shaking those damn notes. You'll shake enough when you get old. Play it straight.'

"Buchanan's old teacher was Joe Gustav, who was head of the trumpet section in the St. Louis Symphony and a very domineering type. He insisted on all his students using Heim mouthpieces. They were wafer thin with deep cups. Miles got hold of one of them. He loved it. I could never play it, because I think my chops are too thick. Miles had thinner chops. He had a knack for making that thing sound. Even in later years, he'd say to me, 'Hey, man, can you find me a Heim mouthpiece?' I found four or five Heims for him.

"Now I always figured that the fact that Buch made him play without vibrato, plus the use of Heim mouthpieces, helped him develop that pure sound. Nobody sounds like Miles. This kid Wallace Roney does about as good as you can hope for. And Miles liked Harry James' sound.

"I loved Harry James too. Harry was a *bitch*. And Harry was so real. I had a picture of him and me and his wife Betty Grable and Duke sitting in a club. Somebody copped that picture. When he won the *Down Beat* poll, Harry said, 'No, this should be for Louis Armstrong,' and he gave it to Louis."

"I'm sure you know that line of Dizzy's about Louis Armstrong: no him, no me."

"That's right. No him, no us. Harry came out of Louis Armstrong too. Roy, Dizzy, all of us. Harry was a phenomenal cat,

man. In his latter years, when the band was just playing weekends, he'd put the horn up and come back the next week and
pick it up and—" Clark sang the opening phrase of *Ciribiribin*.
"He had some chops. He was from that carnival scene. You'd
have to blow from sunup to sundown, and take a break, come
back and bally four or five times, then do a show, and bally some
more and do a show—"

"Bally?"

"Yeah. That's what the barker did. *Step right up, ladies and
gentleman, there's a show going on* . . . Lure the people in."

"Does it come from 'ballyhoo'?"

"I guess so."

"You came from that carnival scene too."

"Yeah," Clark said. "I was with the Reubin and Cherry carnival."

"And you got into the Duval Building in Jacksonville."

"I had gone to a small carnival, called a gilly show. I don't know
where the word comes from. It was a truck show. They carried
everything they owned on trucks, whereas Reubin and Cherry
was a railroad show. They carried everything by train. We
had berths on the train. But we were on this little gilly show,
and we went to winter quarters, which was the end of the season.
We were in Jacksonville, Florida. We'd just come from Pennsyl-
vania.

"We went to a five and ten cent store to buy some tee-shirts,
which were five and ten cents apiece in those days. I was hanging
with a bass player named William Oval Austin, we called him
Fats Austin. We'd come from cold weather right into Florida,
and we had nothing to put on. We had no money anyhow. So we
went to the five and ten cent store. It was a Saturday, and it
was crowded. Now Fats was a big, fat cat, man. Naturally, going
through a crowd, he gotta touch people. He slightly brushed
against an old woman with a cane, and she screamed, 'Aaaaaah,

git that nigger, he tried to knock me down! Catch that nigger!'
I looked around and said, 'Hey, Fats, there ain't nobody in the
store but us. Let's get the hell out of here.' You could hear, 'Nigger, nigger,' all through the store.

"We ran. Now I was just out of high school, and I had the
record for the low hurdles and the 220 and 100 yard, and I looked
around, and Fats was right on my ass." He laughed. "Behind, a
mob was gathering as we ran, and they were throwing bricks and
rocks and things.

"We managed to run up into this area where they were putting
up a round building. And it was Saturday and they weren't working. So we were running around." He drummed his fingers on a
coffee table, like running feet. "And they were after us." More
running feet. "We got almost back around and we jumped into
an area of excavation. I pulled Fats down and we hid, and we
heard them." More drumming. "Luckily, they had no dogs.

"We stayed there until dark, and we sneaked out, and got back
to safety."

"And then there was the incident in Mississippi you told me
about."

"The carnival stopped in Meridian, Mississippi," Clark said. "It
was the end of the tour. Marvin Wright was the drummer. He
ended up being a high school principal in East St. Louis. He was
a good drummer. On Saturday, you had to pack up your drums,
because Sunday you traveled.

"Marvin was packing up his drums and I was waiting for him
on the midway, right outside the tent, and I was with his girl-
friend. Now she was a very fair lady. A child of miscegenation.
The Mills Blue Rhythm Band was playing a dance that night.
Lucky Millinder. We were going over to this dance. All of a sud-
den here comes a little . . . a little . . . a little *motherfucker*.
'Whatchyall doin' hangin' around thish heah midway, boy?'"
Clark mimicked the man with chilling verisimilitude.

" 'I'm waiting for my buddy to pack his drums, and we'll be off.'

" 'You with thish heah show?'

" 'Yeah.'

"He said, 'What? Do you realize you just said "Yes" to a white man?'

"I said, 'What am I supposed to say, No? I *am* with the show.'

"He pulled out a blackjack, one of those leather things loaded with lead, and started beating me about the head."

If you have never seen a spring-loaded sap used by someone skilled with it—and I saw a police detective use one on a man in the restaurant of the Seelbach Hotel in Louisville—you have no idea how brutally efficient this implement is.

"It had been raining," Clark continued, "and he left me face down in the water, to drown. And he went away. And the train crew, which was all Caucasian, came out and picked me up and took me back to the show train. They put some towels on me. By this time he'd come back, with fifteen or twenty more guys with axes and hammers and chains, and he said, 'Where's that nigger I left here?'

"And the train crew which, I repeat, was all Caucasian, said to him, 'Ah, he was a smart ass. We kicked the shit out of him and sent him out that way.' Whereas in reality they'd taken me back to the train and were taking care of me.

"And from that time, I never generalize about race, creed, color, nationality, or anything else. Never."

"You know, over the years of knowing you and Dizzy, you seem like miracles to me. I don't know how anyone who comes up through that experience can even *speak* to white people."

"Yeah, but that incident affected me. When I think of that Caucasian crew that saved my ass, I'd be stupid to generalize. I've never forgotten that."

"I don't know how *anybody* deals with it, day after day."

"It's a very difficult thing to do," Clark said. "Except you reach a point where you have a choice. You can lower yourself to that standard or you can elevate yourself in the hope that you can put an end to all that shit. You know, my first wife could not look a Caucasian in the face. She couldn't talk to one. Because when she was a little girl, they took this kid, a little boy, her cousin, out from her bedroom, he was staying over. They took him out on the porch and hanged him."

For a time Clark worked in Illinois in a Danville group led by a man named Toby Dyer. Another local band was led by Jimmy Raschel. Its personnel included Booty Wood and Milt Buckner.

"Lionel Hampton wanted Milt to join his band," Clark recalled. "Milt was afraid to go, so we got him drunk and made him get on the train for Chicago to join Hamp. Hamp right away took him off vibes and put him on piano. He was a *marvelous* vibes player. So Hamp stymied his career on vibes, although Milt was a great rhythmic player on piano."

Clark hung out in a club in Peoria called the Grenada, owned by Sweets Edison's uncle, Bruce Collins. "They used to gamble in the back and there was a bar in the front. I'll never forget that Seagram's Five Crown whiskey was in those days five dollars a fifth. I was in Peoria on Pearl Harbor day in 1941. I went into the Navy in 1942."

After boot camp, Clark went on leave, visiting a cousin named William Scott who lived on Morningside Avenue in Harlem. Like so many other servicemen later known as major jazz musicians, Clark, on hitting town, headed for Fifty-second Street and its many jazz clubs. He encountered Stuff Smith and Jimmy Jones at one club, Ben Webster and Tony Scott at another. Clark stood at the bar in his sailor's uniform, holding his trumpet case. Tony Scott spoke up on the microphone, "Hey, there's a sailor over there with a trumpet. Come on up here, sailor. You want to play something?" Terrified, Clark mounted the bandstand and played. Scott got him a job at the 845 Club in the Bronx. Then Clark went back to the Navy and a position in one of the bands in training at Great Lakes Naval Station, a cradle of great jazz musicians. Clark and Tony Scott would remain friends.

"At Great Lakes," Clark remembered, "there was a whole bunch of people like Willie Smith, guys from the Jeter-Pillars Band in St. Louis, like Charles Pillars. Al Grey was there. And Lou Donaldson."

The bands were kept strictly segregated at Great Lakes. "Our camp was called Camp Robert Smalls," as Clark described it. "It was in barracks 1812. They really had two branches of the Navy in a sense, as far as we were concerned. All the black people were relegated to being over there. They wanted Willie Smith to come over on the main side, because he could pass. They even offered him a commission. He turned it down, said, 'I'm going to stay over here with my gang.' He was a beautiful cat."

"When I was growing up," I told him, "he was *my* alto player."

"Oh, mine too, baby. He came into Duke's band when Johnny Hodges was out sick or something. Man, nobody remembered Hodges was in the band while Willie was there.

"So that was a great band we had at Great Lakes. We had a concert band, a marching band, and three jazz bands, the A band, the B band, and the C band. We played engagements in Chicago for special affairs.

"When a new guy would come into the band, most of us were old guys—maybe twenty-three years old! There were some eighteen, nineteen, even seventeen-year-olds coming in, and they wanted to play in the band. And we'd play a joke on them. We slept in hammocks in those days, and you had to lash the hammock a certain way. If you didn't do it right, there was no way in hell you could make that last hitch. We'd teach these kids the secret. We'd tell them, 'What you have to do is go over and get the rope stretcher. Go over to Camp Moffat and get it, room 305.' And the cat over there would tell them, 'Oh shoot, you just missed it,' and send them somewhere else. The kid would be looking for it all day, and he'd come back, and we'd say, 'Did you get the rope stretcher?' 'No, I couldn't catch up with it.' It took him a long time to figure out he'd been had.

"When the war ended, I went back to St. Louis. I started working with George Hudson's band. We became popular through the acts we played for at the Club Plantation. We'd take the music home and rehearse the parts. The acts would go back and say, 'Man, you've got to play St. Louis and get that George Hudson band to play your *music!* You've never heard it *played* like that before!' As I'm sure many of them hadn't. We rehearsed it like we were going to be playing it forever.

"We went to New York and played the Apollo Theater on a bill with Illinois Jacquet. He had a marvelous band with Shadow Wilson and Sir Charles Thompson and his brother, Russell Jacquet, and Joe Newman and himself. They were real big. He hired our band as an opening act. We had a bad tenor player with us named Willie Parker. We called him Weasel, because he was a little cat. One of the top writers in St. Louis, Bugs Roberts, wrote a bad chart on *Body and Soul.* It went into double time on the end.

"We went on first, since Jacquet was the star. We opened, and we ended with that number. Weasel was featured on this one. Opening show in the Apollo, he had people standing up on the chairs after that thing. Jacquet came running back and said, 'Take that number out, get that goddamn thing out!' It was out for the rest of those shows."

"Sounds like Benny Goodman," I remarked. "Benny didn't dig it when other people got the applause."

"He sure didn't," Clark said, laughing.

"Duke and Woody Herman *built* their bands on their soloists."

"They sure did, and gave them beautiful arrangements."

I told Clark the story of the time Stan Getz said to Woody Herman, "You can't play." And Woody came back with, "That's right, that's why I hired you."

"Sounds like Stan," Clark said. "I don't know anybody else who'd have the balls to say something like that to Woody. Woody was a sweetheart of a guy. I loved him."

After the Apollo, "We did the T.O.B.A. circuit," he laughed. The letters stood for Theater Owners Booking Association, but the musicians who played it universally said it stood for Tough On Black Asses.

"It was a rough circuit," Clark continued. "But it kept you employed. You knew you were good for four weeks. The Apollo, the Royal in Baltimore, the Earle in Philadelphia, the Howard in Washington. If you could squeeze in a few more weeks, you had six months.

"Then you'd go down South on a tour. The white audience would sit in one place while the blacks danced. Another night the black audience sat in one place while the whites danced. All the money they spent to segregate!

"After we got home, I played a couple of little stints with Ellington. I subbed for Francis Williams for one night in St. Louis. Duke put me in his phone book, saying, 'We'll have to have you come with us some time.' After that, I subbed again, this time for Al Killian. I stayed with the band maybe four, five days.

"Then I got a call from Charlie Barnet. I'd met Gerald Wilson. Gerald lived in Los Angeles. He said, 'If you ever come out here, stay at my house.' So Charlie made me an offer, and he asked me how I wanted to come out. I'd never gone cross country, so I said, 'I'd like to take a train ride.' Charlie sent me a train ticket, and I took the train and enjoyed the scenery. Gerald met me at

Los Angeles Union Station and took me to his house, 5612 Ascot, on the west side.

"That night Gerald took me out to Hermosa Beach, where the Barnet band was playing. The band was on a coast to coast broadcast. We walked through the crowd. Charlie spotted Gerald. Gerald told him, 'Here's your new trumpet player.' Charlie announced, 'Our new trumpet player has just arrived. You'll be hearing from him in a very short time. Maybe the next tune.' He said, 'Get your horn out.' So he kicked off the tune. In the middle of a broadcast, coast to coast, I joined the band! Luckily, it was a tune I knew the changes to.

"He was crazy. I loved him. Charlie was always good to musicians. He took a special liking to me, for some reason. I was very close to him.

"Doc Severinsen was in the band. Doc is a *marvelous* trumpet player. He's always been. I became close to his mom and his dad. His father was a dentist in Portland, Oregon. Whenever we'd come to town, Doc's mother would make cookies for me. And his father would do our teeth, me and Doc. He'd say, 'You've got the hardest damn teeth!'

"Doc's mother still calls me her son. Every time I go out there, I call her up and say, 'Mom, are you going to come to the concert?' She said, 'Yes, I'd love to.' I said, 'I'll send a car for you.'

"She said, 'Well, no, I've got my own car.'

"I said, 'Mom, you can't drive.'

"She said, 'No, but Carl provides me with a chauffeur.' That's Doc's real name. He's a great musician, and a beautiful cat, too."

Clark stayed with Barnet about a year. That edition of the Barnet band went east to play the Apollo Theater and Town Hall. In addition to Doc Severinsen and Clark, the trumpet section also contained Jimmy Nottingham. Bud Shank was playing tenor. When the lead alto player was unable to make one of the engagements, according to Clark, Bud asked Barnet if he could play that chair, and did. "That was Bud's turning point on alto," Clark said.

Clark's next plateau was the Basie band. "They were holding auditions at the old Nola studio at 1619 Broadway, near the Paramount," Clark recounted. Musicians often make this distinction. Later, Tommy Nola, the owner, moved it to its present location at the top of the Steinway Building on Fifty-seventh Street, near Carnegie Hall; it is one of the prominent recording studios.

"They were rehearsing," Clark went on. "Sweets Edison, Dicky Wells, Earle Warren, Ted Donnelly, Jack Washington, Buddy Tate, and all that bunch. They had a knack for making it difficult for a new cat. Put the new boy through the steamer. Now when I came in they said, 'We'll fix his ass.' So they called *South*. Snooky [Young] had recorded it with the band a few years before that. We got to the out chorus, and I made that high A natural. I'd never made one before and I haven't made one since. But I got the gig.

"At that time, Emmett Berry, Sweets, and Ed Lewis were the trumpet section. Shortly after that, Jimmy Nottingham got out of the Navy. We got Jim in the band.

"There was another trick they used to put on everybody when you first joined the band. My seat on the bus was with Jimmy Rushing. And he took up *all* the seat. And they would laugh their asses off. I'd have to sit there riding with Rush. We got to be real buddies."

He joined Basie in 1948, when the big-band era was waning, and constricting financial pressures made it increasingly difficult for anyone to keep a large group on the road. And Basie had debts. "He sure loved the ponies," as Clark put it.

"After he broke up the band because of financial difficulties, he started a small group. He called me in St. Louis and told me to pick up somebody down there who'd work out in the small group. I told him there were two, the older, established cat named Jimmy Forrest, and a young Caucasian kid named Bob Graf. Right away he said, 'Get the kid.' He'd be cheaper. So I brought Bob to Chicago, downtown in the Loop, the Brass Rail. Jimmy Lewis on bass, Gus Johnson on drums, Freddie Green, Basie of course, and Buddy DeFranco, me, and Bob Graf. Carlos Gastel came in every night to hear us. He was scouting Bob Graf for Woody. After that we got Wardell Gray.

"Freddie Green was the foundation. He was the greatest rhythm guitarist that ever lived. Freddie used to say, 'You have to turn the amp down so you can feel it more than you can hear it.' We used to call him Ching Chang. The second chord was always a little more dominant. Just a little. That was the secret.

"Basie, as a leader, was one of the most beautiful people in the whole world. He was very candid and very down to earth. He'd tell you in a minute, 'Kiss my ass,' anything he felt like saying. But he was loving. We used to call him Holy. Some called him Bill, some called him Count, some called him Basie, but some of us called him Holy. In the Basie band, we had some weird names. Prez started all that. 'Holy' had a connotation of something that was special to you. Your wife was holy, your horn was holy. And Basie was the head man, so he was Holy. I can't think of anyone who could ever leave that band and say anything against Basie. He would listen to the band, he would hang out with the band. We'd be somewhere shooting dice or drinking booze, and he'd be right there with us.

"The small group was going to Boston. When I got to the airport, I got scared again. I've always been afraid of flying. I do it all the time and I'm still afraid of it. I got to the airport, and I said, 'I'm not getting on this plane.' Basie said, 'You've got to get on the plane. We've got to be in Boston. Come on with me.' We went over to the liquor store in the airport. He got a half a pint of gin. He said, 'Come on, drink some of this.' We started taking slugs. He started talking about other things completely. Ham and cabbage was his favorite dish. He'd kill for ham and cabbage. I was telling him how my wife could cook ham and cabbage. And we passed the bottle back and forth, and he said, 'Come on, let's get on this plane before we miss it.' And I got on the plane!"

Clark was with Basie from 1948 until 1951. Then began one of the most important associations of his life: that with Duke Ellington. I asked him how that came about, knowing how much he loved Basie and how wrenching it must have been for him to leave.

"We were working at the Capitol Lounge in Chicago," Clark replied. "Duke called me on the phone and said, 'I'd like to talk to you. We'd like to have you come aboard.'

"So I said, 'Yeah, I'd like to talk to you too.'

"Duke said, 'I'll come by your hotel.'

"I said, 'Fine. I'll meet you at the elevator.' I was at the Southway Hotel, at Sixtieth and South Parkway.

"Duke called from the lobby. Just as the elevator comes up and he gets off and I'm meeting him, the door across from the elevator opens and Freddie Green comes out. Freddie looks and says, 'Ooooh, shit,' and goes back and slams the door.

"Duke and I talked and got our business straight. That night on the gig, I walked in, and Freddie Green was tuning up. Instead of saying, 'Hello,' he turned his eyes up and said, 'You're a fool if you *don't.*'"

It seems to have been the accepted thing, for bandleaders to poach musicians from one another. And Ellington and Basie stayed friends, too, in spite of it. "Apparently they all did it," I mentioned to Clark. "Woody was always raiding the Charlie Barnet band, and yet they remained close. And Willie Smith went back and forth between Ellington and Harry James for years."

"Sure," Clark said. "Duke told me to tell Basie I was sick and go home to St. Louis. He said, 'I'll put you on salary, and when you've gotten well, you might like to come out and get your chops together again.'

"Toward the end of my stay with Basie, I was making $125 a week. He gave me a $15 raise. When I told him I was leaving, he took the raise back.

"Years later, I was at Carnegie Hall. They had a little side elevator. It came up, and Basie got out, and I said, 'Hey, Holy. I've got to talk to you about something that's been bugging me for years. Remember when I left you, I told you I was sick?'

"He said, 'Yeah.'

"I said, 'I wasn't sick, Holy. Duke had made me an offer. I lied to you.'

"He said, 'You think I didn't *know* that? Why the fuck do you think I took the raise back?' I felt like an idiot."

I asked him if he had ever heard the story of how Don Byas resigned from the Basie band.

"Sam? We called him Sam," Clark said. "I don't think I have."

"The story goes that he said to him, 'Basie, in one month I will have been gone two weeks.'"

Clark laughed, and sang some lyrics to me: *"If you don't believe I'm leavin', you can count the days I'm gone!* It's an old blues. Anyway, that's the story of how I left Basie and went with Duke."

The great jazz arrangers and composers have built their music around the individual sounds of specific players—but no one more than Ellington, whose genius in part lay in knowing exactly how to use the idiosyncratic sounds of his men, as different from one another as musicians could possibly be: such accomplished players as Juan Tizol, Tricky Sam Nanton, and Lawrence Brown; Ben Webster and Paul Gonsalves; Ray Nance and Bubber Miley. Clark's inflection, articulation, phrasing, and infectious buoyancy make his one of the most identifiable sounds in all jazz, and Ellington used it to potent effect—and made Clark a major star. His affiliation with Ellington was to last from 1951 to 1959.

"Duke was unique," Clark said, "in that just being around him, you could garner more by osmosis than you ever realized until it was time for you to use it, when you needed it. I've been in many situations where I thought, 'What do I do here now?' and then, 'What would the maestro do?' And I'd push the button once and the answer would come. I learned an awful lot about establishing rapport between the bandstand and the audience. How to handle men psychologically, how to read audiences, how to program music. It's very important to someone in front of a band. You've got to *know* your audience, you've got to know what kind of music to choose. Just from being around Duke, these things would rub off on you.

"One of my favorite sayings, one I just love, came from Ellington. He said, 'I'm very easy to please. Just give me the best.'"

"Clark, did you ever read Mingus's book *Beneath the Underdog*?"

"I read most of it, but it was *so* ridiculous."

Clark was right, but the book (first published in 1971) is marvelous in its way, regardless of whether it's accurate. In one passage of the book Mingus attacks Leonard Feather, Whitney Balliett, Barry Ulanov, John S. Wilson, Marshall Stearns, Bill Coss, and me, placing us at a party together. As Whitney has written, that group was never in the same room at the same time in our lives. The opening paragraph of the book is a sharp definition of Mingus's own troubled personality. "In other words, I am three," he says. "One man stands forever in the middle, unconcerned, unmoved, watching, waiting to be allowed to express what he sees to the other two. The second man is like a frightened animal that attacks for fear of being attacked. Then there's the everloving gentle person who lets people into the uttermost sacred temple of his being and he'll take insults and be trusting and signing contracts without reading them and get talked down to working cheap or for nothing and when he realizes what's been done to him he feels like killing and destroying everything around him including himself for being so stupid. But he can't—he goes back inside himself."

Mingus's contradictions were complex. His book is an impressionistic diatribe, poetic in its way, in which he denounces whites and ruminates on his sexual past. Yet he didn't hesitate to hire white musicians; and one of his best friends was Paul Desmond, whom he visited when Paul was dying. Most musicians who knew him, in my experience, thought Mingus was crazy as hell, and a lot of them were afraid of him. In a conversation we had, Mingus verified what he had said about himself in the book. He told me he attacked "because I'm a coward and I'm afraid," and I not only liked him for that, I admired him for the candor. But that didn't help his victims. I told Clark that I knew one musician who told me that when he worked for Mingus, he carried a .32 automatic behind him in his belt, under his jacket. He was that afraid of the towering rages he might encounter.

"I don't blame him," Clark said.

And Mingus hurt some people. There is nothing as frightening to a brass or reed player as the possibility of injury to his teeth. And, Clark pointed out, "He knocked Jimmy Knepper down and broke his teeth. He knocked out Jackie McLean's teeth."

"And Oscar Peterson came close to laying Mingus out," I told him. "But he gave Mingus a message. He said if he so much as raised his hand to him, 'Death! Nothing less, death!'"

"I came close to decking him," Clark said. "When he first came to New York, he passed out this music, *Mingus Fingers* and those things." *Mingus Fingers* was a piece Mingus had originally written for the Lionel Hampton band. They recorded it on Decca; it was Mingus's first recorded composition.

"The parts were all water-spattered and tattered," according to Clark. "You couldn't tell whether a note was a G or an A. I'm sitting there trying to play it, me and Britt Woodman and lot of people Britt got for him. We're sitting there rehearsing. It reached the point where I just couldn't make it any longer. I was very busy anyway. I put my horn up and I said, 'Mingus, I am not able to determine what some of these notes are, and I don't have much time. I'm going to have to cut out instead of wasting your time.'

"He stands there, breathing heavily, his nose expanding. Like I said, I used to box. And if you've boxed, you can see somebody telegraph what they're going to do. I laid my horn down. I was ready. And he stands there, breathing. Finally, his nose went down and he said, 'Okay, okay.'

"One time Mingus was on the bus with Duke. Tony Scott was in the band. Tony had always wanted to play Ben Webster's book. He was sitting in the bus, I'm behind him, and Mingus was back there. Mingus was talking to somebody sitting next to him. Tony, in front of me, was talking about sex. He said, 'My cock was so hard,' and so and so and so.

"And Mingus said, 'It ain't a cock, it's a dick, a prick! You motherfuckin' ofays always want to change that shit around.' And he jumped up and he grabbed Tony and he was choking him. I thought he was playing! And then I said, 'Wait a minute, this cat is *serious!*' And I had to take them apart."

In *Beneath the Underdog*, Mingus claims that he left the Ellington band as the result of an altercation at the Apollo Theater with Juan Tizol, who, he says, attacked him with a bolo knife. Whether the passage is factually accurate or not—and Clark says it isn't—Mingus deftly captured the lofty, imperial, and wryly florid way in which Ellington could speak when he was of a mind to do so. The passage led me to believe that Mingus had the ear and basic abilities of a great writer, had he chosen to develop them; and if he actually invented this passage, it establishes his gift as even the greater. The passage reads as follows:

" 'Now Charles,' [Duke] says, looking amused, putting Cartier links into the cuffs of his beautiful hand-made shirt, 'you could have forewarned me—you left me out of the act entirely! At least you could have let me cue in a few chords as you ran through that Nijinsky routine. I congratulate you on your performance, but why didn't you and Juan inform me about the adagio you planned so that we could score it? I must say I never saw a large man so agile—I never saw *anybody* make such tremendous leaps! The gambado over the piano carrying your bass was colossal. When you exited after that I thought, "That man's really afraid of Juan's knife and at the speed he's going he's probably home in bed by now." But no, back you came through the same door with your bass still intact. For a moment I was hopeful you'd decided to sit down and play but instead you slashed Juan's chair in two with a fire axe! Really, Charles, that's destructive. Everybody knows Juan has a knife but nobody ever took it seriously— he likes to pull it out and show it to people, you understand. So I'm afraid, Charles—I've never fired anybody—you'll have to quit my band. I don't need any new problems. Juan's an old problem, I can cope with that, but you seem to have a whole bag of new tricks. I must ask you to be kind enough to give your notice, Mingus.'

"The charming way he says it, it's like paying you a compliment. Feeling honored, you shake hands and resign."

"But it wasn't like that," Clark said. "I was there. Juan Tizol had written some music. There was no one in the dressing room but me, Mingus, and Juanito—Juan. Mingus had his bass. Juanito said," and Clark imitated his Puerto Rican accent, " 'Play this for me. I want to show it to Duke and I want to be sure the notes are right.' Mingus played an A-flat at one point, and Juanito says, 'That's an A-natural.' So he played it again and he played the A-flat, and Juanito says, 'I wrote it!' and Mingus said, 'I don't give a shit what you did, I'm playing what's down here!'

"One thing led to another. In those days the walls in theaters

had fire axes. Mingus grabbed the fire axe. And Juanito came
Bing! with his switchblade. And it came out this long! Now I'm
right between a fire axe and a switchblade, and I took them apart.

"When Duke found out about Tizol and Mingus, he yelled to
Al Sully, the manager, 'Hey, Sully, pay him off. Call Oscar.' Oscar
Pettiford. Oscar got there in record time. He came in laughing.
And of course walked in and played his ass off."

"I was told Pettiford knocked Mingus down once."

"Yeah, sure! He cold-cocked him in Birdland one night."

Clark left the Ellington band in 1959. He quickly became a major
jazz star on his own, and one of the regulars of the New York
studio scene.

It is hard for younger musicians, not to mention listeners, to
realize what the music world of New York was like in those days
just before the storm of British rock-and-roll hit American shores.
The big-band era was ended, but any number of jazz musicians
whose reputations had been established by the bands were able
to work in the countless jazz clubs of New York, Chicago, Los
Angeles, San Francisco, Toronto, Montreal, and to a large but
lesser extent other cities. There was a circuit to which such musicians as Clark Terry, Miles Davis, Zoot Sims, John Coltrane, Horace Silver, Art Blakey, and others were able to travel for work.
And in New York and Los Angeles—and, again to a lesser extent,
Chicago—they were able as well to work in the thriving recording industry. Singers of high quality, such as Ethel Ennis, Tommy
Leonetti, and Marilyn Maye, and such highly successful major
stars as Frank Sinatra, Tony Bennett, Peggy Lee, Nat Cole, Vic
Damone, Matt Monro, and more, were recording with large orchestras, frequently including substantial string sections. You
would walk into one of their record sessions and find all sorts of
major jazz musicians doing section or solo work, such as Phil

Woods, Zoot Sims, Al Cohn, Frank Rosolino, Cappy Lewis, Bud Shank, Herb Ellis, and, since the racial barriers were breaking down, Sweets Edison, Joe Wilder, Paul Quinichette, Snooky Young, Ray Brown—and Clark Terry.

Snooky and Clark were among the first to break through the network television racial barrier, joining the Johnny Carson *Tonight Show* band. All this was in addition to Clark's own recording as a leader.

But the daily grind of racial abrasion did not cease. He was looking for a house, and found one in Bayside, Long Island.

"It was listed, I went by to see it," Clark remembered. "I wanted to be as close to NBC as I could. And the cat said, 'You just missed it. We just got a binder on it.'"

A section mate of Clark's in the *Tonight Show* band was Jimmy Maxwell, a veteran of the Jimmy Dorsey and Benny Goodman bands and one of the great lead trumpet players. Big, strong, and bearded, Maxwell is an imposing man.

"Maxwell and I are real tight friends," Clark went on. "I told Maxwell about the house, and he said, 'Let's just check it out.' Maxwell called up and said, 'I'd like to come by and see this house.' So we went by. I sat in the car down the street. Maxwell said, 'When I give you the signal, you come on in.' He asked the cat if the house was for sale, and he said, 'Oh yes.' Maxwell said, 'Is there any tie-up, are there any binders in or anything?'

"'Oh no.'

"Maxwell said, 'If I put some money down, I can have it?'

"'If you want it, you got it.'

"Maxwell whistled, and I came in, and Maxwell said, 'You son of a bitch, you'll sell this house to this man or you're in trouble.'

"And that's how I got the house."

Clark laughed. That anyone can laugh at so painful a memory is part of the mystery of this man. It is this alchemical conversion of pain into joy, I think, that lies at the heart of Clark's great art.

In 1961, Clark Terry and Bob Brookmeyer formed a well-remembered and indeed rather celebrated group. It came about almost by accident, according to Brookmeyer.

The Half Note, at the cobblestoned corner of Spring and Hudson Streets in lower Manhattan, was an Italian restaurant and bar owned by the Canterino family. Sonny and Mike Canterino tended the bar, their father cooked, and Mike's wife Judy ran the coat room. An unforgettable fixture of the place was Al the Waiter, a wiry little man in a worn black suit, white serving towel over his arm, two books of paper matches in his belt. You could not pull out a cigarette without his appearing as if by magic at your side, a match already aflame, and with two books he could light two cigarettes at once, whipping out the matches, as Roger Kellaway put it, like six-guns. And he always said, in reply to your thank you, "My pleasure to serve you." The place is remembered—and with as much affection as Jim and Andy's—for its excellent Italian food and the Canterino family's hospitality to musicians and customers alike. The high bandstand was behind the bar, which was in the middle of the room.

"They were bringing in Tubby Hayes from England," Brookmeyer related. "They were worried about name recognition, and so they asked Clark and me to come in with a group to help out. He and I went through some music, then got Hank Jones, Milton Hinton, and Osie Johnson. We went in for a week. It turned into four weeks, and that turned into four or five bookings a year. We went through every pianist in town, I think, until we got Roger Kellaway, and he became our main man. We got Roger from Chris Connor.

"Clark and I had worked for others all our lives, and now we had our own group. We made four albums, three for Bob Shad at Mainstream and one for Creed Taylor. It was a happy band."

Brookmeyer is one of the most intellectual (although he might take issue with that term) of jazz musicians. Known as an arranger and composer of rare attributes, he has been perhaps even better known as a valve trombonist, but he began his career as a dance-band pianist in Kansas City, Missouri, where he was born December 19, 1929. In 1954, on valve trombone, he replaced Chet Baker in the Gerry Mulligan Quartet, known as the pianoless group, a particular irony in that both Brookmeyer and Mulligan played piano. In 1959, Mulligan formed his thirteen-piece Concert Jazz Band, whose personnel included both Brookmeyer and Clark Terry. Mulligan soon found himself so preoccupied with the problems, business and otherwise, of running a band that he had little time to write for it, even though, as he told me ruefully, he had wanted a band in order to write for it. So the burden of writing fell on Brookmeyer. He wrote the arrangement on Django Reinhardt's *Manoir de mes Rêves,* one of the most gorgeous charts in all jazz. Clark was one of the band's soloists.

Brookmeyer's playing could take on a casual, amiable, witty, almost country-boy air, but this was deceptive. Trained at the Kansas City Conservatory, he played in a highly compositional way. This, however, he attributed in one of our conversations not to the conservatory but to his guitarist friend Jimmy Raney. Jim Hall once similarly attested to Raney's influence. Roger Kellaway, another highly compositional improviser, in turn attributes this quality in his own work to Brookmeyer. Thus there is an unsung influence of Jimmy Raney, one of the first bebop guitarists, on other musicians.

These factors, I think, contribute to one's understanding of the Clark Terry–Bob Brookmeyer Quintet. "I was perhaps more experimental than Clark, but that was all right with him," in Bob's words.

"We really loved each other. We had an unusual rapport, both as musicians and as men, a rare empathy as players. We still do."

While Clark and Bob had that group, Clark became heavily involved in music education—as Brookmeyer later would too. One early experience was to be bitterly disappointing, and apparently continues to haunt Clark. It was typical, however, that it did not deter him.

"In my hometown, St. Louis," he recounted, "it was customary for the old farts to send the young musicians in wrong directions, to keep 'em from becoming a threat to their livelihood. If you asked them a question, they'd give you a wrong answer. Then they'd call each other up and gloat about it.

"I asked an old dude once how to improve my tone in the lower register. So he said, 'Son, you got a mirror at home?'

"'Yes sir,' I said. I didn't know. I wanted to learn.

"He said, 'Well son, you go home and sit in front of the mirror with the correct posture. Make sure you sit up straight so you have room in your diaphragm.' That part was correct information. He said, 'Look in the mirror and grit your teeth and wiggle your left ear. *Not the right ear!* The left ear.'

"I don't know how you'd do that anyhow. But I was naive enough to believe it, and tried so hard to do it that people would say, 'Have you seen that kid who can wiggle his ear?' But it was cruel, what he did."

I said, "Ray Brown told me that when he was coming up, he went to one of the older bass players and asked him a question, and the guy said, 'Kid, we figured it out. *You* figure it out.' And remember how in the old days trumpet players would put a handkerchief over the right hand so you couldn't see the fingering?"

"Yes! They did that! Yeah. And from that experience in St. Louis, I made up my mind that if I ever had an opportunity to impart knowledge to kids coming up, I'd bend over backwards to do it."

During the period with Brookmeyer, Clark wanted to try to get Harlem kids off the streets through music, not the passive listening to it, but the active making of it. It is interesting that his old friend Archie Moore was doing something similar through boxing.

Clark bought instruments for kids. "I got 'em in pawn shops, I got 'em anywhere I could. And we found a place to rehearse in a five-flight walkup. No heat. Cold water. Near 125th Street and Fifth Avenue. In summertime you'd burn up, in wintertime you'd freeze. Gene Ghee, I bought his first instrument, a raggedy old baritone I got in a pawn shop. And now he's head of the jazz program at Boys' High in Brooklyn, where Aaron Copland, Max Roach, Randy Weston went to school.

"We had a book by a cat named Fred Wayne, extremely talented. Could write his ass off, and *fast*, like Billy Byers. He'd give you an arrangement in two hours. Copied and everything. He kept us supplied with charts. We had sixty-some charts for the kids.

"We'd meet every week, and if I couldn't be there, I'd get somebody to direct the kids for me, Kenny Dorham, Ernie Wilkins, whoever was available.

"Don Stratton was a friend of mine. Good trumpet player. He went to school with Charlie Mariano, Nat Pierce, and those guys in Boston. I first met them all when I was with Basie, playing a place in Boston called the High Note. Don became dean of men at Manhattan School of Music, which was up in Harlem. He made it possible for us to have facilities at the school. Suddenly we had school rooms, we had blackboards, we had chalk, we had music paper, we had listening equipment.

"I had to be away for a long time. Don took over for me, teaching the kids. A Caucasian, and the kids were black. While I was gone, the kids started dropping off. Not showing up. When I got back, Don said, 'I think I know the reason.' So I called a meeting of the band. One little motherfucker had the nerve to say, 'Well, man, we don't want Whitey teaching us about *our* music.' Now here's a bunch of kids who would probably never, ever again set foot in a major establishment of learning. Never.

"I said, 'If that's the way you feel, I don't want anything to do with it.' And I walked out. I don't even know where that library of charts is any more.

"Shortly after that, the Jazzmobile was born. They took my idea of getting all these kids off the streets and supplying them with instruments, finding a place to rehearse. They got grants and they got salaries." The Jazzmobile was started in 1964.

Having fought white racism all his life, Clark in essence found himself in a two-front war, and his experience with those kids was one of the battles he lost. Another confrontation occurred in the early 1970s, when he had a band that played at Club Baron in Harlem. Clark has recounted the incident to me a couple of times, but an especially interesting account occurs in a 1987 interview he did with Hank O'Neal of Chiaroscuro records:

"It was a big band, about seventeen pieces, and it just so happens it was about half and half, blacks and whites. One night three big black Mafia guys, black Muslims, came into the club and they cornered me, saying, 'What are you doing playing with all these whites in Harlem?'

"I know they mean business and I'm a little frightened, but I know I've gotta be stern, so I say, 'Harlem has always been responsible for great jazz, all kinds of jazz, and big-band jazz has been missing for a number of years. There's been no big band up here for years, right?'

"They looked at me and said, 'Yeah, we have no big bands around.'

"Then I said, 'Well I feel it's my duty to bring big bands back to Harlem. And in doing so I choose the best musicians I can find and I don't listen with my eyes.' I think they're getting the message, and then one of them says, 'Well we got a kid here, a little black kid, and he wants to play, and we want to hear him play.'

"I said, 'That's okay. I've spent half my life making it possible for young musicians to be heard, so we'll bring him up on the beginning of the set and turn him loose.'

"So we start the set, and I asked Lew Soloff, who had the jazz chair, 'Lew, would you mind staying off and let this kid sit in?' He didn't have a problem and Lew got off and the kid came up. I kicked off with a medium tempo tune, one of Chris Woods' tunes, a very simple tune, very easy to play on, nice changes. The kid started when I kicked it off one, two, three, four, and I said, 'Hey, man, you play the music and when you get down to letter D, that's when you come in.' We started again, one, two, three, four, and he started in again. I stopped the band again and said, 'Hey, baby, no, you misunderstood me. When we start, you play the music. When you get down to letter D, then your solo comes, and we're gonna even open it up so you can play long.'

"He said, 'I just want to express, I want to express!'

"I said, 'Well, you're going to get plenty of chances to express.' So we kicked it off again. And he comes in wrong again. I was fed up and said, 'Express your ass off my stage.' I didn't care what the cats with the guns said. When we came off, I went straight up to them and said, 'Now you see what you've done? You stuck your necks out to represent this dude to do something that he's not qualified to do, he's not prepared, he didn't do his homework, he can't read music!'

"In a low grumbly voice, one of them said, 'The little son of a bitch didn't tell us that.'"

At one point the French government invited Clark and several other American musicians to do some clinics. One of them told the young musicians there was no hope for them anyway—they were white, they were French, they would never get the hang of jazz. Clark was furious, telling the man they had been paid to come and he had no right to discourage young people who had hardly begun.

When he finished that story, his face clouded over and he said, in an almost ominous tone, "They can fuck with me, I don't care, *but nobody fucks with my kids!*"

"One of the ways I got into jazz education on a broader scale was through Billy Taylor and his group," Clark explained. "He was doing clinics. At the same time, Doc Severinsen, Jim Maxwell, and Ernie Royal and a bunch of us would go around to a few schools and do trumpet clinics. So I got my feet wet. And I really dug it.

"What it did for me was to make me realize that it was important to the kids that those of us who have been blessed with capabilities pass along this thing called jazz. You can't document it on paper alone. Much of it, you have to sit there and let them soak it up by osmosis. I've been pretty much ensconced in that scene for some time. *Besides!* It keeps you *alert!* The kids ask you a lot of questions. And you've got to have some answers!

"I have a good buddy at the University of Iowa named Cliff McMurray. We've been friends for years and years and years. He plays drums, and he has knowledge of *all* the instruments. I met him when he was a student at Doane College in Iowa. He went on to teach in Anthon, Iowa. He had an all-girl trumpet section. He taught them all how to use plungers! It was so beautiful. I said, 'This cat is really something special.' And he liked the way I would teach kids. I use a system that is simple. It has nothing to do with theory, harmony, composition. It's just simple—basic common sense.

"For instance, I'd take a tune. The blues was the main vehicle. If they played the one chord—the tonic, the minor third, the flatted fifth—they didn't know that it constituted half diminished. They didn't care what you called it. They called them the blue notes.

"We'd have the kids listen to the rhythm section and explain to them what the blues are, explain the chords, get the feeling of the blues instilled in them. Then just take any one of those notes, one at a time, use it. Create any kind of rhythmic pattern using that one note, start with the tonic. Taking advantage of space and time, which is the lesson that Basie taught *everybody:* the utilization of space and time.

"Then put the two notes together, the tonic and the minor third. Then the tonic and minor third and flat five. This is the system that we got so many people involved in. Later the kids would find out that these are the notes of the blues scale. They had a tendency to be able to really hear these things, hear the simplicity of it. And there's something Ellington taught all of us: Simplicity is the most complex form.

"It has to be difficult and complicated for some people to understand. 'Flat five, flat nine, baby.' But a simple one-three-five fucks 'em up.

"So we taught the kids how to do that.

"I get along with kids. First of all, you've got to realize kids are people. Somebody loves them, somebody's paying for their education.

"We have big problems with a lot of people in jazz education because they can play their asses off but they can't teach. They get positions. Because they can play, people want them exposed to their kids. But they can't communicate.

"I remember an incident with a trombone player. The kids wanted some facts about depth of the cup of the mouthpiece and the rim and the depth of the backbore and so forth. He said, 'Well, I've got this horn and I—'" Clark imitated a fast rising and falling passage. "That doesn't help the kids.

"Now Tom Harrell's good at teaching. He has feeling for kids. He knows they belong to somebody. You can't just fart 'em off, like I heard one cat say to a kid, 'What the hell did you do with the money your mother gave you to learn how to play that damn thing?'

"That's jazz education? Then I heard one motherfucker say to five little girls in a trumpet section, eleven, twelve, thirteen years old, he said, 'Come on, haven't you got any balls back there?' And one little girl said, 'What's balls?' That's jazz education?

"Instead of explaining to them how to use the air column more, and use a diaphragmatic approach. You have to have a way of explaining to the kids what you want of them. If you'll explain it to them, they'll try it, and most of them will do it. They'll break their buns trying to do what you teach them, if you know how to teach them. But if you embarrass them, they may quit right there.

"So it's a very very interesting thing, jazz education, and we're lucky that we do have some knowledgeable and very sympathetic people in it. We've got tens of thousands of professors in colleges who can teach the kids the square root of a B-flat chord. But we don't have a whole hell of a lot of sympathetic people who know what jazz is all about, who have participated in it for a number of years, who know all the ins and outs, and then can explain to the kids how to give vent to their feelings and get involved in this music.

"Everybody has to be taught, somewhere along the way. In the beginning they all say, 'Where do we start?' And you say, 'Listen.' That was the only disciplinary word Ellington ever used. He'd say, 'Listen!' All he wanted us to do was pay attention. He later explained that this is complex. If you're playing in a section, you have to listen to what your lead player is playing, listen to the dynamics that he's using, listen to what the other sections are playing that contribute to the overall performance, all these things. Teach 'em how to listen. If they can listen, they can learn.

"Some of the kids have gone to the extreme of using this beautiful music for the wrong purposes, such as rebellion and hatred. I think it's all love and respect for the people who support it and the people who are involved in it and the perpetuation of the craft. A lot of the kids just got into that bag, for whatever reason; they feel like they're justified.

"They're making their statements through their instruments. They don't have an opportunity to say it any other way, so they do it that way. But that's not artistic. I made a statement years ago, and I got a little flak for it. I said, 'The piano keyboard is made of white keys and black keys. And a note don't give a fuck who plays it so long as he plays it well.'

"That's the bottom line. That's basic."

I told him of a conversation I'd had with Sweets Edison, who insisted, "Jazz is no folk music. It's too hard to play."

"Sweets was right," Clark said. "Louis Armstrong was being interviewed on the Johnny Carson show. Johnny Carson said, 'Mr. Armstrong, do you play folk music?'" Clark did a precise imitation of Armstrong's graveled voice: "Pops said, 'Sure I play folk music! All music is folk music. Folks play it, don't they? You don't see no trees playin' it.'

"That always reminds me of the stupid question people ask, 'Where is jazz going?' I always want to say, 'I saw him coming out of Jim and Andy's the other day, and he was going up to the union to pick up some checks.'

"I don't believe in categorizations. There's only two kinds of music, as Ellington said, there's good music and bad music. What do they mean by folk music, anyhow?"

Clark is famous for his "mumbles" singing. He'll start out singing a blues with words that make sense and then the syllables degenerate into incomprehensibility, although they always sound as if he's saying something outrageous. Conversely, using a rubber plunger on his trumpet, Clark will do a blues that sounds as if he's talking, and what he's saying is obscene, and it's very funny. Blues *sacré et profane*.

Singing is part of his act. Many trumpeters have made singing part of their work, Louis Armstrong, Dizzy Gillespie, Doc Cheatham, Roy Eldridge, Ray Nance, Red Allen among them. It long ago struck me that, given the sustained evening-long endurance required in jazz trumpet, singing provides a way to rest the chops. Dizzy Gillespie, even more so toward the end of his life, would sing a couple of tunes, clown with the audience, and then go into that foot-forward stance of his, put the horn to his mouth, and burn the place down.

So I put the question to Clark. Is that the reason? To rest the chops?

"Absolutely," Clark replied. "Pops said so." The press may have referred to Louis Armstrong as Satchmo but his friends always called him Pops. "Diz and I used to go by and visit with him. Constantly. At one time several of us lived in a small radius in Queens. Pops' house was on 107th, Diz was on 106th, I was on 111th, Charlie Shavers was on 110th. Helen Humes. 'Bama Warwick. We all lived in the same area. Diz and I would call each other and say, 'Let's go bug Pops.' So we'd meet on the corner, and go and ring the bell."

There's an image to conjure with: Dizzy Gillespie and Clark Terry at Louis Armstrong's door, ringing the bell.

Again the evocative imitation of Armstrong: " 'Yeah, come on in, come on in, Daddys.'

"We'd say, 'We come on by to get our batteries charged.' Which he kinda liked. He'd say, 'All right. Sit down there, I'll tell you all about the history of jazz.'

"One time I went to tell him that Quinnipiac College and Howard University wanted to give him honorary doctorates. They sent me, because I lived close by. I rang the bell. He said, 'Come on in.' I said, 'Pops, aside from getting my battery charged, I'm here on a special mission. Quinnipiac and Howard both want to give you honorary doctorates. And Quinnipiac wants to do their festival this year in your honor.'

"He says, 'Fuck 'em. Where were they forty years ago when I needed 'em?' But we talked a while, and he was always so nice and he'd put on that big smile, make you feel comfortable. He'd say, 'Yeah, Daddy, you know you're m'man. I got to tell you one thing, though, Daddy.' I said, 'What's that, Pops?' He said, 'You gotta sing more.'

"I said, 'Yeah?'

"He said, 'Y'see, people, all the people, like singin'. Besides, it's good for your chops.'

"He knew that years ago! It lets the blood come back. You know, you can blow your chops to hell if you're not careful. Ray Copeland did that, blew his chops out completely. He was on first call. They wanted all the high notes, and the hard lead parts—Ernie Royal and him. Ernie had the knack for that, him and Maynard Ferguson. These are phenomenal people, unusual people. That's the thing Ray and Ernie were called on to do, play high lead parts. The other times they would rest and play fourth and cool it until they came to another one of those show stoppers and they'd give them the ball again."

"Now," I said, "another point. As we were saying the other day, in the early days, these people were in the entertainment business. But somewhere along the way it began to be evident that jazz was evolving into an art form. When do they think that occurred? Do you think Louis Armstrong was aware of it as an art?"

"I'm sure he was," Clark replied. "He must have been aware. He loved it so much that it became a natural part of him. He enjoyed it so much that people enjoyed the way *he* enjoyed playing. The entertaining thing to them was to see and hear him do consecutive high C's. They'd count them. A hundred and five high C's without stopping. Everybody was excited, and this became the pulse. It became an integral part of him, and he in turn inspired all the serious trumpet players from that point all the way down.

"And they all sang. Yeah. Pops says to me, 'Daddy, you gotta sing.'"

We Are Like Atlas

On December 19, 2000, Milton John Hinton, of Vicksburg, Mississippi, and Chicago, Illinois, entered the sasha. He had in his ninety years recorded with almost every major jazz musician of the century, and many figures of the popular-music world, such as Frank Sinatra and Julius La Rosa. If music was his primary professional passion, photography was his second, and he documented the lives of the musicians around him, and the world they inhabited, in an estimated sixty thousand images, which have been seen in many gallery exhibits and in two books of his pictures. He held eight honorary doctorates and countless other honors.

But Milt Hinton's real legacy was the influence he had on jazz, particularly on bassists. My memories of him begin with recordings of the Cab Calloway band, which he joined in 1936. The Calloway band outlasted the big-band era, but finally, in 1951, it too broke up.

"Now I had a problem," Milt Hinton told me in 1990. He had

a deep Mississippi enunciation, a Gulf accent, related to that of New Orleans and, for reasons I have never fathomed, that of Brooklyn. "Rehearsed" is pronounced *rehoised*.

"I'd been in Cab Calloway's band sixteen years and I thought it was going to last forever, and it almost *did*. I'd been traveling. I was busy, recording with Teddy Wilson, Billie Holiday, making records on the side. New York was doing seventy-five percent of all recording in America. This was before Motown, Nashville, and all that. We *invented* the TV jingle in New York. And here I am, I don't know anybody, and I'm out of work now.

"I'm walking down the street one day, and I run into Jackie Gleason. I knew Jackie Gleason when he couldn't get arrested. I worked clubs in Jersey when I had to buy him a drink. Bullets Durgom was his manager. And I knew Bullets when he was a song-plugger at the Cotton Club. He'd bring songs to Cab. So Bullets and Jackie Gleason are walking down the street. It was around Fifty-fifth Street." Milt had an uncanny memory for exact locations and dates.

"Jackie says, 'Milt Hinton, where've you been?'

"I said, 'Nowhere.'

"Jackie said, 'Bullets, we're doing this record date tomorrow, I can use Milt.' But they ain't used no black guys in any of those big string bands. You know that.

"Bullets says, 'Jackie, we've got a bass player.'

"Jackie says, 'Yeah? Well we've got two now.'

"I went to the date the next day, and everything was wonderful."

Bobby Hackett was the soloist with a string orchestra, and the recordings turned into a series of hit records produced by Jackie Gleason. "I made every one of them," Milt recounted. "It was called *Music for Lovers Only*. The problem wasn't the musicians. The powers that be were the problem. Nobody had ever bothered to change things. I showed up, I've got a good bass, and I can play and I can read music. We had sixty-five men there. And all the big contractors were there. They heard me play, and the string players were interested in my bass, an Italian bass made in 1740. Wonderful bass. And so the guys all came over to me and were talking to me and the contractors took my name down.

"And that's when I got into the recording business. I did *Funny Girl* with Barbra Streisand, I worked with Percy Faith. And it all started with Gleason.

"At that time Jack Lesberg was the busiest bass player in New York. He was doing *Lucky Strike Hit Parade* and doing a CBS radio show, Galen Drake, on Saturday morning. Bernie Leighton was the pianist, Jack Lesberg was the bassist. They changed the rehearsal time of *Lucky Strike Hit Parade,* so Jack Lesberg couldn't make the show and he recommended me. In radio it was *cool* . . ."

"Yeah, you were invisible."

"Yeah!" Milt laughed. "Invisible. I got the show, and it paid ninety dollars. It was manna from heaven. Jack Lesberg gave me that show. Then I did the *Woolworth Hour* with Percy Faith, radio show on Sunday afternoon. Percy was a beautiful man. That was the beginning of life for me. By now I've made more records than any bass player living or dead.

"Pretty soon we were the New York rhythm section: Hank Jones, piano, Barry Galbraith, guitar, Osie Johnson, drums, and me. And we dealt in service. We want to make you sound good. We'll give you anything you want. We worked ten to one, two to five, and seven to ten, every day. We made all those Eddie Fisher records when he was hot."

One of Milt's countless bassist friends was Bill Crow. Bill commented: "After those Jackie Gleason dates, the New York contractors were lining up to book him for dates. At the height of the recording boom in the '50s and '60s, Milt and Osie Johnson were the rhythm team of choice around New York. Many con-

Milt Hinton, Chicago, 1961 (Photo by Ted Williams)

tractors waited to get their availability before booking studio time.

"Milt had a helper running basses to different recording studios around town in advance, so he could hurry from one date to the next and have an instrument waiting for him. He took every date seriously, no matter how inconsequential the music. On the simplest jingle date, Milt would listen critically to the playback and work to improve his part on the next take. He would help you find gigs, would send you in to sub for him in important situations, and would share anything he knew about basses, technique, lore, and the ins and outs of the music business. It was his kindness that connected me with the conductor who hired me for two of the major Broadway shows I played for eleven years.

"I treasure his friendship."

To which bassist and composer John Clayton added: "Milt is our maestro. He is the leader who has taught us, first, how to be loving, compassionate human beings. *And* he has helped us set our goals by supplying us with such a high level of bass playing."

All of this reminded me of something Oscar Peterson once told me: "Bass players are very protective of each other. I would find it almost unbelievable if you told me you'd ever heard a bass player say something about another bass player that wasn't good. If you look at the history of the instrument in jazz, you can see why. The public never used to notice bass players. They were always the guys who came into the group and were given one order, 'Walk!' Once in a while they'd be thrown a bone, like, 'Walk—one chorus solo.' Finally they managed to break away, because of the proficient players who came along."

I mentioned to Milt how Oscar had said you'd never hear one bass player say anything against another.

"Never!" Milt agreed emphatically, and laughed. "It's like family. You might have nine or ten brothers and sisters, but your Mama is your Mama. We come one to a customer in jazz. There's only one bass player in a band. I'm the best bass player of any band I'm in. And I don't have to worry about playing first or second. Saxophone players, this one wants to play first, this guy doesn't want to play second, this guy don't want to play third, and they put each other down. We don't have that problem. We *share work*. I just told you what Jack Lesberg did for me. We've always done that. We still do it."

So I asked him who his favorite bass players were, knowing full well that he would never say.

"All of them. I'm older than most of them that are living. And they all revere me, they treat me like I'm their father. It makes me feel great. I saw this great accomplishment. I saw Ray do what he did. Ray Brown to me is the guru of bass players. He sacrificed. He's a quarterback, he knows music, he's a finished musician, a pretty good piano player. He dedicated himself to playing that bass.

"I saw Oscar Pettiford do that. It was a natural thing; he was not a schooled musician. I saw him first time in St. Paul, Minnesota. I went to a nightclub when I was with Cab Calloway's band, 1937, to be exact. And this kid is playin' his ass off in there. I said, 'Holy cow!' and I introduced myself. Ben Webster was with me. I said, 'We're down at the Orpheum Theater. Come down tomorrow. I want the guys to hear you.' He came down, and all the guys heard him. All through our lives we were friends.

"I saw Richard Davis when he was right out of high school, when he came to New York. He looked me up. And look what he's done.

"I'd invite the new young bass players to come to my home. Some of them stayed at our house. We'd make a big pot of chicken and rice and some chili. If there was a gig, I'd recommend them. So it's gone like that, and we keep that going. I got Brian Torff his first job.

"There's no color to that.

"Scott LaFaro was fantastic. When he was killed, I finished a recording gig with Stan Getz at Webster Hall for him. He was amazing! I saw his great progress. The same thing when Blanton came along. The harmonic expansion, the solos, and still maintaining the prime requisite of a bass player, which is to support. I've seen Richard Davis do that, then Ron Carter, and Rufus Reid. John Clayton is fabulous. He's won awards in classical bass *and* jazz.

"We have a Milt Hinton Scholarship for bass players. We've got enough money to give three, four scholarships a year, on the interest, without even touching the money. They submit a tape, and we sit down, people like Bill Crow, Arvell Shaw, Brian Torff, Jay Leonhart, Rufus Reid, and Charnett Moffet, and listen to all these tapes, and decide who is deserving of this scholarship. I don't even get a vote unless there's a tie. We allocate the scholarships according to that.

"On my eightieth, a hundred bass players went down to Lincoln Center and played *Happy Birthday.*"

Milt's ninetieth was celebrated June 13, 2000, with a concert at the Danny Kaye Theater. Forty musicians played. According to the *New York Times* no concert ever went more smoothly. Produced by David Berger, it was directed by John Clayton. Milt and his wife Mona—as much loved in the business as Milt—were in the audience with his friend Jack Lesberg, who was eighty years old.

The players included Russell Malone, Benny Green, Howard Alden, Art Baron, Jimmy Heath, Frank Wess, Joe Bushkin, James Williams, Renee Rosnes, George Wein, Dick Hyman, Randy Sandke, Jon Faddis, Kenny Davern, Dennis Mackrel, Jackie Williams, and Warren Vaché. At one point there were eighteen bassists on stage, including Bill Crow, Ron Carter, Christian McBride, Jay Leonhart, Brian Torff, Kyle Eastwood, and Richard Davis. All the musicians were chosen by Milt.

"We all had a wonderful time," Bill Crow said. "Everybody had a chance to play something for Milt and Mona. And the packed house seemed enchanted."

There was never a more revered figure on any instrument than Milton John Hinton, almost universally known as the Judge. The nickname came from the punch line of a joke even he could not remember, but he started greeting friends with "Good morning, Judge," or "Good evening, Judge." In time musicians began applying the sobriquet to him. Yet he was the least judgmental of men, this most generous man, this miracle of a man, this giver of knowledge, this phenomenal musician. No other bassist—and only one other musician, namely Benny Carter—has comparably transcended the eras of jazz, comfortable in all of them, since the days when Louis Armstrong put the refining touches to the definition of this music in Chicago in the 1920s.

"I was born June 23, 1910, in Vicksburg, Mississippi," Milt began. "It was the era of blacks migrating from the South. It's a most interesting era that people seem historically to overlook.

"My grandmother was a slave on a plantation. At Emancipation, you took the name of the overseer, the man who was in charge of the plantation. And the man who was in charge was named Carter, so she took the name of Hetty Carter. She married a man named Matt Robinson. He was a pretty enterprising sort of a guy, and he got a horse and a buggy and started what we call a hack, to carry people around. He did *very* well. He had thirteen children. My mother was one. Most of 'em died.

"My grandmother was the idol of my entire life, because this lady had the fortitude, the strength, the know-how to survive. Her last child was born five months after her husband was dead. He had dropsy, they called it in those days. You can imagine a black woman in the South with nine or ten kids and no husband.

"She got a job working for a white family, a Jewish family named Baer, that had a department store. They liked her and gave her three and a half dollars a week, which was a good salary.

They gave her carte blanche to take care of the house, to cook, wash, iron, buy all the food. And she bought enough food for them *and* her children. She cooked for them, and she had enough left for her children to come to the back door and get the food and take the dirty clothes back to the shack they lived in, put the dirty clothes in that big pot out the back with a fire under it to boil those clothes, and the children could eat while she finished doing what she had to do in the house.

"She went to this man Baer, who seemed to like her very much, and she asked him if he would permit her to open a little stand down by his store. People coming to work in the morning needed coffee. She set up her coffee stand, where she sold a cup of coffee and two biscuits for a nickel. And she augmented her salary like that to keep her kids going.

"My grandmother learned to read. She was very religious, of course. She led us all to dignity and morality and peace. She didn't want any of her children to even argue among themselves. She lived until I was in Cab Calloway's band. She made a hundred and three years, so I got the first-hand information about this.

"She told me about smallpox and other diseases. They didn't care about black people with smallpox, and the black community was just ravaged. They quarantined her shack with her children in it and she couldn't even go home to help them. She'd have to push food under the gate and they'd come and get it. She took one of my uncles, who was a baby, to what they called a pest house. It was supposedly like a hospital for black people, and they didn't even have any water. She said they told her the water was no good. People were laying there, dying, and drinking out of the urinals because they had no water.

"Do you know what a dray is? It's a two-wheel cart. Black people were being piled up on a dray like cordwood, and still groaning, and they would take them to the graveyard because there

was no hope for them. And she survived all that. She had pock-
marks in her face, and most of her children did. My mother escaped that. Of the thirteen children, there were five left after
that great scourge, my mother, two sisters, and two brothers.

"The boys never had a chance to go to school. The three girls
got to go to school. My mother seemed to be the most militant
of the three. She got a fairly decent education in some kinda way.

"There was a piano in our house. She must have got the Baer
family to let her have a piano, and God knows what she must
have paid for it. My mother got to learn how to play piano. She
was in the church, and choir rehearsals were held in our house.
The two boys, my uncles, would go down to the railroad tracks
when the trains came by and make faces so the engineers would
call, 'Little black bastards,' and throw coal at them. They would
put it in a sack and take it downtown and sell it. That's how they
made their survival.

"The house sat up on stilts so the Mississippi could run under
it. There were bayous in the sunken part of the land. The Mississippi River starts up in Minnesota. When it gets down to Louisi-
ana, it's going with such force that it pushes the bay water ninety
miles out to sea. And when it backs up, all sorts of sea animals,
sea urchins, come back with it into these bayous, and when it
recedes, they can't get away. We had big sea turtles and fish from
the ocean. My uncles and I would go down there and get 'em
and sell 'em. There were water moccasins, and they were deadly
poison. I remember skinny dipping there. You'd hit the top of
the water and they would go away from you. Kids didn't have
any better sense. But we survived. That's the kind of thing we did.

"By 1910, the year I was born, the minister in this church my
mother was organist of was preaching to the black folks: 'There's
no future for you here. Conditions are terrible, they're not going
to get any better. So, young people, try to get out of here, try to
get North, where you get opportunities to be somebody.' So the

young people were finding ways to get out to Chicago, which was the center of the United States. And it needed all kinds of unskilled labor, which the black folks had. They needed porters in the railroad stations, redcaps, they needed laborers in the stockyards. There was a big strike among white laborers in the stockyards, and in order to break the strike, they sent down South to get a lot of black laborers to come up and take these places. And the ones who could get away got to Chicago. And instead of making three and half a week, they were making twenty or twenty-five dollars a week."

Hank Jones was also from Vicksburg, I pointed out. His family went to Pontiac, Michigan.

"Hank's younger'n I am," Milt replied, "and I didn't know him in Vicksburg. I met him a lot later."

"And who was your father?" I asked.

"My father was an African, a Monrovian bushman. Missionaries brought his family here to educate them. This was in 1900. The kids went to work, but they couldn't stand all that biasedness and the conditions they had been put under in the South. My father married my mother and they had a baby, but he couldn't stand it here and he went back to Africa when I was three months old. My mother's brothers, my uncles, told me about him. I was thirty years old the first time I saw my father."

When Milt was about six, he saw something he could not, would not, ever forget.

His Uncle Matt was taken to a hospital after an automobile accident. Milt went with his Aunt Sissy to see him. The black hospital ward was noisy and dirty. When they left, to make their way home along Clay Street, the main thoroughfare of Vicksburg, passing through the white district, they saw a crowd of excited men. Sissy tried to pull him away, but Milt tugged at her hand

and got closer. A black man was dangling by the neck on a cable from a tree limb. He was covered in blood, apparently already dead. The men, dancing drunkenly around the tree and swigging from whisky jugs, kept firing bullets into the body. Then they pushed a drum filled with gasoline under the body and set it afire. The flames leaped up and Milt saw the body sizzling and turning black like, he remembered, a piece of bacon, and a ghastly stench filled the air. Sissy dragged him home.

Next morning his mother reported that a white woman had claimed to see a black man peeking in her window as she dressed. A pack of men set off in search, with dogs. The dogs barked at a man in the railway station. His was the body Milt saw cooking in the flames.

On his way to school the next morning, he passed the place of the killing. The tree was gone, the stump covered with fresh red paint.

"That was the tradition," Milt said. "After a lynching, they'd cut down the tree and paint the stump red."

"The tradition? The *tradition?*"

"Yeah," Milt said.

His Uncle Bob decided that one way or another he was going to get to Chicago, where all those good wages were supposedly paid.

"With this preacher telling people to go," Milt continued, "the white people decided they can't let this cheap black labor get away. So they blocked the railway stations in Mississippi, and said, 'You can't buy a ticket.' A black man could not buy a ticket from Mississippi in 1910. You had to have permission from your boss. He had to give you a note or go down there with you." It was still slavery, except for a small salary.

"That's right. You couldn't *leave.* And the ones who had left already, who had escaped, are writing back telling how wonderful it was in Chicago, what great opportunities they offer you, and nobody bugs you, if you've got some money, you can get a nice place on the South Side. Black people from Alabama, Mississippi, Georgia, all moving to Chicago.

"My uncle Bob was working in a white barber shop in Vicksburg. And even white folks didn't have bathtubs in their houses in 1910 in Mississippi. So the barber shop was a very important place. Each white barber shop had tubs and places for your mug and razor and towels, so on Saturdays and Sundays people came down to get a bath and a razor for twenty-five cents. And no self-respecting barber would work on Sunday. But the shop had to be open, so the boss would tell the porter, 'You keep them tubs clean, you keep the water hot, keep them brushes clean, and charge them twenty-five cents a person. And when you come in on Monday, you tell me what you sold.' So if my uncle sold forty baths, he told him he counted thirty. And that's how he stashed his little stash."

But how was he to get out of town? Uncle Bob got a friend living in Memphis to send a letter saying that his beloved Aunt Minnie was ill and wanted to see her nephew once more before she died. The barber wrote the requisite permission, Bob bought a round-trip ticket to Memphis (the only kind the station master would sell him), and in Memphis he turned in the return half of the ticket for cash, which he used to buy a ticket to Chicago. There he got a job as a bellboy and began making very good money, as much as fifty dollars a day in tips. But tips were not the only source of money.

"Chicago was a transit city and a convention center," Milt explained. "Salesmen were there, the stock exchange, the stockyards. And all those hotels. Prostitution was rampant. At the hotels, the contact man was a porter. When a salesman arrived and the porter took him to his room, the first thing he wanted was a girl. 'Get me a girl and I'll give you a good tip.'

"The girls were already in the hotel. They'd tell the porter,

'Get me a good john, I'll give you a good tip.' He was getting it from both sides. And he had this homemade gin down in the basement, and he'd take it upstairs and sell it for five dollars a pint."

Uncle Bob was sending home money, carefully wrapped in newspaper. But the money stopped with the advent of World War I. Bob got drafted, and in Vicksburg, Uncle Matt went into the Navy. Once the war was over, Bob returned to Chicago and another good job and again sent money to Vicksburg. Matt joined him in Chicago, where they shared an apartment. They extricated two of their sisters, Milt's mother and his Aunt Pearl, from Vicksburg, leaving only Milt, his grandmother, and his Aunt Sissy there. When the brothers had set up the two sisters in an apartment, they sent money to bring the rest of the family to Chicago.

They were to catch a morning train, but it was raining heavily and they missed it. The three of them were standing in the railway station in the downpour, their baggage around them. One of the neighbors learned of their dilemma and sent a cart for them. They stayed at this friend's house through the day, drying their clothes, desperately hoping that nothing would prevent their leaving. It must have been a lot like trying to escape from Nazi Germany into Switzerland. They waited out the time, went to the station, and got on a six o'clock train. Milt remembers the black railway coach as filthy and smelling of rotting food. But Vicksburg receded behind them. They arrived in Chicago late the next day. It was autumn, and Chicago was cold. Milt's mother bought him a coat in the railway station, and they took a taxi to their new home.

Chicago was a revelation. Milt had always thought that being black meant being poor, and suddenly he was seeing black people who lived in homes far finer than anything in Vicksburg and wore the most elegant of clothes.

"There was a whole segment of town that was changing," Milt said. "The South Side of Chicago, where today black people still live, was a beautiful section. The boulevard was called Grand Boulevard. Mansions were on this street, great mansions. Armour, Cudahy, Swift, had these great mansions there. And as black people began to move into town and working at the stockyards, and it was a little close, these rich white people began to move out, and they changed the name from Grand Boulevard to South Parkway. It's now Martin Luther King Drive. It was Grand Boulevard when I moved there in 1918."

Milt was enrolled in Doolittle Grammar School at Thirty-sixth and Cottage Grove. He had been in grade five in Vicksburg, but the Doolittle authorities, after testing him, set him back three grades. He cried.

Milt's mother taught piano, his sister sang in her church choir, and his Uncle Matt—the two brothers lived nearby, and Milt loved to visit them for, among other benefits, the way their girlfriends gushed over him—played him Louis Armstrong records.

Chicago is largely a city of apartment buildings, and in much of it the buildings are three stories high and built of brick, with limestone windowsills and limestone front-door frames. Their facades are pleasantly dignified. Their backs are a little shabby, facing the alleys that run like veins through the city. The backs of the buildings have flights of wooden stairs connecting the balconies of each apartment. Some of these balconies are enclosed, some are open; and the steps are treacherous in winter when they are slick with ice.

As Milt described it: "I delivered vegetables up and down those stairs for a Mr. Holt, who had a vegetable wagon. He rang a bell when he came into the back alley and people would come to the door, out on the porch, and say, 'Give me a dime's worth of sweet potatoes and ten cents' worth of mustard greens.' He would give me five dollars' worth of change and he would go somewhere and talk to some ladies while I delivered vegetables, running up and down those steps. He'd stay about an hour on that block and move on to the next block."

Milt remembered that every kid in the neighborhood seemed to be studying music, the girls taking piano lessons, the boys studying violin. When he was thirteen his mother bought him a violin. A neighborhood boy named Quinn Wilson taught him to tune it. They remained friends; Quinn Wilson was later an arranger for the Erskine Tate and Earl Hines bands.

Milt had a paper route, delivering the *Herald-Examiner*. One of the homes to which he took papers was that of the mother of violinist Eddie South.

"I see these wonderful pictures on the wall," Milt remembered. "By this time Eddie was in Europe, playing. He was called the Dark Angel of the Violin. He was playing a lot of Hungarian stuff. A black gypsy. He played for all the crowned heads of Europe, and for the Rothschild family, he was the darling of Europe. His mother said, 'Yes, that's my son. And you're studying music?' And I said, 'Yes, I'm studying music and playing it.' And she said, 'I hope some day you'll get to play with my son.'"

South, who had studied at Chicago Musical College, was a formidable musician. His career illustrates a dark irony in the history of American music: the fact that, perversely, the bigotry that excluded blacks from classical music effectually enriched and improved the music we have come to call jazz by driving such men as South into it.

The classic case is that of Will Marion Cook. Born in Washington, D.C., on January 27, 1869, Cook was trained as a violinist, educated at Oberlin College. He became a student of Antonín Dvořák when the Czech composer lived in New York (1892–95) and directed the National Conservatory. Dvořák, himself a part of the nationalist movement among European composers, whose essential tenet was that composers in each nation should use the folk and popular musical elements of their culture to the end of creating a formal art music, held that the United States would not develop a distinct American music until composers explored and incorporated into their work their folk elements, including Negro music. Impressed by Cook, Dvořák arranged for him to study in Europe with the great German violinist Joseph Joachim. During his time abroad, Cook came to know such European musical figures as Brahms.

Returning to America, Cook set out to establish a concert career. After a Boston music critic described him in what he presumably thought were flattering terms as the best Negro violinist in America, Cook entered the man's office, asked if he had written the review, and, on being told yes, shouted, "I am the best *violinist* in the country," and smashed his fiddle on the man's desk. He never played again.

Cook turned his attention to writing for the musical theater. Collaborating with poet Paul Laurence Dunbar, in 1898 he produced the revue *Clorindy, or The Origin of the Cakewalk,* the first important black musical on Broadway. In 1918 he formed what was at first called the New York Syncopated Orchestra but later, perhaps in deference to general public stereotyping, the Southern Syncopated Orchestra. One of its members was Sidney Bechet. Cook took the orchestra to England, where it performed for King George V. (This inspired Sidney Bechet's delicious remark that this was the first time he'd ever met anybody whose picture was on money.) The foray into Europe inspired the essay *Sur un Orchestre Nègre* by the Swiss mathematician and conductor Ernest Ansermet. Though elements of the essay have occasionally been mistranslated, it does make a prediction that this is the way music is likely to go.

In New York, Cook befriended Duke Ellington, passed along Dvořák's exhortations for a distinct American music, and (by Ellington's testimony) taught him elements of harmony and composition. Thus one must consider the influence of Dvořák on what came to be called jazz, and wonder in what ways jazz and American music generally might be different were it not for the faint fragrance of condescension in the writing of a Boston music critic.

The degree to which jazz drew sustenance from this exclusion from "classical" music must be considered in any reflections on the careers of Eddie South, Teddy Wilson, James P. Johnson, Hank Jones, and others, certainly including an aspiring violinist named Milt Hinton.

Milt took Saturday morning lessons at Hull House, the famous community center established by Jane Addams. One of his friends there was a young clarinet student named Benny Goodman.

But the vegetable delivery days were over. Milt had a new job. "It was 1925 or '26," he recalled. "We looked on Al Capone as more or less a Robin Hood in the black community. There was a lot of shifting of power. It didn't concern us in the black community on the South Side until the thing got pretty big and people realized there was a potential of a lot of money.

"Al Capone had decided to come to the South Side of Chicago and sell alcohol to the people who gave house-rent parties."

Rent parties were part of the legend and lore of musical evolution in Chicago. When someone had trouble coming up with the rent money, they'd hire a pianist, throw a big party, and charge admission. Thus they would come up with the needed money.

"My uncle," Milt continued, "knew Pete Ford, who had a

cleaning and pressing place, which was centralized at Thirty-seventh and State Street, and he got me a job there. Al Capone told Pete, 'I'll bring my alcohol over here and I'll sell it to you for twelve dollars a gallon. You sell it to all these houses that have these parties.' We called them skiffle parties. He said, 'You sell it for eighteen dollars a gallon. You make six dollars on the gallon. Just don't buy from nobody but me. I pay all the police protection. I give you the cars to deliver it in, and I pay you good money.'

"He brought us cases of liquor with that green strip across the top of it, which meant it was bonded. We'd take that green strip off the top and pour the whisky in a tub and put alcohol in there and make *three* cases of bonded whisky. We'd put it back in the bottles. And he had some black guy, a guy that had a funny eye, that worked for the government who'd get these sheets as big as the *New York Times* of government bonds. And I used to sit back of the cleaning and pressing place and clip these things in strips, and put them over the bottle and you thought you had a five-dollar bottle of bonded whiskey.

"We would sell that to the house-rent parties. We had three trucks. One was El Paso Cigars. One was Ford Cleaning and Pressing. I can't remember the name of the third truck. We delivered to the people giving house-rent parties all the way from Thirty-first Street out to Sixty-third Street, from State Street to the lake. It was a thriving business. Pete Ford made a fortune. The only thing you needed to do was sit there and take the telephone calls, and deliver.

"And Al Capone came every Thursday or Friday, I can't remember what day it was, in a big car, bullet proof. He'd come with his bodyguards with a bag full of money. And he would park that car and walk in the back of that Ford Cleaning and Pressing place, and the police would be lined up, like they were waiting for a bus. He paid every one of them five dollars, and every sergeant ten. He paid 'em off, so we had no problem with the police at all. You'd never have your house raided.

"Everything was great. There were gang wars, and big funerals with lots of flowers. But then things calmed down because Capone took over the whole city. He had the hotels.

"And all of these flats in Chicago, where people are having these house-rent parties, they were buying alcohol from Pete Ford. Every weekend a different person would have a house-rent party. They'd have a lot of fried chicken. Everybody had a piano. That's why we had what we called ragtime. Ragtime was not band music, it was piano music. They'd get a good piano player to come in and play skiffle, which is what we called boogie-woogie in those days. A guy named Dan Burley was a very important man in jazz history, a good piano player. He was a newspaperman. In fact he went to school with me. We were on the Wendell Phillips High School newspaper, the *Phillipsite*. He taught me how to run a linotype machine. My mother had run a press in Mississippi for a Baptist minister. So I knew how to set type.

"Dan Burley played house-rent piano. He wasn't a good reader or an academic musician. He was a good contact man. He knew where the best house-rent parties were gonna be, and he was there playing for them.

"These piano players made lots of money. They'd get two dollars or five dollars to come in, and you'd get your fried chicken and your drinks and there'd be a lot of girls there.

"It was party time. The guys were making good money. Labor was making twenty-five, thirty-five dollars a week in the stockyards. A loaf of bread was ten cents.

"I was fifteen years old. Every day after school I would come by Ford Cleaning and Pressing. That was the shill. They weren't cleaning any clothes in there. I was getting something like fifty dollars a week. For a kid, it was crazy!

"This one Saturday afternoon, we were delivering all this alcohol to these different apartments. One-gallon tins, with a screw top on it. We loaded up the truck. Pete Ford had on a candy-stripe silk shirt. It was hot in the summertime. He had about fifteen hundred dollars in his shirt pocket. He always carried a lot of money. He was a big guy, nice-looking guy, ate like a horse.

"I was driving the truck. As we were crossing Oakwood Boulevard a lady in a Nash car hit us direct sideways, going full. I went right out the driver's side, out the window. Pete was lying in the street. Alcohol was all over. I thought he was dead. I tried to get up. My arm was broken, my leg was broken, my hand was broken. The finger next to my pinky on my right hand was *off*, hanging by skin. I pulled myself up. My face was cut. I crawled over and grabbed the money out of Pete Ford's pocket.

"The police were all around, but it was Capone's stuff. No problem. They took Pete to one hospital and me to another. I was in terrible shape. By the time they got me to the hospital my legs and hands were starting to swell. I was in excruciating pain. And my finger's hanging. I'm screaming. The doctor said, 'I've gotta take this finger off.' And I was studying *violin*. I said, 'Please don't take my finger off!'

"Now Capone heard about this accident, where two of his men got hurt. Whenever anything happened, he showed up or sent one of his lieutenants. And I'm screaming, 'Please don't take my finger off.'"

In his book *Bass Lines* Milt related that Capone's lieutenant Eddie Pappan came to the hospital. But he told me that Capone himself came. "My mother came. She was crying. Capone says to the doctor, 'If he says don't take it off, then don't take it off.'"

When Laurence Bergreen was researching his biography of Capone, I suggested that he talk to Milt Hinton and gave him Milt's phone number. The book, a massive (and superb) study titled *Capone: The Man and the Era* (1994), contains this quote from Milt: "Al Capone got my mother and brought her down to the hospital. He said to the doctor, 'Don't cut that finger off, don't cut it off.' And what Al Capone said, went."

Possibly both Capone and Pappan were there. One of them certainly issued an order to the doctor.

"And here it is today," Milt said, holding up the finger. "But they put it together wrong. The bone was smashed. But I've never had a moment's trouble with that finger.

"Pete Ford died. I've never driven again to this day."

At the end of his grade school days, Milt became a student at Wendell Phillips High School. Wendell Phillips—named after the famous Boston abolitionist—had an exceptional music department, headed Dr. Mildred Bryant Jones. She was conductor of the school's symphony orchestra. During his time there, Milt was soloist in the Mendelssohn violin concerto. The school also had a brass band, headed by Major N. Clark Smith.

As Milt tells the story: "One of the most popular and famous black newspapers was the *Chicago Defender*. They had an editor named Abbott. He was very much interested in youth. A picnic for young people was organized every year by the *Chicago Defender*.

"When the black people moved into Chicago en masse to those big mansions, as I said, the white people moved out. The first black people to make big money were women who made hair straighteners, because black women were using this stuff to process their hair. These women who produced this stuff got rich. This was before even black men began to use it.

"Madame Walker, out of Indianapolis, Indiana, made a fortune making this stuff. There was another lady named Addie Malone, out of St. Louis. They still have an Addie Malone Day in St. Louis.

"This lady had a product called Poro. My wife Mona was one of her secretaries as a young girl. This woman was a very Christian woman and a very enterprising lady. She opened up a school for black girls in St. Louis to teach cosmetology and hairdressing.

"Now these women, with the money they amassed, began to buy these mansions on Grand Boulevard. Addie Malone bought two. She bought one for a school for her girls. And when Mr. Abbott wanted to organize a youth band for black kids so they could learn to play and go around the country and perform, Mrs. Malone loaned the *Chicago Defender* the other mansion for the rehearsals for these black youths.

"Major N. Clark Smith was in charge. That's where Lionel Hampton, and yours truly, and Hayes Alvis, and Nat Cole, and Scoops Carry, went for band rehearsals. Because we were in his high school band at Wendell Phillips. Every Saturday he would have rehearsals. Lionel was a year or two older than I. He got in the band on drums. He wanted to keep me out because I was in short pants! But I could always read good. I wanted to get in the band because I wanted the chance to learn the bass horn. And when Nat Cole wanted to get into the band, because he wanted to play the lyre, and Nat was younger than I, I tried to keep *him* out!

"My mother loved Nat Cole. He would play piano for her church socials. Even after he was dead, she called him 'dear Nathaniel.'

"Major N. Clark Smith was a very great disciplinarian. A very military person. He wore a uniform all the time. And for reasons not known to me, he had a deep connection with Lyon and Healey, who had a big music store in Chicago. He was commissioned by Lyon and Healey to go around the world and write music about black people and to come back to Chicago and perform it. He did. I still have some of the music. He had us play it. *Pineapple Lament*. He went down into the Caribbean. He was not a jazzman! He was interested in the more academic world, like Sousa or something. And this is the kind of band we grew up in.

"I remember at Wendell Phillips High we had no idea what great influence he had. I remember one day he said to us in class, 'I don't think any of you kids ever heard a symphony orchestra.' He said, 'I think I'll call up Fred Stock . . .'

"We sort of giggled. He's going to call up Frederick Stock, the conductor of the Chicago Symphony!

"He said, 'I think I'll call up Fred Stock and have him bring the orchestra out here.'

"And we giggled some more. The Chicago Symphony Orchestra's going to come out to our school at Thirty-ninth and Prairie Avenue! And in a week or two, they did, and played for us. I remember they played Haydn. *The Surprise Symphony*.

"I was coming along pretty good. I'm playing violin, I'm president of the symphony orchestra at school, and I'm director of the jazz orchestra. First Major N. Clark Smith put me on peckhorn. I always had a fascination for big things. So he gave me a bass saxophone. I liked that. There were only two bass horns in school, and we had two players, and I had to wait for one of them to graduate. Finally one of the guys graduated, Quinn Wilson, and I got a chance at the bass horn. Nat Cole's older brother Eddie played tuba, and then he graduated.

"Major Smith said to me one day, 'Go down to Lyon and Healey's and tell them I said to give you a sarrusaphone.' It's built like a double bassoon, but it's brass. It's five foot tall. And you can't break it down like a bassoon. And it had a big wide double reed on it. I went down to Lyon and Healey, and they *gave* me one. I had to bring this thing back on the bus in this *huge* long case. My mother said, 'What in God's name are you going to do with that thing?' It has a very deep bass sound. It buzzes like a bassoon, and it's fingered like a saxophone.

"Major Smith was a marvelous conductor. He left Wendell Phillips to teach at Sumner High School, a black high school in St. Louis. And Captain Walter Dyett replaced him.

"I was supposed to graduate in 1930 but I graduated in the 1929 class. And they hadn't even finished building DuSable High. Captain Dyett came to Wendell Phillips and he went on to DuSable. He's the one who had Johnny Griffin and Richard Davis and Johnny Hartman. It was really a continuation, the next generation after us. I left Nat Cole in school, I left Ray Nance in school. John Levy was also at Wendell Phillips. I gave him my Sam Browne belt when I graduated. I was a lieutenant in the band by the time I graduated.

"Ed Fox had the Grand Terrace Cafe, and he had Percy Venable, a choreographer from Pittsburgh. Al Capone decided to open up a Cotton Club in Cicero, copied after the one in New York City. Black dancers, black musicians, white audiences. He gave a lot of work to guys. This was about the time I was ready to play. I was doing very well on violin. Every theater in every neighborhood had a violin player, a piano player, and a drummer to play for the screen.

"And that was when Al Jolson was in the first sound movie. When they showed that they didn't need orchestras in the theater, violinists lost their jobs, and here I am, just about ready to enter that business. Things got a little thin. And when Al Capone opened that Cotton Club in Cicero, and used all these black musicians, it was like manna from heaven. All the kids that I went to school with began to get jobs. One of my friends tried to get me to change from violin to trombone, because there weren't any violins in the band. They were using trumpets and saxophones. But I never learned how to play trombone. I was still delivering newspapers. The guys would come by and see me delivering newspapers for nine dollars a week and they were making seventy-five dollars a week in Al Capone's Cotton Club. And they'd say, 'Sporty,' which was my nickname, 'get a horn.' And I was totally embarrassed. Which is why I switched to bass.

"Capone didn't frequent the South Side, except to pay off. But he was in that Cotton Club in Cicero a lot. The guy who produced the show was Lucky Millinder. That's how he got started. His uncle, Percy Venable, was the choreographer for the Grand Terrace. He came from Pittsburgh. And his nephew was Lucky Venable. That was Lucky Millinder's name. When Capone opened his Cotton Club, he wanted to get Percy Venable to produce his shows. And Ed Fox, who owned the Grand Terrace, wouldn't let him go. Percy said, 'Take my nephew.' So Capone took Lucky Venable who changed his name to Lucky Millinder. And that's how he got his start as a bandleader. He was never a musician. But he knew choreography. I was in the band there for a while. There were no arrangements. He'd get the girls together and say, 'Two choruses and a half, take the last eight, tag four,' and that's the way we went out."

Dizzy Gillespie considered Lucky a good bandleader, and I mentioned this to Milt.

"He was. He was not a musician. He exploited the same sort of thing that Cab Calloway had. Have a good flashy guy in front of the band. And Lucky was flashy. The gangsters put Cab in front of the Missourians. Missourians was a corporate band, owned by the musicians. It was a great band. They were all from Missouri. When they got ready to come east to New York, they needed somebody in front of 'em. Cab's sister Blanche Calloway was working in a club in Chicago owned by Joe Glaser's mother."

Joe Glaser was later known as Louis Armstrong's manager and president of the Associated Booking Corporation, which booked, among other bands, that of Duke Ellington. There were always rumors in the jazz world of Glaser's shady connections, but for that matter anyone in the nightclub world of Chicago in the 1920s had connections of some sort with Al Capone: he actually ran the city. In his biography of Capone, Larry Bergreen wrote: "In an earlier incarnation Glaser was an influential fight promoter in Chicago. From his two-room office in the Loop, Glaser ran his boxing empire and zealously protected his turf. When a gambler and part-time journalist named Eddie Borden denounced Glaser in print as a front for the Capone organization, Glaser had him run out of town and swiftly returned to business as usual. Glaser's power to fix fights earned him a reputation as the sage of boxing."

In those days, according to Milt, Cab Calloway "was a young kid, a basketball player, who'd come around to see his sister Blanche. She wanted to get him into the club, so she taught him how to sing, and he'd come in and play the drums."

Blanche Calloway was five years Cab's senior. She began singing in Baltimore clubs—she and her brother were both born in Maryland—in the 1920s, recorded with Louis Armstrong in 1925, worked with Andy Kirk, and for a time had her own band. Thus she was Cab's entree to show business. The mob people were impressed by the dashing young man.

"So the gangsters," Milt continued, "said to the Missourians, 'Put this kid in front of the band.' And they were a great success. They played the Savoy Ballroom and were doing great. When Duke Ellington was getting ready to leave the Cotton Club in New York, they said, 'Give him the band.' They told the Missourians, 'It's Cab's band now.' The bass player was the leader, so he was naturally fired. They told the guys in the band, 'You can stay, but Cab Calloway is the bandleader, and you're going into the Cotton Club.' And they stayed. I can tell you who they were. Lammar Wright, Walter Thomas, Andy Brown, Doc Cheatham. They stayed and it was a tremendous success.

"Cab was made by radio broadcasts from the Cotton Club two or three times a week. Network radio was starting and people all over the country could hear you.

"When they got Capone on income tax, he said, 'If you think

all of these people that I'm hiring, who are making three or four
hundred dollars a week when everybody else that works a week
long in the stockyards and different places is making twenty-five
and thirty dollars, are going to go back to taking jobs at fifteen
or twenty dollars a week, you're crazy.'

"And that's when chaos broke loose. They broke up all that
alcohol-selling, and those people were not going to go back to
those jobs. And they started robbing and killing and breaking
into places. It changed the whole complexion of the town. The
happiness all left, the clubs all closed, and it was pretty drab there
for a long time after that."

"The first band I ever played in, really," Milt said, "was not a jazz
band. It was a sweet band at the Jeffrey Tavern, a white tavern.
It was like Lester Lanin. The bass player got sick or something,
and somebody recommended me for just one night. I got nineteen dollars. That's the first time I made any money playing bass.
I was still delivering newspapers, two hundred papers every
morning, *Chicago Herald-Examiner*, for $9.75 a week, and going
to Northwestern University. That's how I gradually got into the
gigs, when I got this one job for nineteen dollars, and I worked
late, and I had to deliver my morning papers. Then somebody
else got sick in a band, and I got a call again. My mother said,
'You can't do both things. You've got to make a decision.' I had
no dreams it would be possible to make a living in music. That
was the toughest decision of my life, to give up my paper route.

"I had to wait for some of the older players to get drunk or
get sick. We didn't have too many clubs to go to. There was a guy
named Charlie Levy. He wrote arrangements and played violin in
old road houses. He had a car. This is summertime. He'd put
me in a car and we'd go out to some tavern. There were no juke
boxes in those days. We'd go in and start playing, and they'd give

us nickels and dimes and quarters, and we'd come home with ten dollars apiece.

"I came out of Northwestern University, because I was sleeping in the history classes, and Dr. Jones, who had studied with Coleridge Taylor, asked me what was I doing. Why was I so tired? I explained I was working and I had to help support my mother. He encouraged me not to kill myself just to get a degree, but to continue my studies in music, because I seemed to be talented along those lines.

"Consequently I started working with bands around Chicago. I got to work with Erskine Tate. The Savoy Ballroom got to be very popular. All those bands came through Chicago from the west and from the east. Andy Kirk and Duke Ellington. They all played the Savoy Ballroom. And we had a union there, so they had to have a relief band. So I got the job in the relief band, playing the intermission. I got the chance to hear and see Mary Lou Williams and her husband, John Williams, who was a saxophone player. Ben Webster was in the band at that time. Duke Ellington came through and I got the chance to stand there and watch Wellman Braud, and hope he'd just drop his rosin, so I could hand it to him or something like that. The contribution to me was to be around those wonderful people, and see it.

"In 1929, Eddie South came back from Europe. He had a manager named Sam Skolnick. He was an agent. Eddie had been so successful in Europe, Skolnick had convinced some people they should put him into some of the great white hotels downtown in Chicago, with violins, a society type of band. This guy organized the band while Eddie was still in Europe. He got some great musicians. They got me to play bass in this band. It rehearsed for maybe four or five hours in the afternoon upstairs in a Chinese restaurant called Chu Chin Chow near the Savoy Ballroom. We rehearsed music like *Dancing on the Ceiling* and that kind of beautiful stuff. Eddie was supposed to come in with his quartet from Europe and be augmented by this band. We had the rehearsal, and the powers that be decided they couldn't have a black band in this hotel downtown.

"The agent had signed everybody up to contracts, seventy-five dollars a week, guaranteeing us thirty weeks a year. And then the bubble burst. And Eddie had to buy the contracts back from the musicians. He paid three hundred dollars apiece. It probably depleted what he had earned in Europe. They paid everybody off. And when they got to me, this guy said to Eddie, 'Now wait, we can get you a job in one of the small clubs. You don't have a bass player. So don't give this kid three hundred dollars. Give him a job.'

"That's how I got the job with Eddie South. We worked for Al Capone. He owned the Club Rubaiyat, a small club on the North Side that seated less than a hundred. That's where I began to meet most of the white musicians, because everybody knew about Eddie South. We had a small band, with a piano player named Anthonia Spalding, from Louisville, Kentucky. A very great piano player. He played all kinds of music, things like *Rhapsody in Blue*, all of the French music. This guy played it well. Eddie had Stanley Wilson on guitar, and a drummer named Lester Moreira, from Cuba, who later played for Cugat. And he hired me for bass. And we played these wonderful things. I learned to play all the classical things that Eddie played. And all of the musicians from Ben Pollack's band used to come over to hear Eddie South. Benny Goodman was in that band, and Jack Teagarden. This is where we got to meet all these wonderful musicians and exchange ideas. And later they'd go out and jam together. It was that kind of a thing."

The Democratic National Convention of 1932 was held in Chicago at the Congress Hotel. "The Congress was a fabulous hotel," Milt remembered. "And they decided we couldn't play in the big ballroom, but they put us in the lobby, by the fountain. We were playing music with the water dripping, and that's where I got to see all those congressmen. I saw Al Smith and John Nance Garner, Speaker of the House, and Franklin Delano Roosevelt. That was the convention that nominated Roosevelt for president.

"We got to do a recording session for RCA. One of the big tunes was *Old Man Harlem* at that time. Then we went to California. We went to a beautiful club on Hollywood Boulevard, the Club Ballyhoo. We had a trio, Eddie South, Everett Barksdale on guitar, and I'm playing bass. We were really tight. All strings. We played from hot jazz to classical music. Everett Barksdale was the first black guitarist I ever worked with that really read music and played single-string stuff. He was out of Detroit. He was absolutely fantastic. There was no amplification, of course. All they had for entertainment besides Eddie South was a dance trio, a woman and two men. We had to play tango for them. One of the men was Cesar Romero.

"Now all of the great writers and the good musicians in the studios had heard of Eddie South. That was 1933. We stayed in California. Eddie's career grew. We came to Chicago after that.

"Joe Venuti had always loved Eddie South. He was a great benefactor of Eddie's. You hear all the crazy stories about all the jokes that Joe Venuti did. And of course he did that. He was a raucous guy. I never saw one instance of his having any racial feelings at all. He told me that he and Eddie Lang used to cork their faces and go up to Harlem to jam with black musicians, so that nobody would give them any flak about it. When he was with Paul Whiteman at the College Inn, Eddie South was at the Vendome Theater, Whiteman had a great singer with him named Bee Palmer.

"She was used to being accompanied by Joe Venuti on violin. He played beautifully behind her. Joe was leaving with a group of his own playing country clubs. And this lady was distraught because she didn't have Joe to play jazz behind her. She said,

'What am I going to do?' And Joe Venuti said, 'Get Eddie South.' But of course, you couldn't get a black violin player to play in Whiteman's band *then*. They put her on the stage and put a screen behind her and Eddie South stood behind it and played for her.

"Joe Venuti was so wonderful. When he went on tour with his trio, people asked him, 'Who can we get to follow you in here?' Joe always recommended Eddie South. We began to get these wonderful jobs, playing in these exclusive country clubs. When we got there, there was always a very funny note left on the piano for us from Joe Venuti. He made it possible for Eddie to make a very good living.

"Years later I got the chance to work with Joe Venuti. After working with Eddie South, I loved violin, and it was my first instrument. About a third of my record collection is violin players, from Heifetz on down. So I finally got a chance to work with Joe in New York City. He appreciated me because I understood the violin. We could play contrapuntal things. And I could bow. I had one of the most exciting times of my life with him. I was playing with him at Michael's Pub when he got very sick and died—his last engagement.

"I've always been a sideman. I've never had a band. I've worked once or twice in a little trio. I always decided I wanted to be such a good bass player that people would want me to work for them. I could always work. That's what happened to me with Eddie South. Work slowed down for violin players, but I could get gigs around Chicago. I'm not expensive, I'm a sideman. I'm getting scale, but I can survive on scale. A violinist of Eddie's stature can't work for scale."

"And," I interjected, "a jazz violinist can't work as a sideman."

"No, that's right," Milt answered. "And if you've got any kind of reputation, you can't step into somebody else's band. I'm working around with Erskine Tate and Johnny Long and Joe Williams, we're working on the South Side. Eddie South had to sit at home. And he's my *master*. And I'm ending up with a hundred dollars at the end of the week. I had to loan him twenty, because he didn't have the money. He always paid me back when he got a gig. But it was very sad. That's how I really got established, working with Eddie South. In 1934, we got on the RKO circuit with a comedian, and Lee Sims, the pianist, and his wife, Ilomay Bailey, all through theaters in Ohio, and wound up at the Palace Theater in New York City for one week. I made seventy-five bucks.

"I didn't want to go back home. That's just like I'd get back in school or something. So I stayed around New York. For five dollars a week, I got a room in the 135th Street YMCA. I starved, but I didn't care. I could get a fish sandwich with four slices of bread and a whole fish laid across it for twenty cents up in Harlem. I'd cut that sucker in half, put a little hot sauce on it, wrap the other half up and put it in my pocket for later. You could get a big soda for three cents. And I'm trying to get a gig. I go by the Apollo Theater and listen to the rehearsal. I had no dreams: John Kirby was a jazz bass player, Beverly Peer was with Chick Webb. I had no way to survive. I finally had to go back to Chicago.

"In the early 1930s, there was only one big band, besides Les Kincaid's, in Chicago, and that was Earl Hines' band. So there weren't a lot of jobs for bass players. I couldn't get into Earl Hines's band, because he had Quinn Wilson, who graduated ahead of me, and he had Hayes Alvis, a great bass player that used to be a drummer. When the Grand Terrace closed for the summer, the band split up. Some guys would take one half of the band, and some guys would take the other and go to small clubs. I worked my way up to be the second bass player.

"The first time there was ever a coast-to-coast network was when the Lindbergh baby was kidnaped. That night Earl Hines was on the air from midnight at the Grand Terrace. They kept him on the air all night, and they would patch in from Oak Park, Illinois, to Gary, Indiana, to Indianapolis, to relay that message about that baby's kidnaping. It was the first band to ever play coast-to-coast network, a network of stations thirty or forty miles apart.

"Then, in 1935, Zutty Singleton from New Orleans really established me. He was even more respected than Louis Armstrong. He worked with Louis in the Hot Five. And now he's got the job at the Three Deuces down at State and Lake. And he hired me as his bass player. Cozy Cole's brother, Lee Cole, was on piano, Lee Collins was playing trumpet, Everett Barksdale was playing guitar, and Zutty Singleton was playing drums. These guys were New Orleans seniors, and they hired me. There were not too many string bass players around. Zutty was a giant, and when he hired me, that was my stamp of approval into the New Orleans society. Art Tatum was the relief piano player.

"And it was my sad duty, at the end of the night, closing up his set, I had to go play with him. I never caught him yet. He was playing those fantastic changes that I never knew, and I stood there in amazement, trying to catch him all the time. But he was always so nice. We played pinochle together, so the rout wasn't that complete. He'd hold the cards right up to his eye, with the light behind him. A unique man. He would make the waiters set up the room the way it was going to be that night. He knew how to maneuver through the tables without falling or stumbling to the piano.

"I played there with Zutty in 1935. That's when Cab was going out to California to do *The Singing Kid* with Al Jolson. Cab had Al Morgan, this fabulous bass player from New Orleans. Photogenic. Big, tall, looked like he was chiseled out of ebony. Handsome man, exotic clothes, and the ladies loved him. A great shower, and of course he was the biggest showman of the time, and they're making this movie with Al Jolson. And in one of the scenes, Cab Calloway is dancing and shaking his hair, and he looked up. He thought the camera was on him and it was on the bass player, Al Morgan. And of course that didn't sit too good.

"Then Al Morgan beat Cab out of a couple of ladies, and so they weren't too tight together. And then one of the directors told Al Morgan, 'If you're out here in California and we've got a jazz movie, the way you went over, you've got the job.' And so with this altercation between the two of them, Al Morgan *quit* and stayed out in California and joined Les Hite's band. Lionel Hampton was in that band, Lawrence Brown, quite a few guys.

"Cab had to come back east without a bass player for his one-nighters. Well my friend Keg Johnson, Budd Johnson's brother, who had gotten in Cab Calloway's band, said, 'When you're going through Chicago, check out Milt Hinton. He's down at the Three Deuces with Zutty.' Cab Calloway stopped in at the Three Deuces in his coonskin coat on a cold winter night, and he came in the door and everybody saw it was Cab Calloway, and they were making over him. And he never said a word to me. He came up to Zutty Singleton and said, 'I hear that kid's pretty good. How is he?' Zutty said, 'He's fine. He's a good kid. He plays good.'

"And Cab said, 'Well, can I have him?'

"And Zutty said, 'Yeah.' He didn't ask me *anything*. He just gave me away, like a baseball player. Zutty came upstairs, and I was playing cards with Art Tatum, and Zutty said, 'Well kid, you're gone.'

"I said, 'I'm gone *where?*'

" 'Well Cab just asked me for you,' he said with that New Orleans talk.

"I said, 'Zutty, do I have to give you notice or anything?'

"He said, 'Get your ass out of here tonight.'

"We went back and played another set and Cab Hi-de-hoed a couple of choruses with us, and all he said to me, he turned around to me and said, 'The train leaves from the South Street

Station at nine o'clock in the morning. Be there.' And he walked out.

"I had to call home and tell my Mama—and that was one o'clock in the morning, and we played till four—I've got this job with Cab Calloway, and tell her to pack up whatever I have. I only had one suit. She packed up a canvas bag with a change of underwear and a clean shirt. I got on this train in South Street Station, and I'd never been in a Pullman in my life. And you know I didn't come from Mississippi in a Pullman. I got in this train, and all these giants were there. There was Doc Cheatham, Mouse Randolph, Claude Jones—Tommy Dorsey's buddy, great trombone player—Keg Johnson, my friend. And Cab Calloway and Ben Webster had been out in the night in town and got drunk, and *missed* the train.

"But if you missed the train downtown, you could get on at the Sixty-third Street station. Keg Johnson is introducing me to the guys. I musta looked terrible. The train stopped at the Sixty-third Street station, and Cab Calloway and Ben Webster fall in drunk.

"Ben Webster looked at me, and said, 'What is *that*?'

"And Cab said, 'That's the new bass player.'

"And Ben Webster said, 'That is *what*?' I must have weighed a hundred and ten pounds soaking wet. I swore I would never like this man. And he turned out to be one of my dearest friends."

I found myself laughing out loud, having often stood beside Ben, in all his gloomy majesty, talking at the bar of Jim and Andy's in New York. "I think everybody had experiences with Ben," I said. "When he was drunk, get out of the way."

"That's *right*," Milt chuckled. "But he was beautiful. He was good to me.

"I was in the band three months on the road, playing one-nighters, before we hit New York. Cab said, 'We've got a lot of one-nighters. I'll keep you till I get to New York and get me a good bass player.'

"And I stayed with his band sixteen years.

"When we got on the road, the guys liked me. Al Morgan hadn't been much of a good reader, because he was from New Orleans. But he was a handsome bass player, and he knew the book. There *was* no book when I got there!

"But I knew changes, and all of that stuff. Benny Payne, the pianist, was calling changes off to me. And I was doing so well. But the funny part, I've got to tell you . . . Cab turns to the guys—the guys all seemed to be satisfied with me—and said, 'Let's give 'im a blood test.' He called this hard number that Al Morgan was featured in. It was called *Reefer Man.* I had no music. I said to Benny Payne, 'What's that?' He said, 'It features the bass. You start out playing anything you wanna play, and the band'll come in. And it's blues changes when the band comes in.'

"So I started this in F, man, and I played a chromatic deal. I played the F scale upside down and sideways. I squared F, I cubed F. I did every conceivable thing. And when finally the band came in with this big chord, I wanted to drop my bass and go out. Benny Payne says, 'Keep on playing.' Now the band's playing the blues, about ten choruses. And all of a sudden the band stops, and Benny says, 'You got it.'

"That's when I started slapping the bass, and playing all kinds of hip scales and everything. I used to wear my hair in a pompadour, long in front and you plastered it down to your head with grease to make it smooth, and I got hot and the perspiration was running offa me. And the grease ran off and my hair stood straight up!" he said, laughing. "And the musicians in the band were rolling! They were laughing, they could hardly play their horns, and Cab was out of his skull. He was falling out. And they let me go for about ten minutes by myself and I said to Benny

Payne, 'What the hell do I do now?' And Benny said, 'When you get thinking about time, just fall back like you're fainting and I'll catch you.' And that's the way it ended. And the audience cracked up.

"Ben Webster was very kind to me now. He'd take me around with him. We'd get to a town and he'd want to go jamming. He taught me how to approach things, how to lead into a chorus, and all that sort of stuff. I'm making a hundred dollars a week now, after the thirty-five dollars I was making with Zutty, and by the time we get to New York, I've saved up about four, five hundred dollars. That was good bread! That was the Depression. You could get a good meal for thirty-five cents. A suit cost twenty-two fifty.

"And I looked so bad, Ben don't want me to come into New York and hangin' with him, and he's was always dressed impeccably. So Ben and Keg Johnson take me right down to Billy Taub's, one of the clothing stores. He put things up in front of me. And they're dressing me like your Mom would. 'How does this look on him?' And they picked up a nice green suit, and I put this suit on, and they bought me shirts with my money. So by the time I got to Harlem, I was pretty cool, I was sharp.

"Now this is 1936. I'm in the band, I'm established, everybody loves me, and *I'm playing my ass off*. Everything's going right. The Cotton Club is opening downtown where the Latin Quarter was, used to be Palais Royal where Paul Whiteman used to play. Now they made it the Cotton Club, Owney Madden is closing the one in Harlem and moving it to Forty-eighth and Broadway. The first show is Cab Calloway and Bill Robinson, the Berry Brothers, Fred Coots, and a host of others, including Will Vodery. Nobody mentions Will Vodery any more. It's just terrible."

Vodery was an arranger and orchestrator for Florenz Ziegfeld. He worked for Jerome Kern, orchestrated *Show Boat,* and he was the first black composer and arranger to penetrate the film industry. Milt was astonished that I'd heard of him.

"He orchestrated the very first Cotton Club show downtown. And he was so damn sure of himself, he scored in ink. I had never seen a man like Vodery. A dignified man. A brown-skinned man. He had trouble with hearing in one of his ears. He lived up in Harlem, but he had a place in Saratoga too. He rehearsed us. J. Fred Coots was writing tunes."

Among Coots's tunes were *For All We Know, Love Letters in the Sand,* and *You Go to My Head.*

"Harold Arlen did some of the tunes later," Milt said. "Vodery rehearsed us. Nobody's heard of some of these people.

"Why do you think that Antonín Dvořák wrote the *New World Symphony?*

"When he came here from Czechoslovakia to teach, he had a black singer in his class named Harry T. Burleigh. Nobody's heard of him either. Dvořák asked him to sing some of the spirituals. And that's when Dvořák wrote the *New World Symphony,* based on *Going Home.* Harry T. Burleigh became a great singer and sang in the big white churches in New York City. He was a big name. Now nobody mentions him."

I'd heard Burleigh's name but knew little about him. I asked my friend Dr. Dominique de Lerma at Lawrence University— one of the great scholars of black music, including all that preceded jazz—about Burleigh, telling him about the case Milt had just made. Dominique wrote me a letter:

"Harry T. Burleigh (1866–1949) was a voice student at the National Conservatory of Music, there on a scholarship encouraged by the mother of Edward MacDowell (who had been registrar). She had met him at a winter evening musicale being given at a fancy-ass home in Erie where Rafael Joseffy was performing. Burleigh was outside in the snow, trying to listen through the window. The hostess saw him, called him inside, and supposedly gave him some servant's clothes as a disguise.

"My sources say that Burleigh studied with Dvořák. He did not. He was a voice major. But Dvořák got him often to his residence—way up on something like Fifteenth Street in New York!—to sing all the spirituals Burleigh knew. When in that year, 1893, Dvořák wrote his final symphony to show Americans what (he thought) American music was like, he gave the Second Movement's initial theme to the English horn because, he is said to have remarked, it was most like the sound of Burleigh's voice. Today he might have given the solo to the tenor sax.

"Dvořák encouraged his students to write American music, not pseudo-German music, and as you well know, Will Marion Cook was one of his students. So was William Arms Fischer (1861–1948). Fischer later became associated with Oliver Ditson (1897–1937) in Boston. It was there Fischer set Dvořák's melody to a so-called spiritual text, *Goin' Home*. That was in 1924. The tune is in ballad form, AABA, like *Over the Rainbow, Take the 'A' Train,* and *Swanee River.* I know no spiritual in that form.

"*Goin' Home* was often thought to be a real spiritual from the start, but it isn't. Dvořák quoted no spiritual in any work of his.

"Burleigh, a real dicty dude, taught at the school for a bit, even tried his hand at a minstrel show—which I'm sure disgusted him. He became baritone soloist at New York's all-white St. George's Church, high Episcopal, because J. P. Morgan said so. He remained there for a half century, even after Morgan's death, as requested in Morgan's will.

"Since he was free on Saturdays, he was also soloist at Temple Emanu-El from 1900 to 1930, doing such things as singing *Deep River* in Hebrew. I'm on the trail of a recording of Burleigh. Those I've known who actually heard him raved about his voice.

"By 1913, he was editor for Ricordi, in which capacity he published also his own settings of the spirituals, giving the Harlem Renaissance some important literature."

Little wonder, then, that Milt Hinton didn't want Burleigh forgotten.

"I got married in 1939," Milt said. "Mona was in my mother's choir.

"I was in the Cotton Club. The World's Fair was going on. The Trylon and Perisphere. I got a call that my grandmother had died, a hundred and three years old. I left my bass right on the bandstand and I got to Chicago, and all these Mississippi folks had a wake. There was chicken and whisky and talkin' and consoling the family. The house was loaded. And I'm a star. I come in sharp. There were a lot of young girls there, pretty chicks. And my mother gave me hell. She said, 'You come to Mama's funeral and you're looking these girls over. Leave these girls alone!'

"And I saw Mona over there and I hit on Mona. I said, 'Look, I'll be back later. Let's keep in contact.'

"A few weeks later, we were coming back to Indianapolis, Indiana. I called up Mona on the phone. I said, 'Look, I'm going to be in Indianapolis for a week, at the Circle Theater. Why don't you come down on the weekend, Friday, Saturday, and Sunday, and hang out with me, and then go on back to Chicago.' She said, 'Okay.' I told her to come backstage at the theater and when you see my bass trunk, tell them you're waiting for me. So she did.

"Now my mother had some friends in Indianapolis. She decided since I'm playing there, she'd come down and see her friends. She walked backstage, and there was Mona sitting on my bass trunk. She raised hell. She said, 'What are you doing here? Get back on the train, and go back to Chicago.'

"And when I come offstage, she says, 'She's gone back to Chicago.' As if that would stop it. We've been married ever since."

Thus 1939 was a major year in Milt's life. Then another major figure came into it. Dizzy Gillespie joined the Cab Calloway band.

"Cab was one of our greatest leaders," Milt said. "He was kind to us, he paid us more money. He even paid more money than Duke paid. He was born on Christmas Day. We stopped work December 23. Wherever we stopped work, he gave us our salary and a hundred dollars for Christmas, a ticket home to wherever you lived, and a ticket back to Chicago. We had a contract for years to play New Year's Eve at the College Inn.

"He paid for the prenatal care for my daughter. He said, 'Have this one on me.' It's never been told what kind of man this was, except by people like Dizzy and me. We kept that band together after it broke up, like family. Anybody got broke, got sick, was out of money, we always chipped in. When Benny Payne died in California, we got some money together. It's *still* that way, those of us who are left."

A year after Mona and Milt were married, another figure came into his life: his father.

"He came back to the United States. He was an educated man. His field was agriculture, like Booker T. Washington at Tuskegee. After slavery, we weren't trying to get brain surgeons. We were trying to get people who knew how to be servants, porters, cooks. That's why Tuskegee was built. This was right after slavery. People knew *nothin'*.

"My father was well-versed in cotton. When he went back to Africa, Firestone found you could grow rubber trees there in the same conditions you did in South America, and they built the great rubber plantations in Monrovia, and he worked there. But he didn't get on too well with them. From what I hear, he wasn't a very easy man to get along with, and he didn't take anything from anybody. And he got in trouble there, and he came back to the United States—to Memphis, Tennessee. He got to be a cotton sampler, and that was the best job a black man could have in the South. Every cotton buyer would have a cotton sampler, a black man who knew cotton, Grade A, Grade B. And he would buy according to that man's opinion.

"We were playing Memphis. Benny Payne, the piano player, says, 'I hear your father's in town. Have you seen him yet?' I said, 'No.' I'd just played a bass solo. Benny said, 'He's standing over there.' And he was. He was standing backstage. I looked just like the guy. I didn't know what to say to this man. But he said the right words. He looked at me, and he said, 'Your mother's done a wonderful job.' And when he said that, I hugged him. And I said, 'Let's go have a drink.' And Cozy Cole, Cab Calloway, Chu Berry, and my father and I went to the nearest bar and got stoned.

"I went to the telephone and called my mother in Chicago, and I handed him the phone. His voice was the same as mine, with the half hoarseness, half harshness, and she said, 'Baby, have you got a cold?' And he said, 'No,' and she knew, and she said, 'Put my son on the phone!' She never saw him.

"He stayed in Tennessee. When they started building the atomic bomb in Oak Ridge, Tennessee, they grabbed everybody who knew about cotton, because cotton acetate is the basis for explosives.

"I don't know what he did there, but they gave everybody who worked at Oak Ridge, Tennessee, a citation, because if the thing had gone up, everybody would have been gone. He died when he was sixty-six years old. The only thing I have of my father's is that citation from Oak Ridge and his razor."

Many musicians have taken up photography as a hobby, and some have become highly proficient. Stan Levey even turned professional, giving up music as a career. Les McCann is a superb photographer, and a fine painter as well. Milt is one of the best of them. In 1988, Temple University Press published *Bass Lines,* a coffee-table book of his pictures supported by a text in which he recounts his life and times.

"How did the photography start, Milt?"

"Somebody bought me a camera for my birthday in the late '30s. Traveling with Cab, I just wanted to take pictures of the musicians. I wanted to record what I did, and the places that I'd been and the people in my surroundings. And I found that I can do what photographers can't do because I'm a musician. Because I'm going to take a picture, the guy doesn't tie his tie or get his horn. If he does that, I don't take the picture, because that's not what I'm into. I took a picture of Dizzy sleeping in a bus. I just want to catch a guy in a restaurant, eating a sandwich. I got Chu Berry down in Texas, where it was hot as hell, with a big piece of watermelon and he's enjoying it, and he's soaking wet. Places we've been. I've tried to show the stupidity of prejudice. Like a picture in Atlanta, Georgia, of a railway station, 1939. It says *Colored Entrance.* Cab Calloway's whole band. I said, 'Before you go through, guys, let me get this picture.' Fifty years later, you had a black man running for governor there. It shows you the progress that has been made. There's not nearly enough, but we've come a long ways. I took a picture of a sign in Florida that said *No Jews and Dogs Allowed.* Forget me!

"Ray Brown—he was married to Ella Fitzgerald at the time—and I used to stand out on the corner. He was working in one club and Cab Calloway was playing another club. The club where he worked at night, there was no one there in the afternoon. There was a bass in the back. We'd get a half pint of whisky and take a little sip and he'd play something and show me, and I'd play something and show him.

"One day, I remember, the bar was open in the front, but in the back it's dark. And we heard some cats rehearsing back there.

We couldn't see who it was. We listened to the bass player. You couldn't hear much tone out of it. But Ray Brown said, 'That cat sure is keeping good time, man. We're gonna hear more about him.' And the guitar player was playing! And the trumpet player was out of sight. Years later that bass player took Ray's place with Oscar Peterson. It was Sam Jones. The trumpet player was Blue Mitchell. The guitar player killed a woman and went to jail. The saxophone player, the chicks just ruined him and he never made it."

This incident touched on a point I had been meaning to raise with Milt, so I asked him how he viewed the development of bass playing since the 1920s.

"Oh!" he said with a long sigh. "Bass has made more progress than any other instrument in the last fifty years. Listen to Lynn Seaton, or Ron Carter, or Richard Davis. And John Clayton. Fantastic. The epitome of players! The instrument hasn't changed bodily, but the balance of strings has changed, the teaching has changed.

"I heard Jimmy Blanton with Jeter-Pillars down in St. Louis. Bass horn was still the style down in St. Louis. Anybody that played bass fiddle had to emulate bass horn. We played two beats, boom boom, boom boom, budoom-budoom boom boom. That's the way we were taught to play. That's what the musicians wanted to hear. And nobody wanted to hear a bass player taking a solo. Pops Foster got a chance now and then to do a little something.

"The word *bass* means bottom. It means support. That's the prime requisite of a bass player, support. Architecturally, it has to be the lowest part of the building, and it has to be strong, or the building will not stand. Musically, it is the lowest human voice. It is the lowest musical voice in the orchestra. It's identifying. If it's a B-flat-major chord, I have to play B-flat, or you won't know it's a B-flat-major chord. We are like Atlas, standing in support.

Now what we're doing today in most instances is not really supporting. We're bypassing that, doing other things as well as supporting. Which is possible to do. Bridges don't need to have col-
umns, we have suspension bridges with cables coming from
them. And we're doing the same thing musically with the bass."

As a bass player, Milt managed to adjust his playing to all the
different styles of the 1930s and '40s, though few others did. And
he played in contemporary styles, too.

"I try. But I'm still using some of the old things that I heard.
Like the slap bass, which I got from those guys. Steve Brown
was one of my idols. He was fabulous. I listened to his records.
He was a better slap-bass player than even Pops Foster, and
more exposed because he was with Jean Goldkette and Paul
Whiteman. He was a big man. I never met him, but I always
loved him. He was on *Rhapsody in Blue* and all those things with
Whiteman, and you had to be a proficient bass player for that
music. He was the best slap-bass player I ever heard in my life,
amazing. The best in the world. I try to double that, like these
young people who double what Blanton did, and all that sort of
stuff. Now they're coming to me to find out about this slap-bass
thing.

"But I'm amazed at *them,* and I'm still trying to find out and
continue. Education will make you do that, that you don't shut
your mind to any one thing. Not to be facetious about it, all the
bass players in all of the big bands down through the years, you
don't remember who they were. All they did was that one thing
and they didn't keep abreast of the other things. Nobody remembers who was Jimmie Lunceford's bass player. All he had to do
was play that two beats, and he never got past that. His name
was Mose Allen.

"And that goes for all the other bands. So when the complexion
of the dance orchestra changed, Blanton was one of the innovators. He was *also* a violin player. Blanton's innovation was the

violin, improvising. The academic knowledge, having the dexterity, the knowledge of the instrument harmonically. I have some records of him before Ellington, the Jeter-Pillars band out of St. Louis, and the guys in the band didn't *like* him, because he was playing all that stuff, and that was not what they wanted out of a bass player. But he was modern, and he wasn't very successful. He was improvising and doing little things in between. They weren't accustomed to that. It was because of Ivie Anderson, who was a very modern lady singer with Duke Ellington, they went down to St. Louis and heard him, and thought it was marvelous. *She* introduced him to Duke Ellington. And Duke Ellington was always looking for the new.

"And they started with those duos. *Pitter Panther Patter*. I've got the write-ups from when that came out. They panned Duke like hell for that. They said, 'What does Duke mean doing this kind of thing, duets?' I call them bass booets. And then the musicians heard it, and could see a vision of what he was about, and they fell in love with it. And other bass players began to emulate it, and as they got more advanced began to do it.

"I was in Cab Calloway's band, and when I heard him, I thought I'd hang up my bass and leave. There was nothing else for us to do. Billy Taylor was with Duke. Duke never fired anybody—he just added Jimmy Blanton. And Billy Taylor couldn't take that, standing there every night and hearing all that wonderful playing. He just quit.

"You have to keep on top of things, keep abreast, keep listening and find out what you can do, and how it works, and appreciating it. And these kids appreciate *me*, they're coming to me and saying, 'Milt, how do you do that slap-bass thing?' And I'm only too happy to try to show them. But it's gonna take practice to do it."

Yet another bassist who began as a violinist was Milt's friend George Duvivier. He studied at the Conservatory of Music and

Art and became concert master of the Central Manhattan Symphony when he was sixteen. When Duvivier died in 1985, Ray Brown wrote a piece in his memory to be played by seven bassists: himself, Bob Haggart, John Clayton, Major Holley, Carson Smith, Milt, and John Heard.

According to John Heard: "We all played our solos. And then came Milt's turn. He did his animal number. He played slapped bass, he did everything, and he wiped everybody out! It was great."

"Clark Terry and I," Milt said, "have gone to black universities, like Morgan State, and the faculty teaching don't know about people like Harry T. Burleigh, and we tell them these things, the black kids particularly, to give them some impetus about their heritage, some inspiration. Kids have to have role models. There's a book by a man named James M. Trotter called *Musical People of Color*. It goes back to 1845 and tells about the time of slavery, when free blacks became great singers and great writers and opera singers. Joseph White, a great violin player, went to Cuba and France and won medals and was a friend of Rossini's. And our black kids don't *know* about these things. James Holland, whose music for guitar is on the market to this very day. And Blind Tom. This book has got the reviews he got from all over the world. This is a wonderful book. We need this to give the kids something to aspire to.

"In the Jewish religion, the kids learn about the Maccabees and Eliazar, the great priests who held up the faith, and defied kings. Jewish children can read about these things. And we don't have that kind of thing in our race, and it's important.

"I love doing clinics. Sharing my expertise. And not teaching but advising, encouraging, setting a role model. Telling the kids from where we've come, where it is now, and where *you've* got to go, because these young ones have got to do *better*. If you don't do better than what's happening now, you haven't made any progress. I try to tell them how you should carry yourself, and what's required of a professional musician.

"This music came up on the North American continent. That includes Canada, because it is part of this continent. Everybody's contributed to this music, whether Indian, Canadian, black, white. We have to use the academics that people get and put it together with the creativity of other people, and we form something that is truly American.

"It's like plastics. I took a course in plastics. Plastics can be made from waste material, and under heat and pressure it becomes another substance with none of the properties of what it came from. If you wanted to make plastic in Iowa, you would use corn cobs, the parts you throw away, and under heat and pressure you make a plastic sheet material that has none of the properties of corn.

"This is what was done in music in America. All of this has been under the heat and pressure of the North American continent, and we concocted music that has European and African and Asiatic background, and it becomes American classical music. And it is constantly changing, according to what waste materials we use.

"I'm a descendant of slave Africans and black Africans, but it's African. Other people come from the intermarriage of American Indians and black people. Because they were on the low part of the totem pole, they kind of hooked up together there.

"But what we really want to do is be Americans. We're all on this American continent together, man."

Milt slowed in the last few years of his life. His step faltered more and more, and then he had a leg amputated. He died in

Queens at about 11:30 P.M. on December 19, twelve days before the start of the twenty-first century, loved by everyone who knew him.

Given that some of the musicians he inspired and helped and taught were still in their twenties, or even younger, he will be a long time passing into the zamani.

Mona said, "I refuse to complain. I had sixty-one years with one of the best men I ever met."

King Cole

Nat Cole came to Louisville in April 1956.

This was only days after five white supremacists had tried to abduct him from a stage in Birmingham, Alabama. The head of the North Alabama White Citizens Council had issued an edict declaring that "Negro music appeals to the base in man, bringing out animalism and vulgarity," and the white supremacists acted on it, oblivious of course to the animalism, vulgarity, and baseness in themselves. What the five men planned to do with Cole had their abduction succeeded remains unknown, but a friendly entreaty somewhere on a back-country road that he forswear singing "Negro music" is hardly among the possibilities.

Cole was touring with June Christy, the Four Freshmen, and the Ted Heath band from Britain. Two performances were planned for the evening of Tuesday, April 10, in the Birmingham Municipal Auditorium. One was for a white audience, the other black. That is the way things were in the South.

The men clambered up onto that stage in Birmingham. One

of them took a punch at Cole, knocking him back against a piano bench, which shattered as he fell over it. The police subdued his assailants, but he had a swollen lip as he limped offstage.

Bob Flanigan, who as a member of the Four Freshmen was present, remembers, "It was awful. He was hit in the mouth with a microphone. Somebody in the audience asked that he come back, so they could apologize, and he did! He went back out on-stage. That took a lot of balls." Then the mayor came to Cole's dressing room, and augmented the apology.

But the performance for the white audience was suspended, and Cole sang only briefly for the black audience that came to the auditorium later that evening. He went to Chicago, where he had grown up, presumably to settle his nerves. The reporters were ready for him; in the case of some of the members of the black press, you might say they were lying in ambush.

He said, "I was a guinea pig for some hoodlums who thought they could hurt me and frighten me and keep other Negro entertainers from performing in the South. But what they did has backfired on them, because thousands of white people in the audience could see how terrible it is for an innocent man to be subjected to such barbaric treatment."

Then, when a reporter asked him if he would again perform for segregated audiences in the South, he answered: "Sure I will. I'm not a political figure or some controversial person. I'm just an entertainer, and it's my job to perform for them. If I stop because of some state law, I'm deserting the people who are important to me. In my way I may be helping to bring harmony between people through music."

He was castigated for saying it. Tavern operators in Harlem took his records out of their jukeboxes. He was particularly attacked in the *Chicago Defender,* a black newspaper. The argument raged on, and Cole was hurt by it. He had refused to play for a segregated audience in Kansas City in 1944, but this was

Oscar Moore, Nat Cole, and Johnny Miller, probably 1943 (Photo © William P.
Gottlieb, from the Library of Congress Collection)

forgotten in the turmoil over the statements he made about the
Birmingham incident. "The whole thing backfired," Bob Flanigan
said, "because Nat was such a gentleman."

Although I could wrestle with these events intellectually, they were as alien to me as any I might find in the doings of the inhabitants of another planet. I was at that point eleven months out of Canada.

After a few days off, Cole rejoined the tour with the Ted Heath band, which moved on to Louisville. Louisville was different from the rest of the South: he didn't have to play to segregated audiences there. By then he was able to book a room at the Seelbach, one of the city's two good hotels, where I interviewed him over lunch in his room.

Ironically, Nat Cole is remembered by the general public only as a singer, though he was one of the greatest pianists in jazz history, and one of the most influential. Horace Silver once told me that when he first played the Newport Jazz Festival, impresario George Wein stood offstage calling out, "Earl Fatha Hines, Earl Fatha Hines!" This baffled Horace, since he had never listened to Hines. But later, he said, he realized that he had listened a lot to Nat Cole, and *he* had listened to Hines.

And that Cole assuredly did, in Chicago, when he was growing up. He would stand outside the Grand Terrace listening to Hines, absorbing all he could. Hines is a headwater of jazz piano—perhaps one should say *the* headwater—because of the influence he had on pianists who were themselves immensely influential, none more so than Teddy Wilson, Bud Powell, and Bill Evans.

The assault in Alabama must have been only the more bitter to Cole because he was born there, in Montgomery, on March 17, 1919. He was, however, culturally and emotionally a son of Chicago. Nathaniel Adams Coles was born of Perlina and Edward Coles, a wholesale grocer who aspired to be a clergyman. Nat's brothers were Eddie, Isaac, called Ike, and Freddy. There were also two sisters, Eddie Mae, who died when Nat was young, and

Evelyn. The youngest in the family, Lionel Frederick, called Freddy, was born in Chicago in 1931.

Freddy Cole has enunciation similar to Nat's, not only in singing but in speech as well. It is a distinct family resemblance. Leslie Gourse, in her book *Unforgettable: The Life and Mystique of Nat King Cole* (1991), says, "Ike thought with pride that all the brothers sounded as alike in the expressive qualities of their voices as the Kennedy brothers, even though Eddie had a gravelly tone to his singing voice, and Ike's voice was deeper and huskier than Nat's." (There have been a number of such vocal similarities in siblings, including Jim and Don Ameche, Bing and Bob Crosby, James Arness and Peter Graves, Bob and Ray Eberly, or Eberle, and Betty and Marion Hutton.)

Nat Cole had an African voice (and so does Freddy), as surely as Tony Bennett, Ben Gazzara, Peter Rodino, Brenda Vaccaro, Aldo Ray, Robert Loggia, and many others have Italian voices. Not all Italians have that husky, woody sound, any more than all Swedes are blue-eyed and blond, but many do. There are oriental voices, both Chinese and Japanese, and they are slightly different, but they tend to be light and high. We may have superb Japanese and Chinese violinists, but I doubt that our opera companies are likely to recruit many oriental bassos. And many Americans have African voices, airy, soft, sometimes fibrous in timbre. You hear the sound as surely in actor Danny Glover's voice as in that of Nat or Freddy Cole. The African and Italian are among the most attractive vocal sounds in my experience, which may in part be why blacks and Italians have so predominated in American popular music in the post–Morton Downey–Buddy Clark period. And while we are on the subject, Nat Cole had African hands, with long, supple, graceful fingers that almost seem to have been designed for the piano. Oscar Peterson has similar hands.

But where did the Cole brothers get their clear enunciation?

"I guess we got it from our father," Freddy told me in 1990 in Chicago. "My dad insisted that you enunciate. I remember one time I came in from school, trying to be hip and slurring words. That was a no-no.

"Even my older brother, Eddie, spoke that way. Eddie was a fantastic musician. In fact, Nat was in his band—Eddie Cole and the Solid Swingers.

"My mother was choir director in my dad's church. She had great musical feel. Good piano player. She just had a knack for touching the right gospel song in church. She was an extraordinary musician. If she were judged by today's standards, she'd be right up there among the tops.

"She had an Uncle Fess. I understand he was a musician. His name was Adams. That was my mother's maiden name. So I guess our musical genes came from my mother's side of the family."

Edward Coles moved his family to the South Side of Chicago, where he established himself as a Baptist pastor, in 1923. Nat was playing organ in his father's church by the time he was twelve, and his sister Evelyn played in the church too.

"My father's full name was Edward James Coles," Freddy continued. "He used to be at a church in Chicago called True Light Baptist Church over at Forty-fifth and Federal. We moved from there, when Ike and I were very young, out to Waukegan, and this is where we grew up. I was respectful of my father. We all were."

The Coles family was a relatively close one, and the children were immersed in music at home. "We all played piano," Freddy said. "Eddie also played bass. All of us had piano lessons, but I was the only one who went to university. I went to Roosevelt University for a while. I left there and went to Juilliard and then to the New England Conservatory. I was in music education. I lack six hours of a master's."

Nat Cole first learned piano from his mother, then studied

with Milton Hinton's mother. Milton was not interested in the piano, to his mother's chagrin, so she sent him to another teacher to learn. Nat studied music at Wendell Phillips High School, one of the many musicians who came under the influence of Captain Walter Dyett. Nat was therefore shaped by the disciplines of two severe men, his father and Walter Dyett.

Freddy said: "Nat was a very accomplished musician. He could read music like—" A snap of the fingers.

There is more than ample evidence in his playing that Nat Cole had solid classical discipline. "I recall that one of Nat's teachers was a man named Professor Fry," Freddy told me. "He and my brother Eddie both studied with him." Gourse says in her book that Nat studied everything from Bach to Rachmaninoff "with a teacher named Professor Thomas."

Nat certainly studied the "legitimate" repertoire with somebody: his tone and touch were not the least of the evidence. The ease and elegance with which he played lines in thirds is another: he really had that fingering down, as in the polished and scrupulously rehearsed passage he would later use in *Embraceable You*. He would quote classical pieces in his recordings, such as *In the Hall of the Mountain King*, which he always played in block chords in *Body and Soul*, and he recorded a version of MacDowell's *To a Wild Rose* and Rachmaninoff's *Prelude in C-sharp Minor*, although such things were simply in the air in the 1930s, heard on "light classical" network radio shows, such as *The Voice of Firestone*, *The Cities Service Hour*, *The Bell Telephone Hour*, and many others, some of them originating in Chicago. He had a taste, it would seem, for the kind of salon piano pieces popular at the time, and it is virtually certain that he listened to the radio broadcasts of Lee Sims.

But the biggest influence, both by the evidence in his playing and his own statements, was Earl Hines, then in his famous sojourn at the Grand Terrace ballroom. In 1957, Nat told Jack Tynan, West Coast editor of *Down Beat,* "That was the driving force that appealed to me. I first heard Hines in Chicago when I was a kid. He was regarded as the Louis Armstrong of piano players. His was a new, revolutionary kind of playing, because he broke away from the Eastern style. He broke the barrier of what we called stride piano where the left hand kept up in a steady, striding pattern. I latched on to that new Hines style. Guess I still show that influence to this day."

Nat Cole made his recording debut on the Decca label in 1936, in a band led by his brother Eddie. That year the band played engagements in good Chicago locales, including the Congress Hotel.

Eddie and Nat, and later Freddy, dropped the *s* from Coles. Show-business name changes are common, of course, some as radical as Samuel Goldberg to Buddy Clark, others more casual, such as that of Red Norville into Norvo after a critic, giving him his first publicity, misspelled it that way. Conrad Kirnon got his name changed for him in Birdland when Pee Wee Marquette, unable to remember or pronounce it (possibly because he didn't get a payoff), introduced him repeatedly as Connie Kay.

In October 1936, Eddie and Nat joined the orchestra in Noble Sissle's musical *Shuffle Along.* Nat at seventeen was already a minor celebrity in South Side Chicago, courting a beautiful dancer named Nadine Robinson, nine years his senior. In January 1937, while Nat still was in *Shuffle Along,* he and Nadine were married. In May, the show opened in Los Angeles, then collapsed in Long Beach when, apparently, somebody absconded with its payroll. Nat ended up living the rest of his life in Los Angeles, but the first two or three years were tough ones.

For a time Nat was playing solo piano. He was approached by Bob Lewis, who owned a nightclub called the Swanee Inn. Lewis asked him to organize a small group and bring it into his club. Nat engaged Wesley Prince, a bassist he'd heard with Lionel Hampton, and the Texas-born guitarist Oscar Moore. There are conflicting theories on why he didn't also use drums. One is that Lee Young didn't show up on opening night. This is unlikely: Lee Young was as responsible and punctilious as his brother Lester was elusive. One story is that Lee thought the bandstand was too small for a quartet with drums. In any event, Cole went in with a trio, and if it was not unprecedented, piano-guitar-bass had not evolved to the heights of integration and sophistication he, Moore (later Irving Ashby), and Prince (later Johnny Miller) would take that instrumentation. They stayed at the Swanee Inn for six months, honing their material in the luxury of a secure situation.

In September 1938, the trio began to make records for Standard Transcriptions. "Transcriptions" were recordings made only for radio broadcast, not for public sale. Johnny Mercer, who had come out to Hollywood from New York to write lyrics for movies, heard the group about that time, and, given Mercer's lifelong taste for great pianists, it is little wonder that he was enthralled by Cole.

Before I knew his name, I became captivated by Nat Cole. I first heard him on two Lionel Hampton records, *Central Avenue Breakdown* and *Jack the Bellboy,* on the RCA Victor label. Those old 78 rpm records bore no personnel lists, and certainly nothing resembling liner notes. Somehow I learned that Hampton was playing that fast piano with two fingers, probably the two index fingers or maybe the index finger crossed with the middle finger for strength, for he certainly banged hard on the keyboard. How did he play like that with only two fingers? He was a drummer and vibes player, and he had fast hands, playing piano the way some of the old-time newspaper reporters played typewriter. I had no idea where Central Avenue was. It was of course in the black neighborhood of Los Angeles. The record was made in Los Angeles. Hampton was born in Louisville on April 20, 1908 or 1909, but his family, like Nat Cole's, moved to Chicago when he was a boy. He too was an alumnus of Wendell Phillips High.

When Cole was organizing his trio with Oscar Moore, it was Hampton, apparently, who recommended Wesley Prince on bass. Then Hampton tried to hire the whole trio to go on the road with him. Cole declined the offer, but the trio recorded eight sides with Hampton, seven of which were long afterward reissued on a CD titled *Tempo and Swing* (Bluebird 66039-2). *Central Avenue Breakdown* and *Jack the Bellboy*, recorded May 10, 1940, were among these. What I felt but certainly did not understand was that the power and drive of *Breakdown* came from the rich-toned boogie-woogie accompaniment provided by the anonymous Nat Cole. Coming from Chicago, he had no doubt been exposed early in his life to some of the boogie-woogie masters, such as Meade Lux Lewis and Jimmy Yancey, who were born there. *Jack the Bellboy* was presumably named for the Detroit disc jockey Ed Mackenzie, who used that moniker. It was fashionable in jazz to flatter disc jockeys (who as far as I can remember were not yet called that) by naming tunes for them. This number is a showpiece for Hampton's drums, but it is notable for the strong sense of identity the Cole trio already had, and how superbly Cole played piano.

Dough-Ray-Me, recorded a couple of months later, is a "silly" song with a unison vocal. Except for the presence of drums, it sounds exactly like the King Cole Trio of not-far-off Capitol Records fame. It was just the kind of frivolous, trivial song on which Cole's early fame was built. And Cole's voice, with its distinctive timbre and enunciation, defines the vocal sound as surely as Johnny Hodges colored the Ellington sax section.

Also on that session, July 17, 1940, was *Jivin' with Jarvis*, a riff tune (and that title is all the lyric there is) named for the Los Angeles disc jockey Al Jarvis. Cole's piano has all the bounce and rhythmic vitality we came to expect of him. On a ballad called *Blue Because of You* Cole plays a solo that defines him as clearly as Bill Evans's solo on George Russell's *All About Rosie* defined him a generation later. Cole's later characteristics are evident in the Hampton sessions, the banged-out low-note punctuations, the insouciant use of triplets, even the right-hand melody passages in oriental-sounding parallel fourths, the beautiful touch and technique, and that ultimately indefinable quality: his exquisite taste. It never failed him in his playing, only in his choice of songs.

The 1940 recordings with Hampton are significant for their evidence of how far Cole had evolved, how well he already knew who he was and how he wanted to play. When one hears apologias for some of the less than original young lions now in well-publicized prominence, it is instructive to reflect on Nat Cole on those Hampton recordings. He was twenty-three.

The Nat Cole trio in its early days had recorded for Decca, largely such tunes as *I Like to Riff; That Ain't Right; Hit That Jive, Jack; Scotchin' with the Soda,* and *Early Morning Blues*. The group built its reputation as it toured to New York, Chicago, Washington, and elsewhere. The first recording strike by the American Federation of Musicians was about to hit the industry, and Johnny Mercer's newly formed label Capitol acquired some Cole sides from the small Excelsior label, including *Vim Vom Veedle* and *All for You*. It soon signed him to a contract. Other than some of those earlier records and transcriptions, and a few extracurricular dates for Norman Granz later, Cole's entire body of recorded work was for Capitol. The chemistry of Cole-and-Capitol would propel him to a stardom that has not ended, although he has been dead since 1965.

The body of that work is among the most significant in American musical history. In 1991, Mosaic, the independent reissue label notable for the reverent quality of its releases, acquired all the Capitol records on which Cole played piano and put them out in a boxed set. The arrangement covered such performances with orchestra as *Nature Boy* and *The Christmas Song* on which he played piano, but not those orchestral performances on which he only sang.

This Mosaic set of eighteen CDs constitutes some of the most significant jazz documentation we have. Alas, you can't get it. It came out as a limited edition that has long been sold out. With nineteen or twenty takes on each CD, the collection contains 347 tracks, including alternate takes. By my count, sixty-four of these are instrumentals, mostly by the trio.

I would be inclined to include among the instrumentals the twelve tracks recorded in September 1956 and issued on an album called *After Midnight*. Although Cole sings the heads on all the tunes, that album is about blowing, with Stuff Smith, Willie Smith, Sweets Edison, and Juan Tizol as soloists along with one of the most underrated of drummers, Lee Young. And it contains a lot of quietly fervent Cole piano. That album was made when Cole was at the pinnacle of his stardom as a singer.

Cole came under fire from some of the critics for "abandoning" jazz for his hugely lucrative career as a singer. Jazz critics, for the most part, had a certain condescension (shared by a lot of musicians) toward singers. That Cole was one of the most magnificent singers of songs we have ever had seemed to escape the notice of the purists.

But when Cole was coming up in the 1930s, there was no separation of jazz from American popular music: indeed the main repertoire of jazz was the magnificent body of song that grew up simultaneously and partly in tandem with it. Woody Herman (one of Nat's friends) was wont to say, "Jazz *was* the popular music of the land." *Down Beat* was not a jazz magazine; it was a magazine about bands and popular music, the best of which (that of Harold Arlen, for example) was soaked in jazz. *Down Beat* wrote about Guy Lombardo and Freddy Martin and their bands, as well as Basie and Ellington and Herman and Hines. One of the worst things that ever happened to jazz was its definition by intellectuals or would-be intellectuals as an "art form." Much good has come of this, but much bad too, with some musicians disdaining the very public that was paying them, and a lot of pretentious posturing.

Another problem was that Nat Cole was not one of the "improvising" singers, those eager to show how they can demolish a melody and with it the meaning of lyrics. I am not a fan of scat singing, partly because for the most part only skilled instrumentalists—such as Dizzy Gillespie, Richard Boone, Clark Terry, and Frank Rosolino—have really done it well. If ever a musician had the equipment (the knowledge, the harmonic sense, the inward rhythmic chronometer) to do it superbly, Nat Cole did. And he never indulged in it, reminding me of Mark Twain's definition of a gentleman: "One who knows how to play the accordion but refrains from doing so."

Cole stuck close to melodies, a proclivity he shared with Perry Como. Only singers seem to know how good Como really is. But Cole shared two other qualities with Como. One is a mastery so complete that the singing comes across as lazy. The other is that probably no other really fine singer recorded so many dubious songs as Cole and Como.

In some cases, this seems to be a failure of taste. But in others, there seems to be a subtle, pervasive, historical-social-psychological reason that Cole chose and performed a certain style—if style is the appropriate word—of song. I think that not even Freddy Cole, even if I asked him, could tell me why Nat picked the songs he did, and so I am left to venture into what I hope is reasonable speculation.

Racism contains a sexual component. It lies in the territorial imperative, as found in the tale of the rape (from the Latin *rapere,* to seize and carry off) of the Sabine women, the symbol of all such forays into enemy territory and the seizure of women as plunder. Racism consists in this: We have a right to your women; you do not have a right to ours. A black man in the American South who even looked with what might be construed as lust at a white woman could be, and often was, punished with death. Nat Cole's family came from Alabama, and was culturally rooted in southern mores. A black man there knew, without even having to know, that if he ever even thought sexually of a white woman, he must never let it be seen. And in all of Nat Cole's songs one factor is consistent: an instinctive avoidance of direct sexual provocation.

So he sings *Mona Lisa,* whose subtext could be either a man contemplating the famous painting or a friend expressing his compassion to a misunderstood woman. Another unreal girl-in-a-picture inhabits *Portrait of Jennie.* He sings *Nature Boy,* a song whose ersatz exoticism conceals an authentic banality, the tale of a mere boy who gives you the oh-wow insight that loving and being loved is where it's at, man. My God that's a dumb song. Cole elicits sweet seasonal memories in *The Christmas Song,* a song by Mel Tormé and Bob Wells whose popularity obscures its excellence. He sings of food in *The Frim Fram Sauce.*

Cole sings about partying in *Bring Another Drink.* Or he gives you, in inversion, the same message as *Nature Boy* in *You're Nobody Till Somebody Loves You.* He gives you advice, again, on *your* life, in *It Only Happens Once* and still more friendly third-person counsel in *It Is Better to Be by Yourself.* Or, with Cole Porter, he asks *What Is This Thing Called Love?* And, just in case any white man should frown at even the hint of a relationship here, says, "You took my heart, and threw it away."

Or he looks at the girl, but won't move on her, in *But She's*

My Buddy's Chick. When he dares to have a moment of uppity vanity, he loses the girl to another in *The Best Man*. This theme recurs in *You're Looking at Me*. After he asks, "Who had the girls turning handsprings? Crazy to love him, claimed he . . . Where is the boy who was certain his charms couldn't fail? Who woke to find his dream shattered? You're looking at me." (Good song, by the way; like *Route 66*, it is one of Bobby Troup's little jewels.) The singer gets his comeuppance, again, for sexual vanity. Translate that to: that's what happens when you forget your *place*. In these songs, the singer is always defeated; thus he poses no threat.

Don't Hurt the Girl is an interesting alloy of *Mona Lisa* compassion toward women and rebuke of *Best Man* male vanity. There are at least three ways to look at this song. It could be the entreaty of a decent man (the one in *Mona Lisa*) to a rounder friend. Or it might be the internal monologue of one who has commanded more than his share of women and is undergoing a sexual epiphany: "If you hurt that girl, you'll be hurting me." And when you realize the song was written by a woman, Margaret Johnson, it takes on still another aspect. As far as I know, no woman has ever recorded it.

There is more pop philosophy in Irving Berlin's *After You Get What You Want, You Don't Want It* and in *You Can't Make Money Dreaming* (a duet with Johnny Mercer), as well as in *Those Things Money Can't Buy*, *If You Stub Your Toe on the Moon*, and *Paint Me a Rainbow*. He is outside the story in *A Boy from Texas, a Girl from Tennessee*, and in (of all the improbable songs for Cole) *Mule Train*. He paints an American landscape in *Moonlight in Vermont*, another in *'Tis Autumn*—the naturist, once again standing outside the experience. He tells you how to drive across this America in Bobby Troup's *Route 66*. That song became such a part of the culture that when I moved to California in 1974, once I had determined the main highway on the map I hardly ever had to look at it again after Chicago: I just ran the

Nat Cole record in my head and aimed for the cities it specified. I doubt that I'm the only person who ever did that.

In his annotation to the Mosaic boxed set, Will Friedwald tries to explain Cole's predilection for silly songs this way: "The answer is in Cole's miraculous capacity for melody. His limitless tool kit of methods of playing, singing and arranging songs for his unusually-instrumented triumverate [sic] took him at once into high art and lowbrow comedy. Like Henry VIII goose-quilling his own motets, this king of the realm doubled as his own court jester. At their greatest, the King Cole Trio distilled the avant-garde technique of a Lester Young or a Bud Powell with the restrained, dignified piety of fellow Capitol recording artist Daffy Duck."

Frank Sinatra, with whom Cole had a slightly uncomfortable (I am told privately) friendship, might flaunt an overt male sexuality, but Cole didn't dare. Not if he wanted to be a success, and indeed not if he wanted to stay alive, as his Alabama attackers made clear. Sidney Poitier is widely regarded as the first black matinee idol, and black actors all give him obeisance, as indeed they should. But beyond Poitier, they should look back to Nat Cole.

Perhaps the best key to a culture is its humor.

During my years in Chicago, I lived almost entirely in a black world. Not just some but most of my friends were black. My best friend of all was photographer Ted Williams. From the moment I arrived, Ted was my guide to the city, and particularly to South Side Chicago. We used to hang out at the Sutherland Lounge, the Club DeLisa, McKee's, backstage at the Regal Theater, talking to or watching Moms Mabley, Slappy White, Nipsey Russell, Redd Foxx. Sometimes, when he was in town, Art Farmer would hang with us. I heard jokes the white audience didn't dream of.

Redd Foxx said he wanted to be a lifeguard. He wanted to rescue a drowning white man, haul him unconscious to the beach, and—here he cupped his hands around his mouth to make a sepulchral sound—say, "Byeeee, baby!"

This is one that went around in the black community. (If you're not familiar with the city, you need to know that Cottage Grove and Sixty-third is the heart of black Chicago.) In Alabama, a young black man is accused of looking at a white woman, and is dragged off into the woods by torchlight. As the mob is throwing a rope over a tree limb, he breaks free and runs into the brush. He flees through the night, finally eluding his pursuers. He emerges on a highway and frantically waves his thumb at a motorist. The motorist, who is white, stops. "Help me!" the young man says. "They're gonna lynch me."

Opening the trunk, the driver says, "All right, boy, get in here."

The car proceeds north. The driver stops and again opens the trunk. He says, "You can get out now, boy."

"Where are we?"

"Tennessee."

"No no! I ain't safe yet. Let's keep going!"

The same thing happens in Kentucky, and in Indiana. The car finally reaches Chicago. The man opens the trunk and says, "You can get out now, boy."

"Where we at?"

"Cottage Grove and Sixty-third," replies the driver.

The young man gets out, dusts himself off, straightens up, and says, "Who you callin' 'boy'?"

Nat Cole came out of that culture, and when he was of a mind to, according to Julius La Rosa (who said Cole could be hilariously funny), he could tell a story in the thickest southern dialect. You can hear the South in his singing. In that very first Capitol release, *All for You,* he drops a final *r,* in "When you raise yo' eyes . . ." As with many southerners, black and white alike, the giveaway is the tendency to turn *t*'s into *d*'s in certain positions of speech, particularly in the middle of words. Thus "important" comes out "impordant." You'll hear it in the speech of television interviewer Charlie Rose, who is from North Carolina. And Cole does something else, specific to black southerners: he drops terminal consonants (as the French do), in such words as "just," in which the *t* would be omitted. Thus, in the last eight of *Naughty Angeline,* he sings "seddle down and jus' be mine." On the other hand, he sings very flat *a*'s in such words as "that." The sound is specific to the midwest, from Michigan on, but most conspicuously Chicago.

Cole was, as we all are, completely conditioned by his background and rearing and the generation he grew up in. And he was a southerner, a product of a society in which the black male learned the survival skill of avoiding direct confrontation. What is amazing is not that he did this well, but that he did it with such enormous, indeed regal, self-containment. And he was a product of the entertainment business, not of the "art" of jazz, just like Louis Armstrong and Woody Herman, and yes, Guy Lombardo. He was walking through a cultural minefield, passing beyond the age of Tomming. He had the skills of charm that came out of that experience, but he used them with impressive discretion and dignity. A smile was a tool of the trade.

Louis Armstrong made it on the massive smile and what, to me, was an embarrassing public self-humiliation. He did not "make it" as a great artist; he made it as the embodiment of a white racist myth, a grinning clown with a horn. Nor do I mean to criticize him for it; he did what he had to in the age he grew up in. Cab Calloway, who was a very good singer, reached his pinnacle in his exaggerated white zoot suit with his hi-de-ho and his (again) toothy grin, a figure the complacent white world could patronize. Even Duke Ellington, one of the major artists in American musical history, wore the white tails and, in his mannered sophistication, still was catering to a white joke. Lionel Hampton grinned and groaned and jumped on the drums and embarrassed the men in his own band, particularly as the personnel grew younger. As late as 1950, when Billy Daniels undertook one of the most erotic of all songs, the Arlen-Mercer *Old Black Magic,* he did it in cap-and-bells, twisting, gyrating, voice cavernous, exaggerating the song to absurdity. It is little remembered that *Alexander's Ragtime Band* bore the title it did because when Irving Berlin wrote it—it came out in 1911—America wasn't even covert about its racism. As Fido was a name for a dog and Rastus for a shuffling black man, Alexander was a name mockingly used for a black man with pretensions. On the original sheet music of Berlin's song, the band in the picture was black; when the song became a hit, they mysteriously turned white. Not that much had changed by the time of the Billy Daniels recording.

And then there is the career of Louis Jordan and his Tympani Five. The very name Tympani Five, with its sly ostentation, is funny. I don't think the scope of his influence has really been assessed. Jordan built his success on such good-time material as *Let the Good Times Roll, Ain't Nobody Here but Us Chickens, Knock Me a Kiss, What's the Use of Getting Sober, Beans and Corn Bread*—comedy songs that reinforced the stereotype of the black man. But did you ever hear Louis Jordan sing a ballad? He did so extremely well, but he did it very little, and the public didn't embrace him for that dimension of his talent. The point was surely not lost on Cole; the King Cole Trio worked opposite Jordan at the Capitol Lounge in Chicago in 1941. Cole and Jordan were friends.

Blacks had been confined in American entertainment to clown roles, even the women. In the movies, they were always silly, lightheaded, and obsequious. Billie Holiday was cast as a maid. Railway porters could all break into perfect harmony. All black men were shiftless or cowardly or both. A picture I completely detest is *Cabin in the Sky* for its embodiment of every image of the darky a racist society harbored: all its characters, the gambler, the slut, the slickster, the pious wife, are embodiments of white bias. The picture came out in 1943, just when Nat Cole's career was taking off. The social and moral climate of the period should be kept in mind in considering his life and work.

Cole began to emerge (more than a decade before Denzel Washington was born) as the first black male romantic idol in America. I think that's important to note: not just a "sex symbol," Cole was a *romantic* figure. He too grinned, sitting nonchalantly sideways at the piano (a manner of presentation he got from Earl Hines), doing so with enormous dignified charm, singing *Ke-Mo-Ki-Mo* and *Straighten Up and Fly Right* and *Nature Boy* and other songs designed to keep any ofay bastard from thinking the singer was after his sexual property. A respect for the territorial boundaries of possession is in many of the songs. In *That's My Girl*, it's "She looks just like an angel / but she's human just the same. / So I'm not taking chances, / I won't tell her address or even her name." Then there's, "But she's my buddy's chick . . ." I promise, honest, I won't go after your girl, even if I am handsome and more talented than you can dream. There was a sense of discreet sexual territoriality in many of those songs.

Is this a fanciful exegesis? I don't think so. A performer's selection of material is—and this is inevitable—a Rorschach of his or her own personality, just as the judgments of a critic constitute an unwitting and even unwilling self-portrait.

And the general tenor of the show-business times should also be kept in mind. In the years before World War II, the singers clowned (Al Jolson) and the clowns sang (Eddie Cantor, Fanny Brice, Jimmy Durante). The styles of singing (Sophie Tucker) and acting alike (John Barrymore) were largely declamatory. The contained introspection of Frank Sinatra and Peggy Lee and, later, in film, Clift and Brando and Dean, lay in the future. Cole came at the transition point, and the playful clowning deflected the fire of white resentment. Whether he ever gave this one conscious thought, I have no idea. But whether by plan or visceral intuition, this *is* how he handled his burgeoning stardom.

One other factor, I think, should be considered. To a large extent black performers accepted as a given that you had to have *your* white man, running interference, taking care of the business, dealing with the white world, bailing you out when the white society closed in on you. Louis Armstrong had his Joe Glaser, and he needed him. Duke Ellington had Glaser's Associated Booking as well as Irving Mills, whom he allowed to put his name as co-writer on Ellington tunes that Mills had nothing to do with. Even Oscar Peterson followed the pattern: he acquired Norman Granz who, in Jazz at the Philharmonic, ran what Lester Young (Bobby Scott told me) called a flying plantation.

To be sure, Cole sang romantic ballads in those early trio days, a few of them. But he did so in the context of a certain general tomfoolery. The out-in-front repertoire was playful, even childlike; humorous, ingratiating, and unthreatening. And, he also acquired Carlos Gastel.

Anyone who read *Down Beat* in the middle 1940s knew the name Carlos Gastel. Probably no other peripheral figure in jazz and popular music, not even John Hammond, had such high visibility. Gastel's photo was often in the magazine and in *The Capitol,* the odd little pocket-sized handout publicity magazine that Dave Dexter edited for that company, available free in record stores throughout America. Gastel would be seen standing beside clients of his like Sonny Dunham and Stan Kenton, even back when both were struggling, Dunham to go under, Kenton to become a major success.

According to Peggy Lee, who also became one of his clients, he was called The Honduran. He was born in Honduras of a Honduran father and a German mother, but he had gone to a

California military academy and was at ease and at home in the United States and in show business. Six-foot-two and 250 pounds, he was a jolly, joking, partying man with a taste for jazz, liquor, and women. He reminded disc jockey and later producer Gene Norman of Fat Stuff in the *Smilin' Jack* comic strip, the pudgy figure whose buttons were always popping off his shirt.

Peggy said to me once, "I have some idea how much he took me for. I wonder how much he took Nat for."

Nat pursued Gastel, who was six years his senior (that is a lot when you're in your early twenties) to be his manager, and Gastel eventually acquiesced. In 1943 Gastel negotiated Nat's deal with Capitol, getting him a seven-year contract and the highest (at that time) royalty rate, five percent. And he rapidly raised Cole's asking price.

At one time, the major record companies, Victor, Decca, and Columbia and their subsidiaries, practiced a fairly rigid segregation. Black artists were confined to what were called "race records" aimed primarily at black audiences. White kids who discovered this music often had to go to record stores in black neighborhoods to find what they wanted. From the day of its inception, Capitol would have nothing to do with such a policy, and it pushed Nat Cole's career with all its strength. Gradually Cole came to do more and more romantic ballads, and by about 1947 he was sometimes standing up from the piano to sing. More and more, he was seen as a romantic figure. And more and more he recorded with full orchestra.

In his 1974 book *The Great American Popular Singers*, the late Henry Pleasants wrote: "To a dedicated jazz musician, jazz critic, or jazz fan, there was more than a suggestion of apostasy about Nat King Cole's career. The more than promising jazz pianist, winner of the *Esquire* gold medal as pianist in 1946, the heir apparent to the mantle of Earl Fatha Hines . . . achieves fame and fortune as a pop singer! That's putting it crassly, to be sure.

He was more than that. Even as a pop singer he was an original. No one had ever sung quite like that before. He and Billy Eckstine, three years his senior, were, moreover the first black male singers to hit the top in 'the white time.'"

"According to just about everyone who knew him or ever worked with him, or was otherwise associated with him," Henry continued, "he was a born gentleman, just 'one hell of a nice, decent guy.'"

William E. Anderson, the editor of *Stereo Review,* described Nat's voice this way (as quoted by Pleasants): "A piano, even at its most legato, is a percussion instrument, and my sense of Cole's singing, even at *his* most legato, is of isolated, crystal tones, linked only in the aural imagination of the listener, and not in breathed slurs by the performer."

In Henry's description: "It was, as I hear it, a light bass-baritone. I infer as much from the richness and warmth of the tone in the area between the low G and the C a fourth above, an area similarly congenial to the mature voices of both Bing Crosby and Frank Sinatra. A bass-baritone disposition is further suggested by the fact that the 'passage' in his voice, as he moved up the scale and out of his natural range, would appear to have lain around D-flat or D, a semitone or two below the corresponding ticklish area in a true baritone.

"Nat rarely ventured below that low G, and he had little to show for it when he did. Nor did he have any upward extension to speak of. On the records I have checked he never sings above an E. Both the E-flat and the E, while secure enough, were consistently uncharacteristic in timbre, not thin and tenuous as the voices of Ethel Waters and Bessie Smith were when they sang beyond the 'passage,' but somehow ill-matched to the rest of the voice and rather conventional in sound, recalling from time to time the sound of the young Bing Crosby in the same area.

"Big, wide-ranging voices are a dime a dozen—better voices

than Nat Cole's, or, at least, voices of more lavish endowment. But a lavish vocal endowment does not make a great singer. The trick lies in determining, or sensing, where the gold lies in the vocal ore, and in mining it expertly and appreciatively. Or one can think of the vocal cords as violin strings, of the resonating properties of throat, mouth and head as the violin, and of the breath as a bow. In Nat Cole's case, the strings responded most eloquently to a light bow. The tone coarsened under pressure, or when urged, either upward or downward, beyond the G–D range of an octave and a fifth.

"At his best and most characteristic, Nat Cole was not so much a singer as a whisperer, or, as one might put it, a confider."

It was widely said that Cole never sang until a drunk in a bar in Los Angeles demanded it. I asked Freddy Cole whether this was true.

"Yeah!" Freddy said, laughing. "It's true. I talked with him about it. In fact, one time in Los Angeles, he drove me by the place where it happened. We were coming home from the ball game or something. It was a little barbecue joint by that time."

Nat said he'd always sung a little. Indeed, this was nothing rare for musicians. Though they seldom did it in public, Cannonball Adderley, Gerry Mulligan, Zoot Sims, and Milt Jackson all sang very nicely, and the older trumpet players almost all sang. And, as Freddy said, "During that time, musicians were taught to learn the words to songs. Because you would know how to play them better, to learn how to improvise better. Jo Jones. Lester Young. They could get up and tell you every lyric."

And Nat told an interviewer, "I was lucky that I could sing a little, so I did, for variety. The vocals caught on." And on another occasion: "To break the monotony, I would sing a few songs here and there between the playing. I noticed thereafter people started requesting more singing and it was just one of those things."

One has a choice of all these versions of how and why Nat Cole came to be known as a singer. Perhaps they are all to some extent true. Perhaps that drunk reinforced what he already knew he would have to do. To get employment, he would have to sing, like so many pianists before and after him, including Sarah Vaughan, Carmen McRae, Jeri Southern, Shirley Horn, Audrey Morris, Dave Mackay, Bob Dorough, Dave Frishberg, and Diana Krall, for the simple reason that a pianist who sings gets more work. And besides, a lot of them like to do it.

By the middle 1940s, when Cole was making more money in a week than he had in a year in the early days, his marriage to Nadine was wearing thin. He was approaching thirty, she her fortieth birthday. A ten-year gap of that kind may seem insignificant in earlier years, but not later: a woman at forty is entering middle age and maybe menopause, and she is aware of it; a man hasn't even reached his maturity. She is worrying about age and time when he doesn't even want to think about it.

Cole met Marie Hawkins Ellington in May 1946, during an engagement the trio played at the Zanzibar club in New York. She was born in Boston on August 1, 1922, the second of three sisters, all of them beautiful. Their father was a mail carrier, a good job for a black American in those days. Their aunt founded the Palmer Memorial Institute in Sedalia, North Carolina, a black prep school. Marie and her sister Charlotte spent winters with their aunt, known as Aunt Lottie, in a large house with nurses, two bathrooms, and a telephone. She told Daniel Mark Epstein, who quotes her in *Nat King Cole* (1999), "We never plaited our own pigtails until I was thirteen." Eleanor Roosevelt and Langston Hughes, among others, visited their home. They lived on a high social scale, but young black girls and boys still were not normally allowed to try on clothes in stores, were forced to sit in a special balcony at the movie theater, and could not go to restaurants. Epstein says of Marie: "Reading the movie magazines and dreaming in the theater's darkness, she longed to be rich, famous, to have a career in show business."

In 1943 she married a fighter pilot of the all-black 332d Squadron, a young lieutenant named Neal Spurgeon Ellington, who flew against the Germans in Italy. Her sister Charlotte gave a recording of Marie's voice to guitarist Freddie Guy, who gave it to Billy Strayhorn, who hired her in 1945 to sing with the Duke Ellington band, which she did for a few months. Her husband had survived the war and come home with medals, including the Distinguished Flying Cross, only to be killed on a routine flight in Alabama.

She was finishing up a singing engagement at the Club Zanzibar. Nat Cole had been engaged to play a gig there too. She remembered seeing him in the audience, watching her.

Cole was quite smitten by Marie. According to Leslie Gourse, he told a friend, "I've never heard a Negro woman speak so well before." Note the sense of acceptance of one's own inferiority implicit in that remark. *That* is the ultimate rape of the black American.

Soon he was escorting her home to the Dunbar, an exclusive residence in Harlem. Epstein says: "Oscar [Moore] and Johnny [Miller] joked with her that Nat had cut his old friends for *her*, not realizing how serious the joke was. She would be around when they were long gone."

Various friends, including Woody Herman, tried to talk Nat out of divorcing Nadine. Cole's family had grown fond of her. Oscar Moore and Johnny Miller, making light of it as best they could, urged Cole to forget Marie. "If you don't like it," he told them, "you can quit."

Nat asked her to go on the road with him. She knew by now that he was married, but she went anyway. Marie had by this time changed her name to Maria. Epstein's book does not paint a pretty picture of her. He writes: "Maria had refined taste in clothing. She began to steer Nat toward suits and ties with less flash and more substance, more sartorial elegance. He was an eager pupil. Gently she began to influence his speech, mostly by example. He spoke well but not yet with the crystal clarity of diction that would soon make him a musical story-teller who could never be misunderstood. Cole still had the faintest remnant of a lisp and a bit more of the South Side transplanted Alabama hipster drawl than he needed to play the Radio City Music Hall or the Civic Light Opera in Chicago. It was Maria of Boston who would put the final touches on Nathaniel's famous phrasing."

Doug Ramsey saw an early film of Cole. He said there is no lisp. I called Freddy Cole. He said Nat had no lisp. I called Jo Stafford, who had him known since the early 1940s. She recalled no lisp.

Epstein's justification for saying that Cole had a lisp is in Nat's reading of *Sweet Lorraine* recorded on December 15, 1943. He quotes the first eight:

I just found joy.
I'm as happy as a baby boy
With another brand-new choo choo choy,
When I met my sweet Lorraine.

"The third line is not a typo," Epstein writes. "That is the way the young crooner sings it, twice, unable to pronounce the hard letter *t*. But even the mistake has a boyish charm."

And a mysterious one at that: in the same recording, Cole has no problem with "And *to* think that I'm the lucky one . . ." He has no trouble with the word "time" in *Vim Vom Veedle*, recorded more than a year earlier, on October 11, 1942, nor with any other *t* between then and *Sweet Lorraine*. All the young fans who rushed to get *Sweet Lorraine* took "choy" for a playful affectation, and I think it was. Cole sings "choy" in his 1956 performance of the song in the *After Midnight* album.

Even before Nat's divorce from Nadine was final, Epstein tells us, Maria went about restructuring his life and career. The party, as Oscar, Johnny, and Nat had known it, was over, Epstein says. "And of course a number of old friends, particularly women who had been close to Nadine, simply could not abide the young fiancée. They disliked her cleverness, her haughty accent and fine manners. Out of a sense of loyalty to Nadine, if nothing else, these dropped out of Nat's life, some temporarily and some forever." One of those who disapproved of the relationship with Maria was Nat's father.

"Maria let it be known to Nat and Carlos and anyone else who cared to listen to her in 1947 that Nat King Cole was the star of the Trio, the reason for their spectacular success, and that Oscar and Johnny were making too much money," Epstein continues. "The fact is that Nat King Cole had outgrown Oscar Moore, as brilliant as he was, just as he had outgrown his first wife. And it hurt Oscar almost as bad [*sic*]. No doubt Nat understood the extent of the guitarist's contribution to their achievement and their triumph. But now the scene had changed, and business was business.

"Maria Ellington gave the leader the emotional support needed to do what he was too tenderhearted to do on his own. He informed his sidemen they were welcome to continue to share his good fortune, but with a smaller slice of the pie. Judging from later contracts this amounted to cutting their salaries in half.

"Oscar gave his notice in the late summer of 1947."

Johnny Miller followed him a few months later. And problems with the Internal Revenue Service lay in Nat Cole's future; cutting the salaries of his sidemen can be seen in retrospect as nothing less than stupid, even if Maria Cole wanted it that way. Irving

Ashby replaced Moore. How important was Oscar Moore? "I *studied* Oscar Moore," Mundell Lowe says.

On Easter Sunday, Nat and Maria were married in the Abyssinian Baptist Church in New York. Adam Clayton Powell, then married to pianist Hazel Scott, performed the ceremony.

In her book, Leslie Gourse says that Nat's friend Marvin Cane, then a song plugger for the Shapiro, Bernstein publishing house, "was aware of the strong color line still in effect in New York. When Nat sang in New York, he still occasionally stayed in the Theresa Hotel in Harlem or at the Capitol Hotel at Fifty-first Street and Eighth Avenue. At one time, he had little choice except for the Harlem YMCA or a Harlem Hotel. The Capitol was in the vanguard of downtown hotels when it came to accepting Negro guests. Cane recognized Nat's position as a black entertainer who was idolized by white audiences. . . . Women of all races screamed and cheered for Nat's singing. . . . Nat insisted on emphasizing his role as an entertainer. Meanwhile, black activists saw the civil rights struggle as the preeminent issue in the country and became angry when Cole shied away from an aggressive stance. Nat had the platform but not the predilection. Virulent criticism of his quiet approach arose in the 1950s."

Marvin Cane wanted the reception to be held at the new Belmont Plaza Hotel on Lexington Avenue in the East Fifties. He persuaded the manager that all Harlem was not going to overrun the hotel, and the manager relented, agreeing to the reception. The entire cast of *Stormy Weather* turned up.

And the King Cole Trio was finished. By the dawn of 1948, Nat was doing a stand-up more and more. Henceforth the billing would be Nat King Cole and the Trio. Indeed the trio days were over even before the wedding in New York. The last true trio session came on November 29, 1947, when he made his recording of the lovely *Lost April*. When he did the song again on December 21, 1948, strings had been added. The next day he recorded *Portrait of Jennie* with strings, but that take was never issued. The final version was recorded January 14, 1949.

Until I set myself to listen to all the tracks of the Mosaic boxed set, in sequence, I had not realized that the cutoff from the trio was so sharp. Cole took on Jack Costanzo on bongos, succumbing to an "Afro-Cuban" fashion of the time. His colleagues in the trio objected to the addition. They thought the bongos thickened the texture of the trio and clogged the swing. (I think they were right.) When Dizzy Gillespie used Caribbean or Brazilian percussion, he did so in the idiom from which these instruments were drawn. Cole simply added them to the 4/4 rhythm of the trio, and all you get is a sort of tick-pop tick-pop extraneous beat. It is a different story, of course, when he used Lee Young on drums. Young was playing in the jazz idiom, not trying to graft another vocabulary on to it.

There are few small-group recordings of any kind thenceforth. The dates from then on are all orchestral. On March 29, 1949, comes *Lush Life*, a brilliant song that Billy Strayhorn wrote when he was not yet out of his teens. Cole was by now probably the biggest male singer in America. Frank Sinatra's career was at its nadir. He lost his Columbia contract and seemed well on his way to oblivion. Cole continued from one triumph to another. But he still couldn't stay in the major hotels of the big cities. He sued the Mayfair Hotel in Philadelphia, which had refused him a room, and extracted an apology—but no money—for the effort.

Cole and Maria decided to buy a twelve-room Tudor house in the handsome Hancock Park district of Los Angeles, where there was a restrictive covenant against Jews, Negroes, and anyone else deemed undesirable. They used an agent, who made the down payment in cash. When the identity of the true purchaser was revealed, the previous owner of the house and the real estate agent who handled the deal received anonymous threats. Residents of the area formed the Hancock Property Owners Association, whose head told Cole that they would buy back the house from him and give him a profit. In May 1948, the Supreme Court ruled against restrictive covenants. The Coles took residence that August. Someone had posted a sign on their lawn. It read *Nigger Heaven*.

Duke Niles, a publicist who was one of Nat's friends, visited the house when it was being renovated. Gourse writes: "'At first I didn't think it was me,' Cole said. 'But I'm getting used to it,' he added, pointing to a sweeping staircase, which reflected Maria's flair for living with the best of everything."

Cole's ex-wife, Nadine, sued him for nonpayment of alimony. Oscar Moore, who had left the group in 1947, also sued him. Bassist Johnny Miller quit.

On February 6, 1950, Maria presented Nat with a daughter, whom they named Natalie. With adopted children, they ultimately had five.

The IRS assessed him for $146,000 back taxes. (If he did owe this money, it doesn't say much for Carlos Gastel's career management.) The government seized his house, although it could far more easily have filed a lien on his royalties from Capitol Records. It seems highly likely that one or more of the neighbors in Hancock Park, many of whom were lawyers, had put the IRS up to this action to get the Coles out of their house.

There may have been a second motive for the IRS actions, however. Tax collector Robert A. Riddell personally told the *New York Times* about the seizure of Cole's house, tending to corroborate something I found out when researching Woody Herman's life: the IRS *likes* to prosecute famous figures, particularly those in the entertainment world, such as Willie Nelson, because of the publicity it garners, which intimidates the average taxpayer into docility. And the Cole tax prosecution got them plenty of publicity.

Cole managed to make a settlement with the help of advance money from Capitol Records. In this, I see the fine hand of Johnny Mercer, who was still president of the label.

Cole by now was being castigated by critics for turning away from jazz. Barry Ulanov, once one of his most ardent supporters, was one of them. Frank Stacy interviewed Nat, who told him: "I know that a lot of you critics think that I've been fluffing off jazz, but I don't think that you've been looking at the problem correctly. I'm even more interested in it now than I ever was. And the trio is going to play plenty of it. Don't you guys think I ever get sick of playing those dog tunes every night? I'll tell you why. You know how long it took the trio to reach a point where we started making a little prize money and found a little success. For years we did nothing but play for musicians and other hip people. And while we played that, we . . . . practically starved to death. When we did click, it wasn't on the strength of the good jazz that we played, either. We clicked with pop songs, pretty ballads and novelty stuff. You know that. Wouldn't we have been crazy if we'd turned right around after getting a break and started playing pure jazz again? We would have lost the crowd right away."

He told Stacy that he was planning a tour in which he would have a chance to play a lot of jazz. But the tour, when it materialized, featured his usual pop vocals. And Cole was recording a great deal of crap. Along with such pretty things as *Portrait of Jennie* and *Lost April*, he recorded *The Horse Told Me, A Little Yellow Ribbon (In Her Hair)*, and *All I Want for Christmas Is My Two Front Teeth, Mule Train, Poor Jenny Is A Weepin', Twisted Stockings*, and *The Greatest Inventor of Them All*—a bad imitation of Gospel music—along with purely mediocre material such as *A Little Bit Independent*.

In August 1950, he recorded what I think is one of his most dreadful records: *Orange Colored Sky*. Accompanying him is the Stan Kenton Orchestra. Woody Herman had an uneasy relationship with Kenton. Bassist Red Kelly once told me: "They didn't trust each other. Woody didn't trust anything that didn't swing. Stan didn't trust anything that did." Veterans of the Kenton band have told me that Stan would *stop* them from swinging. The band was ponderous, and never more so than in its overblown, gawky accompaniment for Nat Cole and what is a contrived song in the first place.

It was at about this point that Nat advanced the career of a gifted arranger named Nelson Riddle. When I interviewed him in Louisville in 1956, we were talking at some point about arrangers, and Riddle's name came up, probably when we were discussing Frank Sinatra.

"Frank didn't discover Nelson Riddle," Nat said. "I did." In a corridor at Capitol Records in Hollywood, a young man had approached him and said, "Mr. Cole, I'm an arranger, and I'd like to write for you."

Cole, with what I can see in my mind was his manner of unfailing politesse, said, "I'd like to hear your work."

"You've already recorded some of it," the young man replied, "but it didn't have my name on it." He had been ghosting for someone else.

"What's your name?" Nat asked.

"Nelson Riddle."

"Let's have a talk," Nat said. Riddle worked directly for him after that, and then Frank Sinatra signed with Capitol and his career blossomed again, never to fade until he died; and Nelson Riddle became known as *his* arranger.

I could feel that the friendship between Sinatra and Nat Cole was an uneasy one, even though Cole named Frank as his favorite singer in a Leonard Feather survey, and finally (in his soft way) said something a little testy. He said, "Do you want to know the difference between Frank and me? The band swings Frank. I swing the band." Every musician to whom I have ever told that seems to raise his eyebrows a little and say, "That's *right!*"

But while Sinatra, from the time he joined Capitol, set about recording the very finest songs in the American "popular" (to my mind, classic) repertoire, Cole continued to do a lot of bad songs. Not that Sinatra didn't do a certain amount of trash—eventually including *My Way* and *Strangers in the Night*—but the bulk of his work at Capitol and, later, Reprise, comprises the great songs. Nat Cole left no such legacy.

He seemed to have a perpetual hunger for hits. Sinatra had comparatively few real *hits*. His records sold big, but Cole's sales were massive, as he found one commercial hit after another, up to and including such junk as *Those Lazy Hazy Crazy Days of Summer*. It was a repertoire much closer to Perry Como's than Sinatra's.

Rumor in the business always had it that Nat's hunger for hits was the consequence of Maria's hunger for money. Epstein says, "Of course, she loved money and luxury and security, but who doesn't?"

In May 1959, a little over a month after I joined *Down Beat*, Cole departed from his policy of reticence to denounce trends in the record industry. The federal government was in the midst of one of its periodic feckless investigations of corruption in the industry. Cole told my West Coast editor Jack Tynan that he agreed "wholeheartedly with the government's stand" in looking into racketeering in the jukebox business, and he denounced "graft and corruption in the music industry," in particular the practice of payola. He deplored the quality of music being played by disc jockeys, saying, "I know some of these boys and you can't tell me they like the stuff they're playing." And he questioned the inflated sales figures issued by record company publicists.

He said, "So-and-so makes a record and right away it's boomed as a million seller. I've been in the business long enough to know they can't press a million records in the short time they wait after its initial release, not to mention the even longer time it takes to distribute and sell them.

"This isn't sour grapes. I have no reason to complain about my own career, but I feel sorry for the newcomers rushed into the limelight with faked 'million sales' announcements and then are just as quickly dropped.

"Luckily, I got started at the right time. I don't think I could've made it today."

Four or five years later he telephoned Capitol Records and heard a receptionist cheerfully intone, "Capitol Records, home of the Beatles." He was furious. I got that story from both Paul Weston and Johnny Mercer. His sales and those of Peggy Lee had built Capitol. The business was changing fast. With the Beatles, Capitol learned just how much money could be made from records, and the rest of the industry digested the lesson. The age of rock had arrived.

On July 18, 1952, Cole went into the studio with a group that included John Collins on guitar, Charlie Harris on bass, Jack Costanzo on Latin percussion, and Bunny Shawker on drums to make an instrumental album of standards, issued as a ten-inch LP called *Penthouse Serenade*.

It is one of the finest albums Cole ever made. Over the years I have listened to it so much that it lies deep in my subconscious.

I know every note, every chord of it. Donald Byrd said to me many years ago, "After all my years in this business, I have concluded that the hardest thing to do is play straight melody and get some feeling into it." Listening to Bill Evans playing *Danny Boy*, one knows exactly what he meant. And thus it is with *Penthouse Serenade*. It is a gentle, loving, introspective, beautiful examination of the tunes, and all the glories of Cole's piano playing are on display. That old question, "What album would you take to a desert island with you if you could choose only one?" elicits from me without hesitation: Nat Cole's *Penthouse Serenade*. And I have taken it with me, to desert islands of the mind, and into dark nights of the heart. It is a masterpiece, a crown of jewels in the history of jazz, and because of its directness and deceptive simplicity it is terribly overlooked. After *Penthouse Serenade*, Cole's career was devoted almost entirely to singing and attempts to expand his career beyond that.

Steve McQueen said once that there was nothing hard about movie acting. He was probably right. The movie industry has always taken in men and women who have achieved fame in fields other than drama, including swimmers (Esther Williams, Buster Crabbe, Johnny Weissmuller), a skater (Sonja Henie), football players, dancers, and above all singers: Bing Crosby, Rudy Vallee, Dick Powell, Tony Martin, Frank Sinatra, Dick Haymes, Elvis Presley, Pat Boone, Doris Day, among others. This makes a certain amount of sense: a singer's job is to put over the emotional content of words. And some of those singers, particularly Sinatra and Dick Powell, turned into remarkably good actors. Nat Cole aspired to follow their example.

But his position was not unlike that of Billy Eckstine. Eckstine first came to the attention of "the kids" when he recorded with the Earl Hines band. One of the tunes was *Jelly Jelly*, one of the most notoriously sexual of songs, once you knew what "jelly" meant, with the line "jelly stays on my mind." We didn't know, not the white kids anyway. With his striking good looks and rich baritone, Eckstine became a big success on the newly formed MGM label, with which he signed in 1947.

But he said later, not without bitterness, that it was obvious to him that the movies were closed to him because of his color. His appeal to women made many white men uncomfortable. He said that given the attitude of movie-theater owners in the South, no studio would take a chance on casting him as a romantic lead. In case you haven't noticed, to this day television commercials remain segregated. The one black man in a crowd at a party, what Oscar Peterson calls the TTS, standing for Token Television Spook, always has a black wife. And the movies have treated the very idea of a black man and a white woman rarely and cautiously, as witness *Love Field*. Indeed, even the idea of a relationship between a white and an Indian, though such marriages were common in the West, was for years a taboo. It started to crumble with *Broken Arrow* in 1950. Eckstine's career was confined to records and nightclubs. And Nat Cole would soon find there were limitations to his career too.

In 1953, he appeared in the television series *Lux Video Theater* in a role supporting Dick Haymes. He played, logically enough, a piano player. He had a small role in a film called *Small Town Girl*, and then he appeared in a 1955 short about himself called *The Nat King Cole Story*. He stirred no critical acclaim. Leslie Gourse wrote: "He seemed to be too polite and shy to try to emote or plumb the emotional depths of the character he was portraying." That is true of his singing, too. It is dramatic depth that makes Sinatra's singing so compelling; it is not drama but sheer musicality that makes Cole's singing mesmerizing. His daughter Natalie is the better dramatic lyric reader.

Cole appeared as a member of the French Foreign Legion in Indochina in *China Gate*, which starred Gene Barry and Angie Dickinson. (I thought he was rather good in it.) Then he was cast as W. C. Handy in *St. Louis Blues*. Marvin Cane visited him on the set. Nat told him he found moviemaking frustrating because he was not in control, as he was in a recording studio. Marvin answered, "Well, you're in the movie business."

"Yeah, but what the hell am I doing here?" Nat replied.

"You're becoming a movie star."

The film was bad at the root. The script was poor, and far from factual. Bosley Crowther wrote in the *New York Times*, "Mr. Cole simply lumbers through the role of a harassed jazz composer, looking dumb and uncomfortable."

"Cole," Leslie Gourse wrote, "always provided an exquisite relief and lift for the films in which he sang—*Blue Gardenia*, for one. Sometimes his singing was the only bright moment in a film. Throughout *Cat Ballou* in 1965, he and Stubby Kaye augmented the amusing story."

Ultimately, the movies were to prove a deep disappointment, but not so bitter a one as his television experience. Meanwhile, his stardom as a singer just kept growing: he drew an audience of sixty thousand to a football stadium in Brazil.

Dinah Shore wanted to have Nat as a guest on her television show. Chevrolet, her sponsor, would not allow it: they wouldn't have her standing next to a black man. Similarly, Bell Telephone didn't want Herb Ellis and Ella Fitzgerald on camera together in its television show. Norman Granz, her manager, battled them and they agreed to let the two appear together. Technicians put a filter on the lens and covered it with so much gel that you couldn't recognize Ellis. Granz took full-page newspaper ads denouncing the company for it.

But Carlos Gastel negotiated a deal to have Cole star in his own TV series on NBC. The show went on the air in November 1956, a sustaining fifteen-minute broadcast beginning at 7:30 P.M. The advertising salesmen were unenthusiastic, even though Cole was perfect for television. Like Perry Como, a huge success in the medium, he was effective precisely because his projected personality was quiet, warm, and intimate. By 1957, the show was the most successful in television. But still the advertisers held back. The show was expanded to a half hour. Cole delivered himself of a widely quoted epigram: "Madison Avenue is afraid of the dark." His guest stars included Mel Tormé, Tony Martin, Peggy Lee, Ella Fitzgerald, Harry Belafonte, Julius La Rosa, and more, and they appeared for scale—or rather, for *him*.

I asked La Rosa about his appearance on the show. "Nat couldn't have been nicer," he said. "As a thank you, he gave me a lovely white sweater with blue trimming, which I treasured until it almost fell apart. He was such a gentle man. Nelson Riddle was the orchestra leader. Peggy Lee was the other guest! I was performing with three giants I'd paid to see just a few years before! And they made me feel like I belonged, which of course I didn't really."

Throughout 1957, NBC kept the show on the air. Though its ratings steadily improved, the sponsors it needed did not materialize. After losing nearly half a million dollars on the show, NBC decided to move it to the deadly slot of 7 P.M. on Saturday. Cole declined to make the move.

Steve Allen told me that NBC some years ago needed storage space in its New Jersey facility and destroyed the kinescopes of some of its classic shows, including many of his own *Tonight* shows with precious footage of Charlie Parker, Thelonious Monk, and other jazz musicians whose cause he was forever pushing. About a third of his shows survive, and there are thirty segments of *The Nat King Cole Show*, parts of which are seen on TV from time to time. One of the things you notice if you watch them is Cole's remarkable grace of movement. He was a natural for television.

In his statement to the *New York Times* announcing the end of the show, Cole said, "There won't be shows starring Negroes soon." Julius La Rosa offered a footnote to this tale: "By the way, I recall that on a Dinah Shore show, Ella Fitzgerald was the other guest. At one point I put my arms over Dinah's and Ella's shoulders. I got mail denouncing me for putting my arm around 'that nigger.' Incredible, no? And that was in the mid-fifties."

Singer Betty Bennett, in her autobiography *The Ladies Who Sing with the Band* (2000), tells this story: "While the Tommy Dorsey band was in [Omaha], the King Cole Trio was appearing [at a] club. My girlfriend told someone in the Dorsey band that I was a singer. They in turn asked Nat Cole who graciously agreed to accompany me.

"The next night when my friend and I tried to enter the club, [the owner] fixed me with a look of disgust and said, 'We don't want your kind in here.' I made him repeat this because it was beyond my immediate comprehension. I had to be helped up the stairs to the sweet evening air. My friend went back down to ask Murray his reason for barring me. He said it was because I had sung with the 'nigger' band. That was over fifty years ago and it still sickens me. It was my first experience of bigotry and I only wish it had been my last."

She told me that in 1953, during her marriage to André Previn, she and André went to hear Nat at the Sahara in Las Vegas. After the show, he came into the lounge to greet them. He stood at their table to talk. He was not permitted to sit down in that room.

In those days, black entertainers performing at the major Las Vegas hotels were not allowed to reside in them. They had to find rooms in the black part of the city. Sammy Davis Jr. was the first black entertainer to break the barrier and stay in the hotel where he was working.

I have been unable to trace the next story to its root, but I have no doubt of its verity. Such things were common in that period. In the waning days of the big-band era, one of the band buses pulled into a truck stop. As the musicians got off, they were startled to see Nat Cole, standing by his car and eating his lunch off its hood. He could not, of course, eat in the restaurant. He was at that time an idol of musicians, and one of America's biggest stars.

Cole sang for President Eisenhower, and was invited to sing for the queen of England during a pending European tour (and he would soon sing at the inauguration of his friend John F. Kennedy), but the Masonic Auditorium in San Francisco wouldn't let him perform there, its manager telling the press: "No assumption on the man's color. We just don't want the class of people Cole attracts." Though the Civic Auditorium was available to him, Cole canceled San Francisco entirely.

He made a "concept" album called *Wild Is Love*, songs about a man's search for love, or more precisely, sex. Some of his associates didn't like it. Gradually the album evolved into an idea for a Broadway show. Capitol Records put up $75,000, and Cole put at least $75,000 of his money into it. The show, with an interracial cast that included Barbara McNair, opened in Denver on October 17, 1960, to bad reviews. It moved on to San Francisco, where it got even worse reviews. Cole was determined to get it to Broadway, in one form or another, but eventually it went down, taking a great deal of his money with it.

Daniel Mark Epstein takes a considerable interest in Cole's sex life, indeed in seemingly everyone's sex life. His fascination with the quantity of women that a major male star is able to attract infuses the whole book. He says, "As the chief spokesman for romantic love in the early 1960s, it was inevitable that Cole would sample some of what he was selling." And he quotes a press agent who traveled with Cole: "Nat was very discreet. He was not the sort of guy who would say, arriving in a city, 'Hey, let's get some girls and have a party.'"

He doesn't examine a phenomenon that has existed since time immemorial: the sexual flocking, without any trace of pride or dignity, of women around men of celebrity. Leaving aside entirely the lives of actors and athletes, we may note that Liszt gathered great garlands of some of the fairest flowers of Europe; Boston ladies unhitched Offenbach's horses and pulled his carriage through the streets; Paganini plowed through more than his fair share of women; Frank Sinatra and Elvis Presley had herds of girls; they were all around the late Yves Montand; Glenn Miller bought his beautiful belted camel's hair topcoats in triplicate because the girls tore pieces from them when he got caught in crowds; Lady Iris Mountbatten is reliably reputed to have balled the whole Count Basie band; a girl who similarly collected the entire Woody Herman band was known as Mattress Annie to its members; and the rock era gave rise to a new term: groupie. No similar lemminglike behavior has ever been observed in the behavior of men toward famous movie stars or singers.

The Epstein book details Nat's last love affair. It was with a young Swedish chorus girl he had met during a review called *Sights and Sounds* that he did in 1963, hoping still to get to Broadway. Epstein calls her a "dreamy delight." He says she had "the spiritual look of a dream in the twilight between sleep and waking."

Leslie Gourse mentions this relationship in her book, too. "But," Leslie told me, "she asked that I not use her name, and I didn't." Epstein names her. And he says, "Anyway, there were plenty of opportunities for [her] to get Cole alone in a room as the show toured the country late in 1963. And by early spring of 1964, what started as a diversion for Cole, the reliable balm of erotic adventure, had begun to spin out of control and become an obsession. He really loved this girl, who was so different from his wife in every way, so gentle, so simple, so *undemanding*. [She] was funny and she had quiet courage; she had made the great crossover from culture to culture, language to language. And who knows what other changes and challenges she might have the strength of character to endure? In the unreal erotic world of their hours alone together Cole was able to imagine a future free of all that weighted him down—the expectations of his children, parents, the press, his public, his people, who looked to him for leadership, wanted him to be a saint; above all he imagined freedom from his wife, who seemed to him, in his befuddlement, to be the warden of this prison, his life."

Cole by then had lung cancer, and it was progressing rapidly. He played the Copacabana in New York. Epstein says Maria did what "any proud, furious wife with five children and some cash does when her husband is thinking of leaving her for another woman": she put a private detective on the case, and he came away from the girl's apartment "with enough billets-doux and mementos to fry King Cole in the divorce courts, if Maria took a fancy to do it. In California, she and the kids would get everything he had."

Cole at last was hospitalized for cobalt treatments in Los Angeles. Of Maria, Epstein writes: "As magnificent as she had been in love, in devotion, in fighting for her husband's career and their rights to happiness, now she was no less magnificent." In spite of such flattery of her as this, Epstein paints her as a barracuda. She blocked his calls at the hospital's telephone switchboard, he says, to make sure the girl could not speak with the dying man. She compiled a list of everyone she thought might have abetted Nat's love affair and made sure they were never able to speak to their friend, no matter what consolation that might have given him. And then she pulled a master stroke.

Maria Cole got a call from the girl, telling her that she loved Nat and Nat loved her, and asking Maria to give him a divorce. Cole was by now spending his days in a hospital rocking chair. The mail from well-wishers poured in. So did the flowers. "Maria," Epstein writes, "came marching down the corridor of the North Wing on the sixth floor of St. John's Hospital, burst into her husband's room, and lit into him as if the two of them were in their twenties." She demanded the girl's phone number. She dialed it, and handed Nat the phone, and made him tell the girl, in his feeble voice, that it was over between them. Nat Cole's left lung was removed on January 25. He died on the morning of February 15, 1965.

Freddy Cole told me that Nat's death was devastating to him. He said, "Prior to that, two weeks before, my dad died with complications of a heart ailment. So we were all in state of shock for a long while.

"I haven't smoked now in many years, and I don't think about cigarets. I quit before Nat died. I was at the hospital in Santa Monica. I'd been coughing and had a bronchial condition, and Nat said, 'Man, you ought to quit smoking.' And I said I would.

"Later on, I picked Natalie up from the airport. She was coming home from school. She was twelve or thirteen years old. I lit a cigaret, and she said, 'I thought you told Daddy you were going to stop smoking.' So I said, 'Okay,' and threw the cigaret out the window. I haven't smoked since."

Twenty-eight years later, in 1993, Roger Kellaway was sitting at the piano in Studio One at Western in Los Angeles, prior to a record date with Natalie Cole, with charts by Marty Paich. By then she was forty-three years old.

"I was sitting at the piano, just fiddling around," Roger recalled. "These hands touched my shoulders and a warmth filled my entire body. I couldn't believe it. I turned around, and it was her. And that's how we first met. She didn't know me at all. But now that I think about it, wasn't that the logical thing for her to do? Because I was the *pianist*.

"It was her *Take a Look* album. We did the verses to three songs on that one session, just she and I. It was so wonderful to work with a singer who knew those kinds of songs, that concept. I was able to breathe with her, without even knowing her. She invited me to lunch. I congratulated her on being a singer who *understood* verses, and she said, 'Well of course I do. My dad took me everywhere.' That's as close as I'm going to get to Nat Cole."

Listening to the entire Mosaic collection of Nat Cole was a revelatory experience. Now I wanted Roger to listen to some of it with me, along with another pianist friend, Debbie Denke of Santa Barbara. She and Roger and I listened to Cole for two or three hours.

We all marveled at his effortless, unceasing swing. He has the most magnificent time of any musician I've ever heard. Roger said, "You are told in the arts that you have to strive to get out of your own way. He doesn't even have to try."

"And there's the gentleness. The tenderness. He has a way of caressing the piano."

"Nat Cole never shouts," I added. "Not in his singing, not in his playing, not even in his life."

"That's a good way to put it," Roger said. And after a few more minutes of listening: "The musicality is just *there*. It's understood. It's an assumption. His playing sparkles. And it seems effortless. It's not filled with ego and the kinds of thing you've heard for the last thirty-five years, especially the more modern angular players, whether it be anger or wherever they think they're coming from emotionally. The push, and the stress in society that's produced that kind of playing. It's not there."

In Debbie's words: "His singing had a timeless charm—the way he presented his tunes, the way he got the emotion across. There is something so lovable about his voice. And his piano playing really swung. His block chord voicings had a unique sound, a distinct tone. The way he backed himself up as a singer at the piano was so tasteful. The way he would sing and, just at the right time, place the right figure to complement his singing. It sounded effortless. I don't see how it could be done better.

"Another thing I've noticed. I've been researching tunes with *Rhythm* changes for some of my students. Nat Cole did a lot of tunes based on *I Got Rhythm*. He seemed to really do a large tribute to Gershwin. *I'm an Errand Boy for Rhythm*, *Hit that Jive Jack*, the list goes on and on."

I read them some of the 1991 notes, by pianist Dick Katz, for the Mosaic reissue of the Cole Capitol piano records. He wrote: "His deep groove, harmonic awareness, supple phrasing, touch, dynamics, taste, and just plain *delicious* music had a profound effect on . . . Oscar Peterson, Hank Jones, Tommy Flanagan, Al Haig, Bill Evans, Wynton Kelly, Ahmad Jamal, Monty Alexander, and many others, including myself."

"And you," I told Roger.

"But I never heard as much of Nat Cole as I might have wanted. I got his influence through Oscar Peterson, and of course Oscar added all that power." He listened to Nat Cole some more and then said, "When you hear something like this, you think to yourself, 'Boy, would I like to hang out with that person!'"

I can almost see that room in the Seelbach in Louisville. I assumed that Nat had sent for room service, rather than going to the restaurant, in order to assure privacy for our interview. And perhaps that had something to do with it.

But, long afterward, it occurred to me that he probably did it because he knew that even if he could now get into a Louisville hotel, where no one could see him, he and I would still not be allowed into its restaurant, or any other decent restaurant in town.

The privacy was to my advantage, in the end: I had that precious time alone with him, and I stayed the day with him until concert time. I remember being amazed that he would give so much time to me, a nobody.

"He was that way," Freddy Cole told me. "He'd talk to a lamp-post."

I spent two months or so studying his life and his work, sometimes analyzing it at the piano. I have a whole new appreciation of him, and it will never leave me. Devoid of ostentation or pretense, he was truly a genius musician. I idolized him when I was a kid. I guess I still do.

I was not one of those who questioned Cole's turning to singing. I loved his singing. I didn't have the courage to tell him I was secretly writing songs, and one of my regrets is that I never got to hear him do one of mine. (Freddy did one, though.) I do remember asking him why, in his concert and nightclub performances, he rarely accompanied himself now.

"Because when you sing and play at the same time," he said, "you're dividing your attention. You sing better if you don't play, and you play better if you don't sing." Maybe. But he was magnificent at self-accompaniment.

I remember saying that I hoped he would not stop recording jazz albums entirely. And he said, "As a matter of fact, I'm thinking about doing one soon."

After that tour, and that grim experience in Birmingham, he went home to Los Angeles and began to practice. He practiced all through June, and then in July called a session.

"Nat loved to be in the studio," Freddy told me. "He just couldn't sit still. He'd be off for a couple of weeks, and he'd call the guys. That's how that *After Midnight* album came to be made. They were just foolin' around. My favorite in that album is *Blame It on My Youth*. That one and *You're Looking at Me*. *Sometimes I'm Happy* is good too. Stuff Smith and Nat were friends from back in Chicago. I play that album all the time."

The personnel of *After Midnight* comprises Nat, John Collins on guitar, Charlie Harris on bass, and Lee Young on drums. On some tracks, the guest soloist is Stuff Smith on violin, Juan Tizol on trombone, Sweets Edison on trumpet, or Willie Smith on alto saxophone.

The King Cole Trio recordings are set pieces. He did the tunes pretty much the same way each time, even to the vocal phrasing. In one trio session, *I Surrender Dear,* he makes exactly the same allusion at the start of the second eight to *Lover Come Back to Me* as he does in a second take that was unissued. But to hear him blowing, one can turn to the *Jazz at the Philharmonic* recording he did for Norman Granz, an album he made with Lester Young, and *After Midnight.*

After that album, he recorded one more jazz session, in New York, on March 22, 1961. Then his piano falls silent.

His life strikes me, taken in sum, as sad, for all its great moments. He was thwarted at so many turns. Certainly his life was not the field of flowers I would have wished for so magnificent a musician, so humane a man. After the Birmingham incident, his deportment prompted the *Chicago Defender* to thunder: "We wonder if Nat Cole shared the humiliation of the hundreds of his Negro fans who had to stand outdoors and wait while whites inside yelled 'Go home, nigger!' and attacked him as he performed. We hope Cole has learned his lesson."

Cole told a reporter, "I'm not mad at a soul." He caught hell for that one.

Thurgood Marshall, who was then chief counsel for the NAACP, said, "All Cole needs to complete his role as an Uncle Tom is a banjo."

It is a detestable, execrable remark. It is beyond our powers to estimate how much Nat Cole did for "racial relations" in the United States by the graciousness of his comportment, the softness of his manner, and the decency of his example. It still shines.

Four of the men involved in the assault in Alabama were sentenced on April 18, 1956—only days after the incident—to 180 days in jail, and fines. Charges of assault with intent to commit murder were still pending against two other men.

Nat told me that one of the things that bothered him was the impression of America the incident gave to the nineteen British members of the Ted Heath band. That was typical of him, to be concerned about others. "For them," he said, "it was something of a shock." (Most of them would live to see racism arrive in England.)

As for the injuries he had suffered, he told me with a smile (and his smile left a radiant afterimage) that he was feeling "just a few aches and pains."

About the sentences given to his attackers, he said: "I'm happy to see [the courts] take such a stand because it shows progress. It fooled the people who thought they were simply going to ignore it. The newspapers were very kind. The Birmingham paper wrote a wonderful editorial. The *Mobile Press* deplored the incident.

"If what happened to me helped the situation, and since I wasn't hurt badly, then I'm glad it happened.

"The only way to fight this thing is by reasonableness. Sometimes it's hard to turn the other cheek, but reason tells us it is the thing to do."

With my duties as a reporter behind us, we talked for the rest of the day about music, right up until concert time. The normal police contingent for concerts at the Jefferson County Armory was four or five officers. That night, Chief of Police Carl Heustis saw to it that no incident could occur: he assigned forty men to the auditorium, and commanded them personally.

The audience of seventy-three hundred roared its support for Nat. The next day, my review dealt in detail with the Heath band, June Christy, and the Four Freshmen. I wrote Nat Cole off in what seems to me, reading it now, as a deliberately and ironically laconic final sentence: "Cole sang in his inimitable soft style, played a little piano—and brought the house down."

Nat left Louisville later that Thursday, April 19. I never met him again. Whether he ever played Louisville after I left it, I have no idea. But I do know he never set foot in Alabama again.

In January 2001, forty-five years after the attack in Birmingham and thirty-six years after his death, Nat Cole suffered another insult. The nineteen-hour PBS documentary by Ken Burns titled *Jazz* ignored him almost completely. He was in good company. Benny Carter was similarly slighted, and Art Tatum got only a little attention.

In the *New Yorker,* Whitney Balliett wrote: "Many first-rate musicians are tapped only in passing or are ignored altogether. Those who are mentioned briefly, then left on the cutting-room floor, include Charles Mingus, a great bassist and a wildly original composer and bandleader; the Modern Jazz Quartet, for forty years the most lyrical and swinging of jazz chamber groups; and the seminal pianists Earl Hines, Bud Powell, and Bill Evans, who, taken together, invented modern jazz piano.

"The essential musicians who are ignored completely include . . . Nat Cole."

I cannot remember who told me this story:

Cole was playing the Fontainebleu. A little white girl got away from her parents and toddled on to the stage. A kind of hush seized the audience. This was Miami, and Miami was one of the most racist cities in America.

She drew closer to him. Nat had someone bring him a chair. He sat down, took the little girl on his lap, and sang her to sleep.

Index

CPSIA information can be obtained
at www.ICGtesting.com
Printed in the USA
LVHW092253210319
611505LV00004B/41/P